AMERICAN POLITICAL, ECONOMIC, AND SECURITY ISSUES

U.S. EXPORT PROGRAMS AND PROMOTION TOOLS

AMERICAN POLITICAL, ECONOMIC, AND SECURITY ISSUES

Additional books in this series can be found on Nova's website under the Series tab.

Additional E-books in this series can be found on Nova's website under the E-books tab.

AMERICAN POLITICAL, ECONOMIC, AND SECURITY ISSUES

U.S. EXPORT PROGRAMS AND PROMOTION TOOLS

STEVEN D. BRAGHOFF
EDITOR

Nova Science Publishers, Inc.
New York

For permission to use material from this book please contact us:
Telephone 631-231-7269; Fax 631-231-8175
Web Site: http://www.novapublishers.com

Additional color graphics may be available in the e-book version of this book.

LIBRARY OF CONGRESS CATALOGING-IN-PUBLICATION DATA

U.S. export programs and promotion tools / [edited by] Steven D. Braghoff.
p. cm.
"CRS report for Congress prepared for members and committees of Congress."
Includes index.
ISBN 978-1-60741-328-8 (hardcover)
1. Export marketing--United States. 2. Exports--United States. 3. Foreign trade promotion--United States. I. Braghoff, Steven D. II. Library of Congress. Congressional Research Service.
HF1416.5.U17 2011
382'.63--dc22

2011004284

Published by Nova Science Publishers, Inc. † New York

CONTENTS

PREFACE

This new book provides an overview of the federal government agencies that participate in U.S. export promotion efforts, as well as the issues that they raise for Congress. The recent global economic downturn has renewed congressional debate over the role of the federal government in promoting exports. This debate has been heightened with the Obama Administration's introduction of the National Export Initiative (NEI) in the 2010 State of the Union Address. Some Members of Congress have placed greater priority on understanding the coordination, budgets, and functions of federal agencies involved in export promotion. Such an understanding may increase congressional oversight of export promotion policy and related legislative activity.

Chapter 1- This report provides an overview of the federal government agencies that participate in U.S. export promotion efforts and the issues that they raise for Congress. The recent global economic downturn has renewed congressional debate over the role of the federal government in promoting exports. This debate has been heightened with the Obama Administration's introduction of the National Export Initiative (NEI) in the 2010 State of the Union Address. Some Members of Congress have placed greater priority on understanding the coordination, budgets, and functions of federal agencies involved in export promotion. Such an understanding may increase congressional oversight of export promotion policy and related legislative activity.

Chapter 2- The Export-Import Bank (Ex-Im Bank) is the chief U.S. government agency that helps finance American exports of manufactured goods and services with the objective of contributing to the employment of U.S. workers. (For additional information, see the Bank's Internet site: http://www.exim.gov.) With an annual budget of around $200 million, the Bank finances less than 1% of U.S. exports a year. Ex-Im Bank provides loan guarantees and insurance to commercial banks to make trade credits available to U.S. exporters. The Bank also offers direct financing to U.S. exporters, primarily to counter subsidized trade credits offered to foreign exporters by their governments.

Chapter 3- Agricultural exports are important both to farmers and to the U.S. economy. According to the U.S. Department of Agriculture's Economic Research Service (ERS), agricultural exports have exceeded imports since the early 1970s. The most recent outlook for FY2010 has U.S. agricultural exports estimated at $100 billion. While the FY2010 forecast is down from the record level seen in FY2008, the forecast is still the second highest on record.

U.S. agricultural imports are forecast to reach $77.5 billion in FY2010, which would result in a $22.5 billion trade surplus for agricultural goods.

Chapter 4- The President's National Export Initiative has put forth an ambitious goal of doubling exports in the next 5 years. Ex-Im has been identified as having a key role in the initiative, and a recent administration report identifies a number of specific actions for Ex-Im. Our work on Ex-Im's financing with respect to small business found areas where Ex-Im needed to improve its data systems for accurate reporting as well as its tracking of efforts to increase small business financing. Regarding Ex-Im's environmentally beneficial exports financing, we found that the bank could benefit from more consistently following strategic planning practices. Ex-Im has taken a number of steps in response to GAO recommendations, but opportunities for improvement remain. Additional attention to these issues will enable Ex-Im to develop better communication with Congress and other stakeholders regarding the balance between the small business and environmental export targets and the broader priorities in the National Export Initiative.

Chapter 5- Since the recent recession, policymakers have emphasized the role exports can play in strengthening the U.S. economy and in creating higher paying jobs. In March 2010 the President signed an Executive Order creating the National Export Initiative (NEI), with a goal of doubling U.S. exports in 5 years. However, since 2004 the workforce of the U.S. and Foreign Commercial Service (CS) has shrunk, calling into question the ability of this key agency to increase its activities to assist U.S. businesses with their exports.

In response to a conference committee mandate, GAO reviewed (1) how well CS managed its resources from 2004 to 2009, and (2) the completeness of CS's workforce plans and the quality of its fiscal year 2011 budget request. GAO analyzed data from the Departments of Agriculture, Commerce, and State; reviewed agency documents; and interviewed agency officials.

Chapter 6- The 111th Congress may consider legislation to renew, modify, or reauthorize the Export Administration Act (EAA). On July 31, 2009, Representative Sherman introduced the Export Control Improvements Act (H.R. 3515), co-sponsored by Representative Manzullo and Representative A. Smith, that contains provisions on export controls enforcement, integration of export control data in the AES, and diversion control. The House Foreign Affairs Committee is also reportedly working to produce as comprehensive rewrite of the EAA. As part of the Administration's export control review, Defense Secretary Robert M. Gates has proposed creating a unified export control structure merging the dual-use and munitions export control regimes, some aspects of which may require legislative consent.

Chapter 7- On March 11, 2010, President Barack Obama issued an executive order creating the National Export Initiative (NEI), which aims to double U.S. exports over the next five years in support of 2 million jobs here at home.

The NEI recognizes that exports will play a critical role in catalyzing America's near- and long-term economic growth, and it represents the first time the United States will have a government wide export promotion strategy with focused attention from the president and his Cabinet.

Chapter 8- Exports, and trade more broadly, contribute to the U.S. economy in a variety of ways. Trade enables the United States to achieve a higher standard of living through producing and exporting goods and services that are produced here relatively efficiently, and importing goods and services that are produced here relatively inefficiently. An indication of this is that firms engaged in the international marketplace tend to exhibit higher rates of productivity growth and pay higher wages and benefits to their workers than domestically oriented firms of the same size.

In: U.S. Export Programs and Promotion Tools
Editor: Steven D. Braghoff

ISBN: 978-1-60741-328-8

Chapter 1

U.S. GOVERNMENT AGENCIES INVOLVED IN EXPORT PROMOTION: OVERVIEW AND ISSUES FOR CONGRESS

Shayerah Ilias, Charles E. Hanrahan and M. Angeles Villarreal

SUMMARY

This report provides an overview of the federal government agencies that participate in U.S. export promotion efforts and the issues that they raise for Congress. The recent global economic downturn has renewed congressional debate over the role of the federal government in promoting exports. This debate has been heightened with the Obama Administration's introduction of the National Export Initiative (NEI) in the 2010 State of the Union Address. Some Members of Congress have placed greater priority on understanding the coordination, budgets, and functions of federal agencies involved in export promotion. Such an understanding may increase congressional oversight of export promotion policy and related legislative activity.

In 1992, Congress attempted to enhance coordination of U.S. export promotion policy by creating the Trade Promotion Coordinating Committee (TPCC), an interagency task force chaired by the Department of Commerce. The TPCC releases the *National Export Strategy* (NES), an annual report that serves as an effort to guide federal export promotion policy, goals, and activity.

Executive Order 13534, issued in March 2010, formalized the NEI and established the Export Promotion Cabinet, a higher level coordinating body that is to work with the TPCC to make the NEI operational.

Approximately 20 federal government agencies are involved in supporting U.S. exports directly or indirectly. The TPCC has identified nine of these agencies currently as having budgets for programs or activities directly related to export promotion. They are the Department of Agriculture (USDA), Department of Commerce, Export-Import Bank (Ex-Im Bank), Overseas Private Investment Corporation (OPIC), Small Business Administration (SBA), Department of State, Trade and Development Agency (TDA), Office of the U.S.

Trade Representative (USTR), and Department of the Treasury. The USDA has the largest level of export promotion funding, followed by Commerce. Some agencies charge fees for their services.

Federal government agencies perform a wide variety of functions that contribute to export promotion, including providing information, counseling, and export assistance services; funding feasibility studies; financing and insuring U.S. trade; conducting government-to-government advocacy; and negotiating new trade agreements and enforcing existing ones.

The export promotion activities of federal government agencies raise a number of issues for Congress. Among the most prominent are the following:

- the economic arguments for and against the involvement of the U.S. government in promoting exports in the context of issues such as market failures and foreign governments' support for their national exports;
- the effectiveness of interagency export promotion coordination through the TPCC and the newly created Export Promotion Cabinet;
- the level of U.S. government spending on export promotion, its adequacy, and efficiency of use; and
- the extent to which the export promotion activities conducted by federal government agencies may be similar or overlapping.

INTRODUCTION

In times of economic crisis, including the most recent global economic downturn that began in 2007, Congress often has debated on how best to promote U.S. commercial exports as a policy tool for economic growth and job creation. Congressional interest in U.S. export promotion policy has risen with President Obama's announcement of a National Export Initiative (NEI) in his 2010 State of the Union Address. The NEI is a strategy for doubling U.S. exports over the next five years in order to help generate two million new jobs in the United States through increased coordination and funding of federal export promotion activities; greater financing for U.S. exporters; increased government advocacy on behalf of U.S. exporters; and negotiation of new trade agreements and stronger enforcement of existing U.S. trade agreements.

With the increased focus on export promotion efforts, some Members of Congress have placed greater priority on understanding the coordination, budgets, and functions of federal government agencies involved in export promotion. Such an understanding may support increased congressional oversight of U.S. export promotion policy and related legislative activity. It also may assist Members of Congress in supporting the efforts of their constituents to learn about federal export promotion services and to become involved in exporting.

This report provides an overview of the federal agencies that participate in U.S. export promotion efforts and the issues that they raise for Congress. It proceeds first by discussing the coordination, budgets, and functions of federal government agencies involved in promoting exports. Next, the report provides an overview of the missions and activities of key federal government agencies that support exports. The last section of the report discusses agency-related issues for Congress.

While this report focuses on the role of the federal government in promoting exports, it is important to acknowledge that State and local governments, as well as businesses, have an important role in promoting exports.

COORDINATION OF EXPORT PROMOTION ACTIVITIES

Trade Promotion Coordinating Committee

The Trade Promotion Coordinating Committee (TPCC) is an interagency committee whose objective is to coordinate and set priorities for federal agencies involved in export promotion and to propose a unified export promotion budget to the President. Title II of the Export Enhancement Act of 1992 (P.L. 100-412), which added Sections 2312 and 2313 to the Omnibus Trade and Competitiveness Act of 1988 (P.L. 102-429), established the TPCC. Congress enacted the 1992 Act in an attempt to rectify some of the perceived shortfalls in the U.S. export promotion regime, including concerns that existing export promotion programs lacked coordination and an overall strategy.[1]

The TPCC is comprised of twenty member agencies, nine of which are key federal government agencies involved in export promotion. The key agencies are the U.S. Department of Agriculture (USDA), U.S. Department of Commerce, Export-Import Bank of the United States (Ex-Im Bank), Overseas Private Investment Corporation (OPIC), U.S. Trade and Development Agency (TDA), Small Business Administration (SBA), U.S. Department of State, Office of the U.S. Trade Representative (USTR), and U.S. Department of the Treasury. The Department of Commerce chairs the TPCC.

Since 1993, the TPCC has issued an annual report entitled the *National Export Strategy* (NES), which lists U.S. trade promotion priorities and provides estimates of spending levels for trade promotion by agency and function. In general, U.S. commercial export promotion activities are guided by the NES.

The latest NES report, issued in 2008, outlined four major export policy objectives: (1) engaging more companies, especially small businesses and new exporters, in exporting; (2) expanding opportunities through bilateral and regional free trade agreements (FTAs); (3) assisting U.S. exporters in entering "emerging priority markets," identified as China, India, Brazil, and Russia; and (4) assisting U.S. exporters in taking advantage of commercial opportunities in "next generation markets" in the Middle East and Africa, while reducing the risks of entering these markets.[2] The NES was not released in 2009. According to the Director of the TPCC, a NES is not published in transition years between Administrations.[3] The next NES is expected to be released in late 2010.

President's Export Promotion Cabinet

The National Export Initiative, announced by President Obama in the 2010 State of the Union address, introduced a new level of coordination to federal export promotion activities.

Executive Order 13534, which was issued on March 11, 2010, formalized the NEI and, among other provisions, instructs the U.S. government to enhance and organize federal efforts to promote exports through high-level coordination. E.O. 13534 created a President's Export Promotion Cabinet to ensure that export promotion is a high priority for all relevant agencies.[4] Members of the Export Promotion Cabinet include the nine key Secretaries or Directors of the export promotion agencies of the TPCC and senior White House advisors. The Export Promotion Cabinet is to coordinate with the TPCC in order to "operationalize" the NEI.[5]

In September 2010, the Export Promotion Cabinet released a report containing recommendations for implementing the NEI. The Cabinet, through the TPCC, identified eight priority areas: (1) exports by small and medium-sized enterprises (SMEs); (2) federal export assistance; (3) trade missions; (4) commercial advocacy; (5) increasing export credits; (6) macroeconomic rebalancing; (7) reducing barriers to trade; and (8) export promotion of services. Some of these recommendations focus on improving federal services that directly support export assistance efforts. Others focus on efforts to promote exports in broader ways.[6]

The Cabinet noted that four general themes apply to all eight priority areas: (1) strengthen interagency information-sharing and coordination; (2) leverage and enhance technology to reach potential exporters and provide U.S. businesses with the tools necessary to export successfully; (3) leverage combined efforts of State and local governments and public-private partnerships; and (4) have unified goals for TPCC member agencies to support the NEI's implementation.[7]

Since its introduction, the NEI has become the centerpiece of federal export promotion efforts. Going forward, it is unclear how the *National Export Strategy* will fit into or incorporate the priority areas identified in the Export Promotion Cabinet's report on the NEI. This may be an opportunity for the TPCC to clarify export promotion goals identified in the NES and how they relate to broad U.S. priorities.

FUNDING FOR EXPORT PROMOTION ACTIVITIES

The *National Export Strategy* reports government funding levels for the activities of federal agencies deemed to constitute "trade promotion." It includes all or part of the budgets of the TPCC's member agencies, but does not provide details on the programs and activities of each agency that are dedicated to export promotion.

The TPCC does not have an independent budget, nor does it have any specific authority to direct member agencies' allocation of resources. The TPCC secretariat does not review member agency budgets in relation to the annual NES and its budgetary needs. Each federal agency has its own statutory requirements and budgets appropriated by various congressional committees. As a result, each agency submits its annual budget request separately to the President.[8]

Table 1. TPCC Trade Promotion Funding Levels, FY2003-FY2009 (Millions of U.S. Dollars)

Agency	FY03 Enacted	FY04 Enacted	FY05 Enacted	FY06 Enacted	FY07 Enacted	FY08 Enacted	FY09 Requested
U.S. Department of Agriculture (USDA)	1,354	828	979	769	693	644	563
Department of Commerce	316	250	333	335	335	339	350
Department of Energy (DOE)	4	9	9	9	9	9	NA
Department of Labor (DOL)	1	1	1	NA	NA	NA	NA
Department of State	139	155	151	177	174	184	198
Department of Transportation (DOT)	0	0	NA	NA	NA	NA	NA
Department of the Treasury	3	3	3	3	3	3	3
U.S. Agency for International Development (AID)	NA	NA	NA	NA	NA	NA	NA
Environmental Protection Agency (EPA)	0	0	NA	NA	NA	NA	NA
Export-Import Bank (Ex-Im Bank)	578	73	132	123	55	1	3
Overseas Private Investment Corporation (OPIC)[a]	(214)	(199)	(213)	(161)	(113)	(165)	(170)
Small Business Administration (SBA)	9	8	5	6	6	6	6.4
U.S. Trade and Development Agency (TDA)	47	50	51	50	50	51	51
U.S. Trade Representative (USTR)	35	42	41	44	44	44	46
Total	*2,486*	*1,419*	*1,705*	*1,516*	*1,369*	*1,272*	*1,220*

Source: Trade Policy Coordinating Committee (TPCC), *National Export Strategy* (NES) reports from various years.

Notes: This table contains funding levels for export promotion activities only. Agencies that currently have budgets related to export promotion are bolded. According to the TPCC, amounts may be restated to reflect new data or definitions. Funding levels reported may include administrative expenses, transfers, or other adjustments.

a. OPIC fees result in a budget surplus.

The individual agencies and the TPCC determine which programs or activities are considered to constitute trade promotion and therefore included in the annual report of trade promotion budget authority. However, a breakdown of these activities within each agency is not listed. Instead the TPCC publishes overall trade promotion spending by agency. For example, it is unclear which units within the Department of Commerce have programs or activities the TPCC has classified as "trade promotion" in the NES.

Not all of the TPCC member agencies have budget authority for trade promotion activities.[9] Although the NES report lists 20 member agencies as part of the TPCC, nine of these agencies currently have budgets for programs or activities directly related to trade promotion (see **Table 1**).

Between FY2003 and FY2008, the overall export promotion-related budget of federal agencies, as reported in the NES, declined by about 50%, due to lower funding levels for USDA and Ex-Im Bank. The USDA is the agency with the largest funding levels for export promotion activities. However, USDA's budget on export programs has decreased by 42% since FY2004, from $1.1 billion in FY2004 to $644 million in FY2008. Ex-Im Bank's funding levels have decreased primarily because the agency became "self-sustaining" for appropriations purposes in FY2008. Ex-Im Bank funds its administrative and program costs through fee income generated from its financing programs.

After USDA, the Department of Commerce and the State Department have the second and third largest fund levels for export promotion. During the FY2003-2008 time period, funding for the Department of Commerce's export promotion activities increased from $316 million to $339 million, while the State Department's increased from $139 million to $184 million.

Funding levels reported by the TPCC do not necessarily show total U.S. agency spending on export promotion activities. Thus, total budget authority for government agencies and offices may be higher than the spending levels reported in the NES. For example, Ex-Im Bank charges fees to cover its services, and uses offsetting collections to support its activities—spending that is not necessarily reflected in the TPCC budget. Although Ex-Im Bank's FY2009 trade promotion requested budget was $3 billion, it authorized $21 billion in credit and insurance in that year.

Export Promotion Services and Activities

Federal government agencies perform a wide variety of functions that contribute to export promotion. Some of these services directly assist U.S. companies to overcome information and market entry barriers related to exporting. They include:

- **Export assistance services:** The U.S. government provides export assistance services, such as distribution of trade-related information to exporters, foreign country market research, and counseling to both new and seasoned exporters. Key agencies that offer direct export assistance include the USDA, Department of Commerce, Department of State, and SBA.
- **Feasibility studies:** The U.S. government conducts feasibility studies, which evaluate the economic, financial, technical, and other aspects of proposed projects in foreign countries that may generate exports of U.S. goods and services. USDA and TDA both conduct such studies.
- **Export financing and insurance:** U.S. government agencies may finance and insure U.S. exports to foreign countries for a number reasons, including: (1) to assume commercial and political risks that exporters or private financial institutions are unwilling or unable to undertake alone; (2) to overcome maturity and other limitations in private sector export financing; and (3) to counter subsidized trade credits offered to foreign exporters by their governments. USDA takes the lead on

agricultural export financing, while Ex-Im Bank is the lead agency for providing financing and insurance for non-agricultural exports. Export financing for small business exporters is available from Ex-Im Bank and SBA. Related to exports also is OPIC's role in investment insurance for projects in developing countries and emerging markets.

- **Government-to-government advocacy:** In many situations, U.S. companies face direct competition from foreign enterprises with access to greater foreign financing, subsidies, and other forms of support from their governments. The United States may use diplomatic tools to advocate on behalf of U.S. companies to ensure that they can compete on a level playing field with foreign competitors in export markets. Key agencies involved in such efforts are the Department of Commerce, Department of State, and the USTR.

The federal government also promotes exports in broader ways, such as through negotiating new multilateral, regional, and bilateral FTAs and monitoring the implementation and enforcement of existing trade agreements. Such efforts work to address constraints, barriers, and unfair trade practices faced by U.S. exporters, including foreign countries' tariff and other import policies, export subsidies, inadequate protection of intellectual property rights, service barriers, investment barriers, and anti-competitive practices.[10] They also help to develop foreign markets for U.S. goods and services. The lead agency in such efforts is the USTR. Other agencies, including the State Department and Department of Commerce, also play a role in FTA negotiations and enforcement.

In addition, the U.S. government conducts activities that may help to promote exports indirectly. Government programs that are not charged directly with the promotion of U.S. exports may contribute to the expansion of exports through their activities. For example, overseas investment insurance provided by OPIC helps to support U.S. investment in foreign countries to support U.S. foreign policy objectives, which may lead to the sale of U.S. goods and services to these markets.

KEY U.S. GOVERNMENT AGENCIES CHARGED WITH EXPORT PROMOTION

The export promotion functions of the federal government are distributed across a range of agencies. This section focuses on the nine agencies that have dedicated budgets to export promotion, as reported in the NES.

U.S. Department of Agriculture (USDA)

The USDA, through its Foreign Agricultural Service (FAS), carries out five programs to develop export markets for U.S. agricultural products.[11] These programs are authorized in farm bills, the most recent being the 2008 farm bill (P.L. 110-246). FAS also provides information, counseling and assistance to potential U.S. exporters of agricultural products. In addition, USDA can guarantee the commercial bank financing of up to $5.5 billion of U.S.

agricultural exports annually and can make available export subsidies for dairy products. All of USDA's export promotion, export financing and subsidy programs are funded through the borrowing authority of the Commodity Credit Corporation (CCC).[12]

The **Foreign Market Development Program (FMDP)** aims to develop long-term export markets for U.S. agricultural products. FMDP funds are allocated each fiscal year mainly to nonprofit U.S. agricultural and trade organizations that represent an entire industry or are nationwide in membership and scope. FMDP agreements with private organizations also are sometimes approved. FMDP promotes generic U.S. commodities, rather than brand-name products. Activities financed include consumer promotions, market research, technical assistance, and trade servicing. In recent years, the program has been funded at around $34 million annually.

The **Market Access Program (MAP)** helps U.S. producers, exporters, private companies, and other trade organizations to finance promotional activities for U.S. agricultural products, both generic and branded products. Activities financed include consumer promotions, market research, technical assistance, and trade servicing. The 2008 farm bill makes organic produce eligible for the program for the first time, and funds the program at $200 million each fiscal year from FY2008 through FY2012.

Both MAP and FMDP work in partnership with the private sector. Both reimburse program participants for a portion of the cost of carrying out overseas export promotions. One estimate is that government funding accounts for 37% of export promotion under these two programs while private sector funding accounts for 63%.[13]

The **Emerging Markets Program (EMP)** funds technical assistance activities to promote exports of U.S. agricultural commodities and products to emerging markets. An emerging market is any country that "is taking steps toward a market-oriented economy through the food, agriculture, or rural business sectors of the economy of the country," and "has the potential to provide a viable and significant market for United States commodities or products of United States agricultural commodities." Activities funded by the EMP include feasibility studies, market research, sectoral assessments, orientation visits, specialized training, and business workshops. Funding is set at $10 million each fiscal year from FY2008 through FY2012.

The **Quality Samples Program (QSP)** helps U.S. agricultural trade organizations provide small samples of their agricultural products to potential importers in emerging markets overseas. Focusing on industry and manufacturing, as opposed to end-use consumers, EMP allows manufacturers overseas to assess how U.S. food and fiber products can meet their production needs best. Funding for QSP has averaged $2 million annually in recent years.

The **Technical Assistance for Specialty Crops (TASC)** program is designed to assist U.S. organizations by providing funding for projects that address sanitary and phytosanitary (SPS) and technical barriers that prohibit or threaten the export of U.S. specialty crops.[14] Examples of activities TASC may cover include seminars and workshops, study tours, field surveys, pest and disease research, and pre-clearance programs. The 2008 farm bill authorized $7 million for TASC in FY2009.

Separate from these programs, FAS makes available resources, products, and services to help companies explore the potential for international sales of agricultural products.[15] FAS assists both beginning and experienced exporters, targeting especially SMEs.

Table 2. Funding for USDA Market Development and Export Financing Programs: FY2004-FY2011 Program Level (Millions of U.S. Dollars)

Program	FY05	FY06	FY07	FY08	FY09	FY10[a]	FY11[b]
Market Access Program (MAP)	140	200	200	200	200	200	160
Foreign Market Development Program (FMDP)	34	34	34	34	34	34	69
Emerging Markets Program (EMP)	10	10	4	10	10	10	10
Quality Samples	2	2	1	1	2	2	2
Technical Assistance for Specialty Crops (TASC)	2	2	1	4	7	8	18
Export Credit Guarantee Program (GSM- 102)[c]	2,170	1,363	1,445	3,115	5,400	5,500	5,500
Facilities Guarantee Program (FGP)[d]	0	0	0	0	70	100	100
Dairy Export Incentive Program (DEIP)	0	0	0	0	100	10	0
Total	*2,358*	*1,611*	*1,685*	*3,364*	*5,823*	*5,864*	*5,859*

Source: U.S. Department of Agriculture (USDA) Budget Summaries, 2004-2010.

Notes: According to the USDA, program level "represents the gross value of all financial assistance USDA provides to the public. This assistance may be in the form of grants, guaranteed or direct loans, cost-sharing, professional services such as research or technical assistance activities, or in-kind benefits such as commodities."

a. Estimated.

b. Requested.

c. GSM-102 program level is the value of agricultural exports whose financing is guaranteed.

d. FGP program level is the value of U.S. goods and services exports whose financing is guaranteed.

USDA operates two export financing programs for U.S. agricultural exports—the Export Credit Guarantee (GSM-102) Program and the Facilities Guarantee Program (FGP). GSM-102 guarantees against defaults of commercial bank financing of agricultural commodity exports. FGP provides payment guarantees to facilitate the financing of manufactured goods and services exported from the United States to improve or establish agriculture-related facilities in emerging markets. FAS carries out these programs and finances them through the CCC. Both GSM-102 and the FGP are authorized in farm bills, again most recently in the 2008 farm bill. Financing of an estimated $5.5 billion of U.S. agricultural exports was guaranteed in FY2009; and an estimated $70 million of U.S. goods and services exports will be guaranteed under FGP in FY2010 (see **Table 2**).[16] FAS also operates an export subsidy program, the Dairy Export Incentive Program (DEIP), which allows exporters to sell certain U.S. dairy products in foreign markets at prices lower than the exporter's costs of acquiring them.

In addition to USDA programs, U.S. agricultural exporters may receive help in financing the marketing and distribution of their products abroad through the SBA International Trade Loan Program, which provides financing for small businesses to expand their market or upgrade their facilities to improve their competitive position; the Ex-Im Bank, which operates loan, guarantee and insurance programs for exporters; and OPIC, which provides insurance for overseas investments (these agencies are described below).

The President's FY2011 budget request for USDA includes $54 million for the Foreign Agricultural Service, for trade promotion activities as part of the NEI.[17] This includes an increase of $10 million in FAS's budget to cover higher operating costs entailed by additional exporter assistance and in-country export promotion activities. USDA funding for the NEI also includes \$34.5 million additional funding for FMDP and an additional \$9 million for TASC. Additional funding for FMDP and TASC will double the overall funding available to these programs in FY2011. According to USDA, the added funding for FMDP will permit greater participation by cooperators in promotional activities, while additional funding for TASC reflects the increased importance of specialty crops in U.S. agricultural exports and the need to address phytosanitary and technical trade barriers they confront.

U.S. Department of Commerce

The Department of Commerce, through its International Trade Administration (ITA), is the lead agency providing export assistance services for U.S. non-agricultural businesses. ITA resources include: 1) trade specialists in over 100 U.S. Export Assistance Centers (USEACs) and approximately 150 overseas offices; 2) industry experts and market and economic analysts; 3) market access experts; and 4) import policy and trade compliance analysts. The agency is divided into four policy units and an Executive and Administrative Directorate.

The **Trade Promotion and U.S. Commercial Service** is the main trade promotion unit of ITA. It has trade specialists in 107 U.S. cities and in more than 80 countries who work with U.S. companies to help them get started in exporting or increasing sales in foreign markets. Its services include market research; trade events to promote U.S. products and services; introductions of qualified buyers and distributors in foreign countries to U.S. companies; and counseling and advocacy services throughout the export process.[18] The Advocacy Center of this unit serves as an advocate for U.S. companies by assisting them in pursuing foreign business opportunities and dealing with foreign governments. It also has liaisons to five Multilateral Development Banks (World Bank, Inter-American Development Bank, European Bank for Reconstruction and Development, Africa Development Bank and Asia Development Bank) to counsel U.S. companies on working with the Banks and on procurement and contracting issues.

The **Manufacturing and Services** (MAS) unit works to strengthen the global competitiveness of U.S. industry, expand market access for U.S. businesses, and increase U.S. exports. As the research arm of ITA, the MAS undertakes industry economic and trade policy analysis, helps formulate U.S. trade policy, participates in trade negotiations, organizes trade capacity building programs, and evaluates the impact of U.S. and foreign regulations on U.S. manufacturing and service industries. The MAS works with other federal agencies, private sector partners and Congress in developing a public policy environment to help advance the competitiveness of U.S. firms at home and abroad.

The **Market Access and Compliance** (MAC) unit monitors foreign country compliance with trade agreements with the United States, identifies compliance problems and market access obstacles, and informs U.S. firms of foreign business practices and opportunities. The MAC has country desk officers with expertise on the commercial, economic, and political climates in their assigned countries. The desk officers focus on resolving trade complaints and market access issues.

ITA has other functions, such as countering unfair foreign trade practices, in order to boost exports. The Import Administration (IA) unit is ITA's lead unit on enforcing trade laws and agreements. Its primary role is to enforce U.S. anti-dumping and countervailing duty laws and to develop and implement other policies and programs aimed at countering unfair foreign trade practices.[19]

ITA is playing a major role under the NEI's goal of boosting exports. It is increasing certain export promotion activities such as conducting trade missions, bringing foreign buyers to U.S. trade shows, and promoting foreign market access for U.S. companies. The ITA also has introduced a New Market Exporter Initiative (NMEI), which works with the ITA's Strategic Partners to identify customers who sell to at least one international market and support those customers in expanding to additional markets. ITA's Strategic Partners include FedEx, UPS, and the U.S. Postal Service. The effort focuses on U.S. SMEs that already are familiar with exporting.[20]

The Administration is requesting an increase of 131 full-time employees and $78.5 million in additional funding in its FY2011 budget request to support its export expansion strategy under the NEI.[21] Total budget authority for ITA in FY2010 was $456 million, though it is unclear what portion of the budget is directly related to export promotion activities (see **Table 3**). The Department of Commerce's FY2011 budget request states that the increase in requested FY2011 funding related to the NEI would be used to help promote growth in the U.S. economy by export promotion services aimed at increasing the volume of U.S. exports and the number of U.S. firms that export. The Administration hopes that the initiative will help U.S. companies be more competitive in the global market and that jobs created through export growth will be associated with higher wages.[22] The ITA plans to focus on increasing the number of SMEs that are exporting to more than one market by 50% over the next five years; expanding SME exports to Brazil, China, India; and increasing exports in fast-growing sectors, such as environmental goods and services, renewable energy, health care, and biotechnology.[23]

Table 3. ITA Budget Authority: FY2002-FY2010 and Request for FY2011
(Millions of U.S. Dollars)

ITA Unit[a]	FY05	FY06	FY07	FY08	FY09	FY10[b]	FY11[c]
U.S. Commercial Service	227	236	235	242	243	258	320
Manufacturing and Services (MAS)[d]	49	49	48	42	49	50	56
Import Administration (IA)	63	60	61	64	67	68	73
Market Access and Compliance (MAC)	44	45	44	46	45	43	56
Administration and Executive Direction	26	26	26	26	25	27	29
Direct Funding	409	416	414	420	429	446	534
Fees	8	8	8	8	9	9	9
Total Budget Authority[e]	417	424	422	428	438	456	544

Sources:

1) For FY2002-FY2009 amounts: Executive Office of the President, *Budget of the United States Government,* Fiscal Years 2005, 2006, 2007, 2008, 2009, 2010, and 2011.
2) For enacted FY2010 amounts: House Congressional Record, H13653, December 8, 2009.
3) For FY2011 request: Executive Office of the President, *Budget of the United States Government,* Fiscal Year 2011.

Notes:

a. Not all ITA units have a direct role in export promotion activities.

b. Estimated.

c. Requested.

d. Formerly the Trade Development unit (prior to 2004).

e. Estimated totals may not add due to rounding.

Export-Import Bank of the United States (Ex-Im Bank)

Ex-Im Bank is the official export credit agency (ECA) of the U.S. government. It maintains finance and insurance programs to facilitate U.S. exports to developing countries, especially in circumstances when alternative financing is not available, to contribute to U.S. employment. Some Ex-Im Bank programs are used to counter export subsidies of other countries. Its main programs are direct loans, export credit guarantees, working capital guarantees, and export credit insurance, and are backed by the full faith and credit of the U.S. government. Ex-Im Bank participates in the regional network of USEACs. The Bank operates under a renewable charter, the *Export-Import Bank Act of 1945*, as amended, and has been re-authorized through September 30, 2011 (P.L. 109-438).[24] Ex-Im Bank charges fees for its services and collects interest on its loans. It is a "self-sustaining institution," using offsetting collections to cover its operations.[25] Congress does not provide funding to the Bank, but does set an upper limit on the level of the Bank's financial activities as part of the annual appropriations process (see **Table 4**).

Table 4. Budget of the Export-Import Bank, FY2005-2011 (in Millions of U.S. Dollars)

	FY05	FY06	FY07	FY08	FY09	FY10[a]	FY11[b]
Total Subsidy Requested	126	187	26	68	41	58	93
Total Subsidy Appropriated	60	100	NA	68	41	58	—
Total Administrative Budget Requested	73	73	75	78	82	84	106
Total Administrative Budget Appropriated	73	73	NA	78	82	84	—
Budget Authority (gross)	477	198	341	585	685	1,316	263
-Appropriated	132	109	99	487	571	1,121	—
-Other	345	89	242	123	158	195	263

Source: Executive Office of the President, *Budget of the United States Government*, various years.

Notes:

a. Estimated.

b. Requested.

Table 5. Ex-Im Bank's Credit and Insurance Authorizations, FY2008-2009 (Millions of U.S. Dollars)

Program	Number of Authorizations		Amount Authorized	
	FY08	FY09	FY08	FY09
Total Authorizations	**2,704**	**2,891**	**$14,399**	**$21,021**
Loans	2	16	$356	$3,033
Guarantees	673	619	$10,179	$11,475
Insurance	2,029	2,256	$3,864	$6,513
Selected Types of Authorizations				
Small Business	2,328	2,540	$3,190	$4,360
Percent of Total Authorizations	86.1%	87.9%	22.2%	20.7%
Environmentally Beneficial	87	88	$227	$394
Percent of Total Authorizations	3.2%	3.0%	1.5%	1.9%
Renewable Energy Authorizations	7	13	$30	$93
Percent of Total Authorizations	0.3%	0.4%	0.2%	0.4%

Source: Ex-Im Bank Annual Reports.

Though the Ex-Im Bank's export promotion budget level reported by the TPCC is small compared to the other federal agencies, Ex-Im Bank is considered by many to have a key role in federal export promotion efforts. In FY2009, Ex-Im Bank authorized over $21 billion in loans, guarantees, and insurance in support of U.S. exports, the largest level in the Bank's history, with a total exposure of nearly $67 billion (see **Table 5**). Officials from the Bank attribute the surge in authorizations to increased private sector demand for government financing after the international financial crisis.

Ex-Im Bank programs must comply with certain congressional directives. The Bank's Charter requires it to make available not less than 20% of its aggregate loan, guarantee, and insurance authority to finance exports directly by small business. The Charter also requires the Bank to promote the export of goods and services related to renewable energy sources. In recent years, appropriations language further has specified the Bank should make available not less than 10% of its aggregate credit and insurance authority for the financing of exports of renewable energy technologies or energy efficient end-use technologies. In FY2010, Ex-Im Bank continued to provide enhanced levels of support to small business exporters and exporters of renewable energy exporters. Ex-Im Bank also continued to engage in outreach to and advocacy for small businesses, including through its five regional offices.

Ex-Im Bank financing support also must meet several other statutory and policy criteria.[26] Congress requires that Ex-Im Bank projects have no adverse effect on U.S. industry. Chiefly, Ex-Im Bank may not support projects that enable foreign production of an exportable good that would compete with U.S. production of a same, or similar, good and that would cause "substantial injury" to U.S. producers. Ex-Im Bank also may not support projects that result in the foreign production of a good that is substantially the same as a good subject to specified U.S. trade measures, such as anti-dumping or countervailing duty investigations. In addition, the Bank places certain limits on the maximum amount of foreign content that can be included in the transactions it supports. Ex-Im Bank is permitted to deny applications for credit for non-financial or non-commercial considerations only in situations where the President, after consultation with relevant congressional committees, determines that such action would be in the national interest and would advance U.S. policy in areas such as international terrorism, nuclear proliferation, environmental protection, and human rights. The power to make such a determination has been delegated to the Secretary of State.[27]

Overseas Private Investment Corporation (OPIC)

OPIC seeks to promote economic growth in developing and emerging economies by providing investment insurance, project financing, and other services for U.S. businesses in those countries, in support of U.S. foreign policy goals. OPIC's programs are intended to promote U.S. private investment by mitigating risks, such as political risks (including currency inconvertibility, expropriation, political violence, and terrorism), for U.S. firms making qualified investment overseas. OPIC conducts its activities on a self-sustaining basis to mobilize and facilitate private capital investment in developing countries.[28] OPIC operates in 156 developing countries and emerging markets. Based on U.S. development and foreign policy priorities, OPIC has placed special emphasis in its activities on supporting small business and microfinance; renewable energy and clean technologies; and Sub-Saharan Africa, the broader Middle East and North Africa region, and Asia.[29]

OPIC's support for international investment is believed to support U.S. exports. Since its creation in 1971, OPIC has supported $188 billion worth of investments overseas, which it reports has generated 830,000 jobs in host countries and supported $72 billion in U.S. exports and 273,000 U.S. jobs.[30]

OPIC has general statutory requirements that govern its support for international investment projects. Under the *Foreign Assistance Act of 1961* (P.L. 97-195), as amended, OPIC is required to ensure that its projects contribute to the economic and social development of a country and also do not have an adverse effect on the U.S. economy or U.S. employment.[31] Also under the Act, OPIC-supported projects can be implemented only in countries that currently have, or are taking steps to adopt and implement, laws that uphold internationally recognized worker rights.[32] The Act includes a national economic interest waiver on the worker rights provision, which states that OPIC shall not be prohibited "from providing any insurance, reinsurance, guaranty, or financing with respect to a country if the President determines that such activities by OPIC would be in the national economic interests of the United States. Any such determination shall be reported in writing to the Congress, together with the reasons for the determination."[33] OPIC further takes into account developmental, environmental, health, safety, human rights, and other considerations when screening projects.[34]

Small Business Administration (SBA)

SBA provides export financing and promotion services to small businesses. **SBA's Office of International Trade** assists with four stages of export promotion: (1) identifying small businesses interested in export promotion; (2) preparing small businesses to export successfully; (3) connecting small businesses to export opportunities; and (4) supporting small businesses once they find export opportunities. SBA also participates in the regional network of USEACs. In FY2009, the SBA's Office of International Trade approved 1,500 loans, totaling over $600 million, to support small businesses in generating export sales. According to SBA, the loans generated export sales of approximately $1.6 billion.[35]

U.S. Department of State[36]

The State Department promotes exports through U.S. embassies abroad that collect and disseminate trade and economic data, identify trade opportunities, brief U.S. businesses, provide advocacy on behalf of U.S. firms, and participate in trade negotiations and monitoring of trade agreements. The **Bureau of Economic Analysis, Energy, and Business Affairs** (EEB) plays a key role in the State Department's export promotion activities.

EEB's **Trade and Policy Programs** (TPP) section participates in formulating U.S. trade policy and negotiating positions under the coordination of the USTR to ensure that U.S. foreign policy goals are considered in trade policy formulation. It also promotes the use and understanding of agricultural biotechnology overseas, and works to maintain open markets for

U.S. biotechnology products. In addition, TPP's Intellectual Property Enforcement Office promotes intellectual property rights protection worldwide, in coordination with other U.S. agencies such as USTR and the U.S. Patent and Trademark Office (USPTO). The unit also works to ensure that foreign governments comply with their trade commitments, sometimes through foreign missions.

Commercial and Business Affairs (CBA), another section of EEB, provides support to U.S. embassies assisting U.S. business operating abroad. Such assistance includes help with resolving regulatory and investment problems, ensuring U.S. firms are afforded equal opportunity, and providing market analysis and commercial information to maximize U.S. commercial opportunities. For countries without Commercial Service officers, CBA uses the Business Facilitation Incentive Fund to engage in trade promotion activities.

U.S. Embassies and Consulates advocate for U.S. businesses overseas. Embassies can provide U.S. exporters with country-specific market information, assist in commercial and investment disputes, and provide expertise on foreign judicial systems.[37]

U.S. Trade and Development Agency (TDA)

TDA operates under a dual mission of promoting economic development and U.S. commercial interests in developing and middle-income countries. TDA works to achieve its mission primarily by supporting the development of modern infrastructure in economic sectors such as transportation, energy and power, and telecommunications through the funding of feasibility studies, technical assistance, and other activities. TDA provides grants to overseas project sponsors (frequently host country governments) who select U.S. companies to conduct TDA-financed activities in the program areas of: (1) trade capacity-building and sector development; and (2) project definition and analysis. These activities are intended to help U.S. firms gain follow-on contracts on infrastructure and industrial projects and to counter similar assistance offered by other foreign governments.

In FY2009, TDA funded 249 activities in 50 countries.[38] Between 1997 and 2006 (the most recent time period for which data are complete), TDA estimated that $300 million in project spending helped to generate $12.4 billion in U.S. exports.[39]

TDA recently launched the International Business Partnership Program, an initiative to host reverse trade missions that will bring prospective overseas buyers to the United States to meet with U.S. companies that export goods and services. TDA also is increasing engagement with the Department of Commerce's Advocacy Center to identify new reverse trade missions and grant opportunities for U.S. exporters.[40]

Office of the U.S. Trade Representative (USTR)

The USTR, within the Executive Office of the President (EOP), develops and implements the coordination of U.S. trade policy, and leads the United States' bilateral, regional, and multilateral trade negotiations, among other responsibilities. The USTR has sought to reduce both tariff and non-tariff barriers to trade through these negotiations. It also investigates unfair foreign trade practices and enforcement of FTAs affecting U.S. goods and services, and it is authorized statutorily to negotiate the removal of these barriers.

The USTR's primary role in export promotion is to expand international market access for U.S. exporters of goods and services. Presently, the USTR is working to resolve outstanding issues in the pending U.S. FTAs with Korea, Panama, and Colombia; to negotiate the Trans-Pacific Partnership (TPP) Agreement; and to enforce U.S. rights secured through existing trade agreements.

U.S. Department of the Treasury

The Department of the Treasury's **Office of Foreign Assets Control** (OFAC) administers and enforces economic and trade sanctions based on U.S. foreign policy and national security goals against targeted foreign countries, terrorists, international narcotics traffickers, and those engaged in activities related to the proliferation of weapons of mass destruction.

The Department of the Treasury is involved in broader efforts with the Administration to address global economic imbalances and to promote an international economic climate that is more supportive of exports, such as through reforming the U.S. financial system and tackling foreign currency exchange issues. While such macroeconomic efforts may help to promote exports, they may not be included in the TPCC's trade promotion budget for the Treasury. According to the NES, a very small portion of Treasury's budget is directed at export promotion activities.

Local Export Assistance

Led by the Department of Commerce's International Trade Administration, U.S. Export Assistance Centers (USEACs) constitute a key component of support services provided by federal government agencies to U.S. exporters. The Department of Commerce, together with SBA, Ex-Im Bank, and USDA, are part of a nationwide network of USEACs that serve as a "one-stop shop" for firms—primarily small- and medium-sized business— that are new to exporting or want to expand their exporting activities. They provide export counseling, planning, and financing services, such as working with firms to identify target markets, to formulate marketing strategies, and to identify export financing options. Through USEACs, the agencies work to coordinate their export education, promotion, and finance services to U.S. businesses.[41] USEACs coordinate with Foreign Commercial Service posts that provide export assistance services.[42] USEACs also work closely with non-federal export service providers, such as state agencies and world trade centers, to provide export assistance for U.S. businesses. USEACs are located in over 100 U.S. cities. Some USEAC services are free, while others are fee-based.[43]

ISSUES FOR CONGRESS

Congressional interest in federal agencies involved in export promotion centers is rooted in an underlying issue of effectiveness. How effective are federal export promotion efforts at supporting U.S. exports and, in turn, supporting U.S. jobs? What agency-specific issues can be addressed to enhance this effectiveness?

Economic Rationales For and Against Federal Export Promotion

A starting point for congressional debates on export promotion often is the economic rationales for and against the involvement of U.S. government agencies in promoting U.S. exports. Advocates of the federal government's export promotion activities argue that such efforts are critical for addressing market failures, such as imperfect information and barriers to entry. Export assistance services to overcome such barriers may be particularly useful for small business exporters, which tend to face greater challenges than larger firms in entering overseas markets.

Federal export promotion efforts also can help to counter foreign governments' export promotion activities. Some supporters consider international export promotion competition to be significant. For example, according to a 2010 Ex-Im Bank report on international export credit competition, in 2009, medium- and long-term official export credit volumes from the Group of 7 (G-7) countries totaled $77 billion.[44] In 2009, among the G-7 countries, France provided the largest level of support at $28 billion, followed by the United States at $17 billion and Germany at $13.3 billion. Official export credit support by emerging market economies such as Brazil, China, and India—which are not a part of the Organization for Economic Cooperation and Development's international arrangement on export credits—is considered to be sizeable, although data is often difficult to obtain. The Ex-Im Bank report estimated that, in 2008, China's medium- and long-term official export credit volumes totaled $59.6 billion, more than the combined G-7 total of $51 billion in that year.[45]

Others, including some economists, view government-funded trade promotion efforts as a subsidy which distorts free markets, because they encourage commercial activities that are not commercially viable, and in doing so, may encourage an inefficient use of resources. Those critical of the government's involvement in export promotion contend that there is little in the way of evidence suggesting that export promotion by the government can have significant effects on U.S. export levels. While critics concede that federal export assistance may help individual firms, they contend that such activities do not influence the overall level of employment and may, in fact, simply shift production among sectors within the economy. Critics also assert that macroeconomic factors, such as global economic growth and exchange rates, hold greater sway over a nation's level of exports.

While there is no consensus on the economic rationales for and against export promotion, it appears that, in light of the recent global economic downturn, U.S. trade policy has converged around the notion of promoting U.S. exports as a way to support U.S. economic growth and employment. U.S. export promotion also has emerged as a means to achieve a rebalancing of the U.S. economy by depending less on domestic consumption for gross domestic product (GDP) growth and more on other sectors of the economy, including exports.

As such, many policymakers have turned to more agency-specific issues in export promotion that are discussed below.

Coordination of Federal Export Promotion Agencies and Activities

Coordination of the U.S. government's export promotion activities has been a longstanding issue of interest for Congress. Since the inception of the TPCC in 1992, the Government Accountability Office (GAO), at the request of Congress, has conducted several studies on the effectiveness of the TPCC in coordinating the export promotion activities of federal government agencies. The TPCC has a mandate to establish a set of priorities for federal export promotion activities, to coordinate a government-wide export promotion framework, and to propose a unified export promotion budget to the President. In practice, however, its effectiveness in fostering interagency coordination often has been more limited.

Interagency coordination by the TPCC inherently is complicated by the fact that multiple agencies are involved in export promotion. These are independent agencies with their own missions, goals, and priorities. Many of these agencies prioritize the promotion of exports, but often, it is within the context of their own agency missions.

The GAO reports that the TPCC has made progress in improving its coordination of export promotion activities, but continues to report shortcomings. Positive developments include improvements in interagency training, joint outreach by agencies to serve small businesses, and enhanced support for the trade promotion activities conducted at U.S. embassies.[46] While the GAO has reported previously that the objectives and priority markets identified in the NES have changed on an annual basis without reflection of the outcomes of the previous year, in 2009 testimony, the GAO noted that the 2008 NES contained information about the status of priority initiatives identified in the prior year's report.[47]

Nevertheless, the GAO has identified a number of areas of ongoing concern related to the TPCC. For example, according to the GAO, the annual *National Export Strategy* reports have several limitations that affect the TPCC's ability to coordinate trade promotion activities. In March 2009, the GAO testified that the NES continues to lack an overall review of member agencies' allocation of resources relative to government-wide export promotion priorities.[48] This may constrain the TPCC's ability to guide progress toward achievement of export promotion goals. In addition, the GAO has testified that the TPCC continues to have limited influence over its member agencies' allocation of resources for trade promotion.

Through the NEI, there is a cabinet-level interagency development that may further enhance interagency coordination. Some policymakers welcome the concerted effort to coordinate export promotion at the federal level through the creation of the Export Promotion Cabinet. Supporters believe that the elevation of export promotion as a policy issue to the cabinet level will ensure that it is given national priority. Commerce Secretary Locke has characterized it as a shift from export promotion being a "some of the time focus" for cabinet agencies and departments to an "all the time focus."[49] However, some critics contend that the NEI essentially is a bureaucratic maneuver that overlays the newly created National Export Cabinet over the existing TPCC. They contend that it does not bring substantive reforms or improvements to coordination of U.S. export promotion.[50]

Funding for Export Promotion Activities by Federal Agencies

Congress has an ongoing interest in the level of U.S. government spending on export promotion activities by federal agencies, and the extent to which such spending is effective and efficient. Over the years, some policymakers have called for greater federal funding for export promotion activities, such as export financing. Supporters argue that increased resources would improve the ability of the U.S. government to provide support to U.S. exporters. For example, in 2006, the GAO reported that the Commerce Department's budget authority for security at overseas offices has risen in recent years, leaving few resources for trade promotion activities at foreign missions.[51] Supporters also contend that the low level of federal spending on export promotion activities, compared to those of foreign governments, places U.S. firms at a competitive disadvantage in the global marketplace.[52] Greater spending, they argue, would enhance the ability of the federal government to equip U.S. firms with the tools necessary to compete with foreign firms that have access to similar support through their national programs. It also would allow the United States to counter the unfair trading practices of foreign countries and help "level the playing field" for U.S. exporters.

Some critics of policy proposals to increase funding contend that these programs are funded adequately, and that the challenge primarily is about using resources efficiently. For example, some groups may take issue with the fact that while agricultural goods accounted for about 11% of total U.S. exports in 2009, federal support for agricultural exports accounts for nearly half of the TPCC export promotion budget. They may contend that federal government support for agricultural exports is inefficient. Some critics assert that it is difficult to make assessments of which federal export promotion programs should receive greater federal funding. As mentioned before, the GAO continues to find that the NES lacks "an overall review of agencies' allocation of resources relative to government-wide export promotion priorities."[53]

Reorganization or Consolidation of Federal Agencies Involved in Export Promotion

Over the past few decades, Congress has considered several legislative proposals to reorganize trade policy functions, such as consolidating all U.S. export- or trade-related programs under one federal agency to provide the U.S. exporting community with a "one-stop" source of export promotion services. Given the multiple different federal government agencies involved in export promotion, some policymakers are concerned that certain functions and activities of the agencies may be duplicative. Some also are concerned that export promotion responsibilities are spread too diffusely across the U.S. government. In addition, some observers consider the diverse range of policy goals that fall under U.S. export promotion policy challenging to balance. Goals range from increasing the level of exports to lowering the U.S. trade deficit to supporting SME exporters to promoting renewable energy and clean technology exports.

On the one hand, proponents of consolidation proposals believe that they may eliminate duplication of federal export promotion services, provide a more streamlined rationale for U.S. export promotion services based on more clearly defined goals, and reduce overall costs of such programs. They argue that federal export promotion efforts could be enhanced through a more centralized government body.

On the other hand, critics contend that such proposals could result in the creation of a large, costly federal bureaucracy. They also assert that the diffusion of export promotion responsibilities across federal government agencies helps to advance various aspects of U.S. export promotion policy. Advocates of particular types of exporters, such as SMEs or agricultural exporters, may be concerned that such a "one-stop" federal source may not be responsive to their unique needs.

Export Promotion Outlook

With the continued focus on U.S. economic growth and job creation, export promotion issues may figure prominently in the 112th Congress. In its oversight role, Congress may continue to debate the best approaches to coordination, funding, and reorganization of federal government agencies involved in export promotion in order to support U.S. export levels and U.S. jobs, and may consider introducing legislation to address such concerns. Going forward, the National Export Initiative has the potential to have significant bearing on the coordination, budgets, and activities of federal government agencies involved in export promotion.

Acknowledgments

The authors wish to thank the following CRS colleagues who provided helpful input on this report: Raymond J. Ahearn, William H. Cooper, Mary A. Irace, Wayne M. Morrison, and Carolyn C. Smith.

End Notes

[1] P.L. 102-429, approved October 21, 1992.

[2] Trade Promotion Coordinating Committee (TPCC), *2008 National Export Strategy: The New Global Main Street*, October 2008.

[3] U.S. Government Accountability Office (GAO), *Export Promotion: Increases in Commercial Service Workforce Should Be Better Planned*, GAO-10-874, August 2010, p. 17.

[4] "National Export Initiative," Executive Order 13534 of March 11, 2010, 75 *Federal Register* 12433, March 16, 2010.

[5] Department of Commerce, "Commerce Secretary Gary Locke Unveils Details of the National Export Initiative," press release, February 4, 2010, http://trade.gov/press/press_releases/2010/nei_020410.asp.

[6] *Report to the President on the National Export Initiative: The Export Promotion Cabinet's Plan for Doubling U.S. Exports in Five Years*, Washington, D.C., September 2010, pp. 5-7.

[7] Ibid., pp.23-24.

[8] U.S. General Accounting Office, *Export Promotion: Mixed Progress in Achieving a Governmentwide Strategy*, GAO-02-850, September 2002. Patrick Mendis and Leah Green, "Government-Wide Collaboration Boosts National Trade," *The Public Manager*, Spring 2010, pp. 43-47.

[9] GAO, *Export Promotion: Trade Promotion Coordinating Committee's Role Remains Limited*, GAO-06-660T, April 26, 2006.

[10] Office of the U.S. Trade Representative (USTR), *2009 National Trade Estimate Report on Foreign Trade Barriers*.

[11] For extensive detail on each of these market development program, see *FAS Administered Programs—Market Development Programs*, available at http://www.fas.usda.gov/mos/marketdev.asp.

[12] The Commodity Credit Corporation (CCC) is a wholly owned government corporation created in 1933 to stabilize, support, and protect farm income and prices (federally chartered by the CCC Charter Act of 1948, P.L. 80-806). The CCC is essentially a financing institution for USDA's farm price and income commodity support and agricultural export programs. It is authorized to buy, sell, lend, make payments and engage in other activities for the purpose of increasing production, stabilizing prices, assuring adequate supplies, and facilitating the efficient marketing of agricultural commodities. The export programs funded through CCC are administered by the Foreign Agricultural Service. The CCC has the authority to borrow up to $30 billion from the U.S. Treasury to carry out its obligations. Net losses from its operations subsequently are restored through the congressional appropriations process.

[13] U.S. Department of Agriculture, Foreign Agricultural Service, *The Competition in 2002: U.S. and Competitor Expenditures on Export Promotion for Agricultural, Forestry, and Fishery Products*, August, 2004, viewed at http://www.fas.usda.gov/cmp/com-study/2002/2002.pdf.

[14] Specialty crops include fruit, vegetable, tree nut, and nursery crops. Sanitary and phytosanitary (SPS) measures, according to the WTO definition, are measures "taken to protect against risks linked to food safety, animal health and plant protection or to prevent or limit damage within the territory of a Member from the entry, establishment and spread of pests." WTO, Doha Development Agenda, Trade Capacity Building Database, at http://tcbdb.wto.org/trta_subcategory.aspx?cat=33113.

[15] FAS's *Selling Products Overseas* web page has links to various kinds of assistance FAS can provide to potential exporters, at http://www.fas.usda.gov/agx/exporter_assistance.asp.

[16] Program level funding for USDA's Market Development and Export Financing Programs (**Table 2**) differs from TPCC-reported USDA program level funding for trade promotion (**Table 1**). This may be because the former's program level funding includes a broader array of activities than the latter. The USDA-specific use of program level "represents the gross value of all financial assistance USDA provides to the public. This assistance may be in the form of grants, guaranteed or direct loans, cost-sharing, professional services such as research or technical assistance, or in-kind benefits such as commodities."

[17] USDA, *FY2011 Budget Summary and Annual Performance Plan*, p. 45, available at http://www.obpa.usda.gov/budsum/FY11budsum.pdf.

[18] See [https://www.trade.gov] for more information on the Trade Promotion and U.S. Foreign Commercial Service of the International Trade Administration (ITA).

[19] For more information on U.S. anti-dumping and countervailing duty laws, see CRS Report RL32371, *Trade Remedies: A Primer*, by Vivian C. Jones.

[20] Department of Commerce, ITA, "New Market Exporter Initiative," available at http://trade.gov/nei/new-market-exporter-initiative.asp.

[21] ITA, *FY2011 Budget in Brief*, available at http://www.osec.doc.gov/bmi/budget/11BiB/ITA.pdf.

[22] Ibid.

[23] Department of Commerce, "Commerce Secretary Gary Locke Unveils Details of the National Export Initiative," press release, February 4, 2010, http://trade.gov/press/press_releases/2010/nei_020410.asp.

[24] For more information on the Export-Import Bank (Ex-Im Bank), see CRS Report 98-568, *Export-Import Bank: Background and Legislative Issues*, by Shayerah Ilias.

[25] Ex-Im Bank, *Annual Report 2008*.

[26] Additional information about Ex-Im Bank's policies are available at: [http://www.exim.gov/ products/ policies/index.cfm].

[27] U.S. Code Title 12, Chapter 6a, Section 635(b)(1)(B)(ii).

[28] For more information on OPIC, see CRS Report 98-567, *The Overseas Private Investment Corporation: Background and Legislative Issues*, by Shayerah Ilias.

[29] Fiscal Year 2011 Foreign Operations Congressional Budget Justification.

[30] OPIC, *OPIC 2009 Annual Report*, p. 4.

[31] Sec. 231(1) and Sec. 231(3)(e)(2)(k), et seq. of the *Foreign Assistance Act of 1961* (P.L. 97-195), as amended.

[32] Sec. 231A(1) of the *Foreign Assistance Act of 1961* (P.L. 97-195), as amended.

[33] Sec. 231A(3) of the *Foreign Assistance Act of 1961* (P.L. 97-195), as amended.

[34] OPIC, *OPIC Annual Policy Report*, Fiscal Year 2008, March 2008.

[35] Small Business Administration (SBA), *FY2011 Congressional Budget Justification and FY2009 Annual Performance Report*, p. 48, http://www.sba.gov/idc/groups/public/ documents/sba_homepage/ fy_2011_ cbj_09_ apr.pdf.

[36] This section draws on language written by Ian F. Fergusson.

[37] Department of State, Bureau of Public Affairs, "The National Export Initiative: Stimulating Global Economic Growth Through U.S. Exports," press release, March 24, 2010, http://www.state scp/fs/2010/ 134811.htm.

[38] U.S. Trade and Development Agency (TDA), *Congressional Budget Justification of the U.S. Trade and Development Agency: Fiscal Year 2011*, Attachment 1.

[39] TDA, Ibid., p. 8.

[40] TDA, "Statement by Leocadia I. Zak, Director, U.S. Trade and Development Agency, National Export Initiative, Denver, CO," press release, March 22, 2010, http://www.ustda.gov/news/speeches/2010/US/NEI OutreachLZRemarks_032210.pdf.

[41] U.S. General Accounting Office, *U.S. Export Assistance Centers' Efforts to Support U.S. Business*, GAO/T-NSIAD- 99 -252, September 9, 1999. Telephone conversation with Ex-Im Bank official, March 5, 2009.

[42] GAO, *Export Promotion: Increases in Commercial Service Workforce Should Be Better Planned*, GAO-10-874, August 2010, p. 7.

[43] Department of Commerce, CommerceConnect, "U.S. Export Assistance Centers," http://www.commerceconnect.gov/connections/programs/program000078.asp.

[44] The Group of 7 (G-7) countries are Canada, France, Germany, Italy, Japan, the United Kingdom, and the United States.

[45] Ex-Im Bank, *Report to the U.S. Congress on Export Credit Competition and the Export-Import Bank of the United States*, June 2010, pp. 10-11. Emerging economies data for 2009 was not available.

[46] GAO-06-660T, April 26, 2006, pp. 9-11. GAO, *International Trade: Effective Export Programs Can Help in Achieving U.S. Economic Goals*, GAO-09-480T, March 17, 2009, p. 3.

[47] GAO, *International Trade: Effective Export Programs Can Help in Achieving U.S. Economic Goals*, GAO-09-480T, March 17, 2009, p. 3.

[48] GAO-09-480T, March 17, 2009, p. 3.

[49] Diana Ransom, "Obama's Math: More Exports Equals More Jobs," *Wall Street Journal*, February 5, 2010.

[50] Sherle R. Schwenninger and Samuel Sherraden, *Getting Serious About Doubling U.S. Exports*, New America Foundation, Talking Points, March 17, 2010.

[51] GAO-06-660T, April 26, 2006, p. 8.

[52] Kent Hoover, "Business groups praise export plan, but want more," *Washington Business Journal*, February 15, 2010, http://www.bizjournals.com/extraedge/washingtonbureau/archive/2010/02/15/bureau1.html.

[53] GAO-09-480T, March 17, 2009, p. 3.

In: U.S. Export Programs and Promotion Tools
Editor: Steven D. Braghoff
ISBN: 978-1-60741-328-8

Chapter 2

EXPORT-IMPORT BANK: BACKGROUND AND LEGISLATIVE ISSUES

Shayerah Ilias

SUMMARY

The Export-Import Bank (Ex-Im Bank) is the chief U.S. government agency that helps finance American exports of manufactured goods and services with the objective of contributing to the employment of U.S. workers. (For additional information, see the Bank's Internet site: http://www.exim.gov.) With an annual budget of around $200 million, the Bank finances less than 1% of U.S. exports a year. Ex-Im Bank provides loan guarantees and insurance to commercial banks to make trade credits available to U.S. exporters. The Bank also offers direct financing to U.S. exporters, primarily to counter subsidized trade credits offered to foreign exporters by their governments.

On December 20, 2006, President Bush signed P.L. 109-438, to reauthorize the Bank's authority through September 30, 2011. Since the FY2008 appropriations, Ex-Im Bank has been a "self-sustaining" agency for appropriations purposes. The Bank funds it administrative and program costs through fee income generated from its financing programs.

On December 16, 2009, President Obama signed the Consolidated Appropriations Act of 2010 (P.L. 111-17), which authorized a limit of $58 million on the total amount that Ex-Im Bank can spend on its loan, guarantees, and insurance programs and a limit of $83.88 million for the Bank's administrative expenses. In addition, under the legislation, offsetting collections in excess of obligations are to be available for use in the following three fiscal years. For FY2011, the President requested a limit of $92.7 million on the total about the Bank can spend on its loan, guarantees, and insurance programs and a limit of $105.6 million for the Bank's administrative expenses, a significant increase from the FY2010 budget request.

BACKGROUND

The Export-Import Bank (Ex-Im Bank) is an independent U.S. government agency that is charged with financing and promoting exports of U.S. manufactured goods and services with the objective of contributing to the employment of U.S. workers. To accomplish these goals, Ex-Im Bank uses its authority and resources to: assume commercial and political risks that exporters or private financial institutions are unwilling, or unable, to undertake alone; overcome maturity and other limitations in private sector export financing; and assist U.S. exporters to meet foreign, officially sponsored, export credit competition. The Bank operates under a renewable charter, the Export-Import Bank Act of 1945, as amended, and has been authorized through September 30, 2011. The charter requires that all of the Bank's financing have a reasonable assurance of repayment and directs the Bank to supplement, and to not compete with, private capital.

Ex-Im Bank is one of twenty federal government agencies that are a part of the U.S. Trade Promotion Coordinating Committee (TPCC), an interagency committee created by the Export Enhancement Act of 1992 (P.L. 102-429). The TPCC is chaired by the Department of Commerce to coordinate and to set priorities for the federal agencies involved in export promotion.

The international financial crisis and global economic downturn have renewed congressional interest in Ex-Im Bank, and federal export promotion activities more broadly, as a means of generating U.S. jobs and contributing to U.S. economic recovery. In the 2010 State of the Union address, President Obama announced a goal of doubling U.S. exports over the next five years to support two million new jobs in the United States. The President also outlined a National Export Initiative (NEI) that is intended to grow U.S. exports by providing more funding, more focus, and more coordination for federal export promotion activities. The NEI creates an Export Promotion Cabinet consisting of principals from key agencies involved in export promotion (including Ex-Im Bank, Department of Commerce, Department of State, Department of the Treasury, Office of the U.S. Trade Representative, Small Business Administration, and U.S. Department of Agriculture). The Export Promotion Cabinet would coordinate with the TPCC.[1]

BUDGET

When it was initially established, Ex-Im Bank was capitalized by an appropriation of $1 billion from the U.S. Treasury. The Bank also is authorized to borrow up to $6 billion directly from the Treasury, and it may draw upon a substantial line of credit with the Federal Financing Bank (FFB).[2] Ex-Im Bank uses its Treasury borrowings to finance its short-term needs, and repays the Treasury quarterly from loan repayments and by borrowing from the FFB on a medium-and long-term basis. Ex-Im Bank has not borrowed from the FFB after FY1997.[3]

The Omnibus Budget Reconciliation Act of 1990 (P.L. 101-508) included two sections with implications for the Export-Import Bank's budget. Under the terms of the Budget Enforcement Act of 1990 (Title XIII), Congress appropriates the estimated amount of subsidy the Bank expects to expend throughout all of its credit programs, including direct loans, guarantees, and insurance, as indicated in **Table 1**. Congress no longer sets separate limits on the amount of loans, guarantees, and insurance the Bank can authorize, but the Bank continues to provide estimates of the amounts of activity it expects to undertake. Under the Federal Credit Reform Act of 1990 (Title V), for a given fiscal year, the cost of federal credit activities, including those of Ex-Im Bank, is reported on an accrual basis equivalent with other federal spending, rather than on a cash flow basis, as used previously. [4] The Bank's estimates now allocate budgetary resources to reserve against the estimated risk of loss to the Bank.

As of FY2008, the Ex-Im Bank has been "self-sustaining" for appropriations purposes.[5] Since then, in the President's annual budget request, the President has requested, and Congress has approved, that offsetting collections would count against the appropriation of subsidy and administrative expenses from the General Fund and that the appropriation is expected to be $0. In essence, the President requests approval for the level of expenses that Ex-Im Bank would cover on its own.

Table 1. Budget of the Export-Import Bank, FY2005-2011 (in Millions of U.S. Dollars)

	FY05	FY06	FY07	FY08	FY09	FY10	FY11
Total Subsidy Requested	126	187	26	68	41	58	93
Total Subsidy Appropriated	60	100	NA	68	41	58	—
Total Administrative Budget Requested	73	73	75	78	82	84	106
Total Administrative Budget Appropriated	73	73	NA	78	82	84	—
Operating Expenses	661	353	366	590	690	1,261	207
-Direct Loan Subsidy	—	1	—	—	8	17	8
-Guarantee Loan Subsidy	227	185	51	25	30	58	93
-Loan Modifications	14	5	8	2	—	—	—
-Administrative Expenses	73	73	73	78	82	84	106
-Re-estimates of Subsidy Costs	347	189	241	487	570	1,102	—
Budget Authority (gross)	477	198	341	585	685	1,316	263
-Appropriated	132	109	99	487	571	1,121	—
-Other	345	89	242	123	158	195	263
Budget Resources	1,252	812	712	934	1,031	1,641	643
-Budget Authority (gross)	477	188	341	585	685	1,316	263
-Recoveries from previous years	70	22	—	-3	-4	—	—
-Unobligated resources start of year	705	592	371	123	342	325	380
-Unobligated resources end of year	591	371	346	89	325	380	436
Budget Authority (net)	476	198	340	462	527	1,121	—
Outlays (net)	681	318	450	468	511	1,104	-74

Source: Office of Management and Budget. *Budget of the United States Government*, various issues. Washington, U.S. Government Printing Office.

Note: Data for FY2010 and FY2011 are requested or estimated amounts.

In FY2009, the Bank received $292.1 million in offsetting collections, which are receipts in excess of estimated credit losses. Of this amount, the Bank directed $81.5 million to fund its administrative expenses to conduct its credit portfolio; returned $135.6 million to the U.S. Treasury; and retained and carried over $75 million to FY2010. During FY2008, the Bank collected $122.8 million in offsetting collections. Of this amount, $78 million was used to pay the Bank's credit-related administrative expenses and $44.8 million was retained and carried over to FY2009.[6]

For FY2010, the Consolidated Appropriations Act of 2010 (P.L. 111-17) approved a limit of $58 million on the total amount that Ex-Im Bank can spend on its loan, guarantees, and insurance programs and a limit of $83.88 million for the Bank's administrative expenses to conduct its credit and insurance programs. In addition, offsetting collections in excess of obligations are to be available for use in the following three fiscal years. In previous years, appropriations legislation set a limit on the amount of offsetting collections in excess of obligations that could remain available for use in subsequent fiscal years.

For FY2011, the President requested a limit of $92.7 million on the total amount that the Bank can spend on its loan, guarantees, and insurance programs, a 60% increase over the FY2010 amount. The President also requested a limit of $105.6 million for the Bank's administrative expenses to conduct its credit and insurance programs, a more than 25% increase over the FY2010 amount. This is in line with the President's recent emphasis on export promotion activities.

Authorizations and Exposure

In FY2009, Ex-Im Bank approved 2,891 transactions of credit and insurance support. The Bank's authorizations totaled $21 billion, the highest level of authorizations in any fiscal year in the history of the Bank, and is estimated to support about $26 billion in U.S. exports of goods and services. In comparison, in FY2008, Bank approved 2,704 transactions that totaled $14 billion and were estimated to support about $20 billion U.S. exports (see **Table 2**).

The Bank's Charter requires it to make available not less than 20% of its aggregate loan, guarantee, and insurance authority to finance exports directly by small business.[7] The Charter also requires the Bank to promote the export of goods and services related to renewable energy sources.[8] In recent years, appropriations language further has specified the Bank should make available not less than 10% of its aggregate credit and insurance authority for the financing of exports of renewable energy technologies or energy efficient end-use technologies. While Ex-Im Bank can make financing available for certain purposes, if U.S. firms do not have sufficient interests or commercial incentives for exporting in particular markets, then they may not seek out Ex-Im Bank support.

The Bank's authority to lend, guarantee, and insure is limited to a total of $100 billion. The outstanding principal amount of all loans made, guaranteed, or insured by the Ex-Im Bank is charged at the full value against the $100 billion limitation. In FY2009, the Bank had an exposure of nearly $68 billion in more than 165 countries. The Bank's exposure was concentrated, by industrial sector, in air transportation (48.8%) and, geographically, in Asia (41.6%).[9]

Table 2. Ex-Im Bank's Credit and Insurance Authorizations, FY2008-2009 (in Millions of U.S. Dollars)

Program	Number of Authorizations		Amount Authorized	
	2008	2009	2008	2009
Total Authorizations	**2,704**	**2,891**	**$14,399**	**$21,021**
Loans	2	16	$356	$3,033
Guarantees	673	619	$10,179	$11,475
Insurance	2,029	2,256	$3,864	$6,513
Selected Types of Authorizations				
Small Business	2,328	2,540	$3,190	$4,360
Percent of Total Authorizations	86.1%	87.9%	22.2%	20.7%
Environmentally Beneficial	87	88	$227	$394
Percent of Total Authorizations	3.2%	3.0%	1.5%	1.9%
Renewable Energy Authorizations	7	13	$30	$93
Percent of Total Authorizations	0.3%	0.4%	0.2%	0.4%

Source: Ex-Im Bank Annual Reports

PROGRAMS

Ex-Im Bank has three main financial products it uses to support U.S. exports: direct loans, loan guarantees, and export credit insurance. The Bank's financing programs are used primarily to aid U.S. exporters in instances where they face a foreign competitor that is receiving officially subsidized financing by a foreign government, or when private sector financing is unavailable. They are made primarily to counter attempts by foreign governments to sway purchases in favor of their exporters solely on the basis of subsidized financing, rather than on market conditions (price, quality, etc.), and to enforce internationally agreed upon terms and conditions for export financing.

Direct Loans

Prior to 1980, the Bank's direct lending program was its chief financing vehicle, which it used to finance such capital-intensive exports as commercial aircraft and nuclear power plants. Both the budget authority requested by the Administration and the level approved by the Congress for the Bank's direct lending were sharply reduced during the 1980s. The direct loans carry fixed interest rates and generally are made at terms that are the most attractive allowed under the provisions of international agreements. The Bank also has an Intermediary Credit Program it uses to offer medium- and long-term fixed-rate financing to buyers of U.S. exports, but U.S. exporters also must face officially subsidized foreign competition to qualify for this program.

Lately, Ex-Im Bank has worked to increase access to direct loans by engaging with borrowers on a case-by-case basis to structure transactions to adapt to current financial conditions. In FY2009, the Bank authorized 16 direct loans totaling about $3 billion. Direct loan transactions included $913 million to finance exports of General Electric Company goods to Saudi Arabia, $900 million in long-term direct loans to Petróleas Mexicanos (PEMEX) for oil and gas equipment; and $500 million to Textron Financial Corp. to continue financing helicopters and business aircraft exports.[10] This represents a significant increase from FY2008, when the Bank's direct loans totaled $356 million. In FY2008, Ex-Im Bank made two direct loans, one to Brazil for helicopters ($11.8 million) and the other to Ghana for equipment for a rural electrification project ($344.2 million). [11] In comparison, in FY2007, the Bank made no direct loans, and in FY2006 it authorized three.

As part of its direct lending program, the Bank has a tied aid "war chest" it uses to counter specific projects that are receiving foreign officially subsidized export financing. Tied aid credits and mixed credits are two methods whereby governments provide their exporters with official assistance to promote exports. Tied aid credits include loans and grants which reduce financing costs below market rates for exporters and which are tied to the procurement of goods and services from the donor country. Mixed credits combine concessional government financing (funds at below market rates or terms) with commercial or near-commercial funds to produce an overall rate that is lower than market-based interest rates and carries more lenient loan terms. The United States does tie substantial amounts of its agricultural and military aid to U.S. goods, but it generally has avoided using such financing to promote American capital goods exports. Funds for the tied aid war chest are available to the Bank from the Treasury Department and are subtracted from the Bank's direct credit resources. Applications for the tied aid fund are subject to review by the Treasury Department.

Export Credit Guarantees and Insurance

Export credit guarantees and insurance are the main programs the Bank uses to assist American exporters. Both programs reduce some of the risks involved in exporting by insuring against commercial or political uncertainty. There is an important distinction, however, between the two programs. Insurance coverage is more conditional than a guarantee. Insurance coverage carries various conditions that must be met by the insured before the Bank will pay off a claim. In contrast, a guarantee is a commitment made to a commercial bank by the Export-Import Bank that promises full repayment with few, if any, conditions attached.

Ex-Im Bank also offers a working capital guarantee program that it uses to facilitate working capital financing to small- and medium-sized businesses. Businesses that qualify have exporting potential but need working capital funds to produce or market their goods or services for export. Guarantees are offered to qualified lenders (primarily commercial banks) in order to facilitate loans to small businesses.

Recent Developments

Beginning with the collapse of the U.S. housing market in October 2008, the international financial crisis has caused turmoil in the financial markets of both developed and developing countries. It also has been coupled with a global economic turndown. U.S. exporters have been affected by a contraction in the global demand for exports and a tightening of private sector credit and insurance.[12] Ex-Im Bank has reported a significant increase in demand for its services in response to the liquidity shortage in the private sector. The Bank has noted that small businesses especially have faced difficulty accessing credit in light of the financial crisis. A surge in insurance coverage authorizations for small business increased the level of authorizations conducted by the Bank in FY2009. Due to global economic conditions and resulting deterioration of the credit quality of the Bank's existing portfolio, the weighted-average risk rating for the Bank's outstanding portfolio increased from FY2008 to FY2009.[13]

In order to counter the commercial and liquidity shortages associated with the global financial crisis, Ex-Im Bank has taken several actions to enhance its financing products. In October 2008, the Bank started offering U.S. small businesses a 15% premium-rate reduction for certain insurance policies. The Bank also took measures to expand coverage under and to provide flexible financing terms for its working capital guarantee program. In addition, the Bank has worked to increase access to direct loans by engaging with borrowers on a case-by-case basis to structure transactions to adapt to the current financial conditions.[14]

In February 2009, a settlement was reached in an environmental lawsuit brought by Friends of the Earth, Greenpeace, and four cities (Boulder, Colorado and the cities of Arcata, Santa Monica, and Oakland in California) against the Export-Import Bank and another U.S. government agency, the Overseas Private Investment Corporation (OPIC), in 2002.[15] In the lawsuit, the environmental groups and cities alleged that Ex-Im Bank and OPIC provided more than $32 billion in financing and insurance from 1990 to 2003, without assessing the extent to which the projects contributed to climate change in the United States as required by the National Environmental Policy Act (P.L. 91-190). Under the settlement, Ex-Im Bank is able to continue funding fossil fuel projects, but it must disclose the estimated carbon dioxide emissions from potential transactions for such projects on its website; make public its determinations as to whether the National Environmental Policy Act applies to specific transactions involving fossil fuel projects and provide opportunity for comment; develop and implement a carbon policy in cooperation with plaintiff representatives that will include a $250 million renewable energy loan facility; and promote consideration of climate change issues among export credit agencies with the Organization of Economic Development (OECD).[16] Observers point out that the Ex-Im Bank has had a track record of promoting environmentally friendly exports and assessing the environmental impact of its projects since the early 1990s. More recently, in November 2009, the Bank adopted a carbon policy to support U.S. exports of environmentally friendly exports and to enhance transparency in the tracking and reporting of carbon dioxide emissions of projects supported by the Bank.[17]

In November and December of 2008, two groups of Members of Congress sent letters to the Export-Import Bank calling on the Bank to ensure that its projects do not conflict with national security and to end loan guarantees to companies doing key business with Iran. The December 2008 letter requested the Bank to rescind loan guarantees worth $900 million made to the Indian company Reliance Industries Limited (RIL) until the company agrees to stop exporting gasoline to Iran. RIL is reported to provide Iran with up to 30% of its imports of gasoline.[18] The Ex-Im Bank authorized two loan guarantees to RIL, one in July 2007 for supporting the company's petroleum refinery equipment and services ($500 million) and the other in August 2008 for oil and gas development and exploration in India's Bay of Bengal region ($400 million).[19] Members raised concerns about the foreign policy and national security implications of providing loans to RIL. Since the letter, in January 2009, RIL reportedly announced that it will terminate gasoline sales to Iran once its current contractual obligations expire.[20] The Bank is allowed to deny applications for credit on the basis of non-financial and non-commercial considerations in cases where the President, in consultation with the House Financial Services Committee and Senate Banking, Housing and Urban Affairs Committee, determines that the denial of such applications would advance U.S. national interests.[21]

In 2007, several individuals were charged with scheming to defraud Ex-Im Bank. In one case, an exporter, buyer, and broker all allegedly conspired to misappropriate loan proceeds from an Ex-Im Bank-supported loan.[22] Convictions were obtained in 2008 for some individuals charged in connection with fraud schemes.[23] Fraud can waste Bank resources and undermine the Bank's programs. In response to concerns about fraud, Ex-Im Bank adopted new guidelines for its transaction partners (lenders, brokers, and exporters) in January 2008 to reduce the risk of fraud, "Transaction Due Diligence Best Practices." These guidelines consist of a series of questions to help transaction partners undertake effective due diligence and assess the risk of fraud in their transactions. Applicants for Ex-Im Bank assistance are under no legal obligation to follow the guidelines, but they are written to help the applicants prevent financial and legal losses as well as to help Ex-Im Bank prevent fraud. In addition to reducing the risk of fraud, these guidelines aim to decrease the processing time for applications, which has been a concern in the business community.

International Agreements

The United States generally opposes subsidies for exports of commercial products. (Nevertheless, like most countries, the United States has in place procurement policies that seek to assure that most U.S. foreign assistance funds are spent by the recipients on U.S. goods and services.) Since the 1970s, the United States has led efforts within the Organization for Economic Cooperation and Development (OECD) to adopt international protocols which reduce the subsidy level in export credits by raising the interest rates on government-provided export credits to more closely reflect market levels.

The primary agreement governing export credits is the OECD "Arrangement on Officially Supported Export Credits" (the "OECD Arrangement"), which was concluded in November 1991 and has been revised. Participants agreed to tighten further restrictions on the use of tied-aid. The participants agreed that projects would be financially viable, and commercial credits would be prohibited from using tied or partially untied aid credits, except for credits to the least developed countries where per capita income is below $2,465. Moreover, the agreement set up tests and consultation procedures to distinguish between projects that should be financed on market or official export credit terms, and those that legitimately require such aid funds. In addition to agreements on credit terms, OECD member countries have agreed to other guidelines for official export credit. In 2007, OECD member countries agreed to revise guidelines on environmental procedures, referred to as "Common Approaches on Environment and Officially Supported Export Credits" (the "Common Approaches"). These environmental guidelines call for member governments to review projects for potential environmental impacts and to assess them against international standards, such as those of the World Bank. They also call for more public disclosure for environmentally sensitive projects. The OECD also adopted new guidelines on sustainable lending principles that aim to help developing countries avoid a renewed build-up of debt after receiving debt relief.

Another issue of concern is that some countries outside of the OECD, such as China, are becoming major providers of official export credit finance. To the extent that these countries' export credit agencies provide financing on terms that are more advantageous than those allowed within the OECD Arrangement, Ex-Im Bank and other OECD export credit agencies may find it difficult to compete with such export credit programs.

U.S. exporters and others also have expressed doubts about the effectiveness of international efforts to stem officially subsidized trade financing. While the OECD agreement appears to be reducing most direct government subsidies to trade financing, a number of countries have found a way around the agreement through market windows, or subsidized trade financing through ostensibly private financial institutions that are not subject to the agreement. The agreement also has a number of limitations, including the difficulty of defining commercially viable projects; and the presence of an "escape clause" that allows countries to proceed with a tied aid offer, despite objections by other participants, if that country claims that the project is in its national interest. Moreover, the agreement contains no explicit enforcement mechanism. The effectiveness of the agreement also depends on the accuracy and openness of tied aid offers reported to the OECD, but the OECD does not confirm or verify the accuracy of the data provided by its members.[24]

Congressional Oversight

Congress does not directly approve individual Ex-Im Bank transactions, but has a number of oversight responsibilities concerning the Bank and its activities. The Senate confirms Presidential appointments to the Bank's Board of Directors and Congress authorizes the Bank's legal charter for a period of time chosen by Congress. At times, Congress has required an annual reauthorization of the Bank's legal charter, and at other times has authorized the Bank for periods that have varied from two to five years. Congress also approves an annual appropriation for the Bank that sets an upper limit on the level of the Bank's financial activities. In addition, Congress can always amend or alter the Bank's governing legislation as it deems appropriate. Members of Congress and Congressional Committees can request that the Bank's President consult with them or testify before committees, with some qualifications.

President Bush signed P.L. 109-438, the Export-Import Bank Reauthorization Act of 2006, on December 20, 2006. This act reauthorizes the Bank through September 30, 2011. Among its provisions, the act created a Small Business Division within the Bank that is responsible for conducting research, tailoring products to small business needs, and increasing loans to small business concerns. The measure also extends the authority of the Advisory Committee on Sub-Saharan Africa through FY2011. In addition, the measure directs the Bank to submit annually to Congress a list of U.S. commercial sectors and products that could suffer "adverse economic impact" due to Ex-Im Bank support of projects abroad. The measure encourages the Bank to make greater use of its "tied aid" facility, but also provides a mechanism for the Secretary of the Treasury to oppose decisions made by the Bank's board of Directors to match an offer of tied aid by a foreign entity. The measure also requires that the Bank determine whether an entity receiving Ex-Im Bank support could produce goods other than those specified on its application in order to circumvent prohibitions on supporting projects abroad that could compete with U.S. firms.

EXPORT-IMPORT BANK DEBATE

One rationale for the Export-Import Bank is the acknowledged competition among nations' official export financing agencies. Some Ex-Im Bank supporters maintain that the Bank's programs are necessary for U.S. exporters to compete with foreign subsidized export financing and also to pressure foreign governments to eliminate concessionary financing.

However, among some critics of the Bank, there is doubt that a nation can improve its welfare or level of employment over the long run by subsidizing exports. Economists generally maintain that economic policies within individual countries are the prime factors which determine interest rates, capital flows, and exchange rates, and the overall level of a nation's exports. As a result, they hold that subsidizing export financing merely shifts production among sectors within the economy, but does not add to the overall level of economic activity, and subsidizes foreign consumption at the expense of the domestic economy. From this point of view, promoting exports through subsidized financing or through government-backed insurance and guarantees will not permanently raise the level of employment in the economy, but alters the composition of employment among the various sectors of the economy.

In response, some supporters highlight that the Bank is required by its charter to provide U.S. exporters with financing terms that are "fully competitive" with those offered by other trade financing institutions. These and other supporters of the Bank, also stress that deficiencies in financial markets bias those markets against exports of high value, long-term assets.

Some opponents also argue that, by providing financing or insurance for exporters that the market seems unwilling, or unable, to provide, Ex-Im Bank's activities draw from the financial resources within the economy that would be available for other uses. Such "opportunity costs," while impossible to estimate, could be potentially significant. Another opposition argument is that subsidized export financing raises financing costs for all borrowers by drawing on financial resources that otherwise would be available for other uses, thereby possibly crowding out some borrowers from the financial markets. Critics assert that this crowding-out effect might nullify any positive impact subsidized export financing may have on the economy.

For critics of the Ex-Im Bank, another argument is that federal government spending on export promotion programs cuts against the interest of taxpayers and is tantamount to "corporate welfare" or for the support of large corporations. Critics may point out that, by value, 20.7% of the Bank's authorizations went toward assisting small businesses in FY2009. However, supporters may highlight that, by number of transactions, about 87.9% of the Bank's authorizations were directed toward support for small business exporters.[25] Ex-Im Bank is largely a demand-driven agency. While the Bank can make financing available for certain purposes, if U.S. firms do not have sufficient interests or commercial incentives for exporting in particular markets, then they may not seek out Ex-Im Bank support.

Another point of contention is the risk to taxpayers imposed by the Bank's activities. Opponents argue that because Ex-Im Bank's loans are backed by the full faith and credit of the U.S. government, taxpayers are potentially burdened if the Bank's projects fail. Supporters point out that a reasonable assurance of repayment is required by the Bank's charter for all credit authorizations. In addition, the Bank monitors credit and other risks in its portfolio.[26]

End Notes

[1] Department of Commerce, "Commerce Secretary Gary Locke Unveils Details of the National Export Initiative," press release, February 4, 2010, http://www.commerce PROD01_008895.

[2] The Federal Financing Bank (FFB) is a part of the Department of the Treasury and obtains its funds from regular Treasury issues.

[3] FFB, *Financial Statements*, multiple years, http://www.ustreas.gov/ffb/financial-statements/.

[4] CRS Report RL30346, *Federal Credit Reform: Implementation of the Changed Budgetary Treatment of Direct Loans and Loan Guarantees*, by James M. Bickley.

[5] Export-Import Bank of the United States (Ex-Im Bank), *Annual Report 2008*, p. 3.

[6] Ex-Im Bank, *2009 Annual Report*, pp. 51-52.

[7] Ex-Im Bank, *The Charter of the Export-Import Bank of the United States*, as amended through P.L. 109-438, updated December 27, 2006, Sec. 2(b)(1)(E)(v).

[8] Ibid., Sec. 2(b)(1)(K).

[9] Ex-Im Bank, *2009 Annual Report*, p. 33.

[10] Ex-Im Bank, *2009 Annual Report*, p. 28.

[11] Ex-Im Bank, *Annual Report 2008*, pp. 22-23.

[12] For a thorough background and analysis of the international financial crisis, see CRS Report RL34742, *The Global Financial Crisis: Analysis and Policy Implications*, coordinated by Dick K. Nanto.

[13] Ex-Im Bank, *2009 Annual Report*, pp. 24, 38. Ex-Im Bank , "Ex-Im Bank Enhances Small Business Insurance Policies and Lender Benefits," press release, November 16, 2009, http://www.exim.gov/pressrelease.cfm/FEED8B67-0C4C-88F2-27D77192291D17F3/.

[14] Ex-Im Bank, *Annual Report 2009*, pp. 28.

[15] Friends of the Earth v. Mosbacher, 488 F. Supp. 2d 889 (N.D. Cal. 2007).

[16] "Lawsuit Forces U.S. Financing Agencies to Account for Climate," *Environment News Service*, February 7, 2009. Gerald Karey, "ExIm Bank, OPIC agree to provide $500 mil for renewable energy," *Platts Commodity News*, February 6, 2009. Meeting with Export-Import Bank officials, March 9, 2009.

[17] Ex-Im Bank, "Export-Import Bank Adopts Carbon Policy to," press release, November 3, 2009, http://www.exim.gov/pressrelease_print.cfm/BC0AA512-EF10-91BF-A6F1508E016C9E5E/.

[18] "Rep. Sherman Issues Statement on Reported RIL Decision to Stop Selling Refined Petroleum to Iran," *US Fed News Service*, January 7, 2009.

[19] Ex-Im Bank, annual reports for 2007 and 2008.

[20] "Reports of Indian Company's Decision to Halt Gas Shipments to Iran Welcomed by Sherman," *International Trade Daily*, January 8, 2009.

[21] Ex-Im Bank, *The Charter of the Export-Import Bank of the United States*, as amended through P.L. 109-438, December 20, 2006, pp. 10-11.

[22] "Eight Charged in Connection with $80 million Scheme to Defraud Ex-Im Bank," *U.S. Fed News*, October 11, 2007.

[23] Export-Import Bank, "California Man Sentenced to Six Months in Prison in Connection With ," press release, July 18, 2008.

[24] *Competitor's Tied Aid Practices Affect U.S. Exports*. General Accounting Office. Report No. GGD-94-81. May 1994. p. 19-21.

[25] Ex-Im Bank, *2009 Annual Report*, p. 30.

[26] Ibid., pp. 26, 37.

In: U.S. Export Programs and Promotion Tools
Editor: Steven D. Braghoff

ISBN: 978-1-60741-328-8

Chapter 3

AGRICULTURAL EXPORT PROGRAMS: BACKGROUND AND ISSUES

Melissa D. Ho and Charles E. Hanrahan

SUMMARY

Agricultural exports are important both to farmers and to the U.S. economy. According to the U.S. Department of Agriculture's Economic Research Service (ERS), agricultural exports have exceeded imports since the early 1970s. The most recent outlook for FY2010 has U.S. agricultural exports estimated at $100 billion. While the FY2010 forecast is down from the record level seen in FY2008, the forecast is still the second highest on record. U.S. agricultural imports are forecast to reach $77.5 billion in FY2010, which would result in a $22.5 billion trade surplus for agricultural goods.

The trade title of the 2008 farm bill, the Food, Conservation, and Energy Act of 2008 (Title III of P.L. 110-246), authorized, amended and repealed certain U.S. agricultural export programs. USDA's Foreign Agricultural Service (FAS) administers three main types of agricultural export programs, which are funded through the borrowing authority of the Commodity Credit Corporation (CCC). Annual appropriations acts, however, sometimes amend the spending limits on these mandatory programs. USDA agricultural export programs include:

- Direct export subsidy programs: The 2008 farm bill reauthorized the Dairy Export Incentive Program (DEIP), which was reactivated in FY2009 due to falling dairy prices, and repealed authority for the Export Enhancement Program (EEP), which has been inactive since FY2002;
- Export market development programs: FAS administers five market development programs, whose primary aim is to assist U.S. industry efforts to build, maintain, and expand overseas markets for U.S. agricultural products: these are the Market Access Program (MAP); the Foreign Market Development Program (FMDP); the Emerging Markets Program (EMP); the Quality Samples Program (QSP), and the Technical

Assistance for Specialty Crops Program (TASC). The 2008 farm bill made organic products eligible for market development programs and increased funds available to address sanitary and phytosanitary barriers to U.S. specialty crops;

- Export credit guarantee programs: Through the GSM-102 Program and the Facility Guarantee Program, USDA's CCC guarantees loans so that private U.S. financial institutions will extend financing to buyers in emerging markets that want to purchase U.S. agricultural exports. The 2008 farm bill made changes to export credit programs to conform to U.S. commitments in the World Trade Organization (WTO). The 2008 farm bill also repealed two other export guarantee programs.

The President's FY2011 budget request includes an additional $53 5 million for agricultural export programs for the Administration's National Export Initiative. Important factors affecting U.S. agricultural exports include the recent global recession (2007-2008), which led to a sharp curtailment of global trade, including agricultural commodities; the depreciation in value of the U.S. dollar, which makes U.S. agricultural exports increasingly competitive in a global market; and increasing global economic growth, particularly in developing and emerging countries, which will likely increase demand for U.S. agricultural commodities in the coming year. Issues for Congress include determining the role and effectiveness of public vs. private sector for investing in the development of new markets; the Brazil WTO case against the U.S. cotton subsidies and implications for trade relations; and the U.S. Trade Representative's approach for addressing agricultural trade barriers, primarily related to sanitary and phytosanitary issues.

U.S. Agricultural Exports

Agricultural exports are important both to farmers and to the U.S. economy. With the productivity of U.S. agriculture growing faster than domestic demand, U.S. farmers and agricultural firms rely heavily on export markets to sustain prices and revenue. According to the U.S. Department of Agriculture's Economic Research Service (ERS), agricultural exports have exceeded imports since the early 1970s (**Figure 1**). In FY2009, U.S. agricultural exports reached $96.6 billion, a significant decline from the record high of $115.5 billion in FY2008. With agricultural imports of $73.4 billion, the FY2009 agricultural trade surplus was $23.2 billion, which was almost $13 billion lower than that in FY2008. The global recession was the primary factor contributing to the decline (See section on "Recent Developments"). The outlook for FY2010 has exports rebounding to $100 billion.' While the FY2010 forecast is down from the record level seen two years ago, the forecast is still the second highest on record. U.S. agricultural imports are forecast to also rise and reach $77.5 billion in FY2010, which would result in a $22.5 billion trade surplus for agricultural goods.

USDA estimates that production from about a third of the harvested acreage in the United States is exported, including about 50 percent of rice and wheat, 74 percent of cotton, and 34 percent of soybeans.[2] Exports also generate economic activity in the non-farm economy. According to a recent USDA study, each $1 received from agricultural exports stimulated an additional $1.65 in supporting activities to produce those exports, and agricultural exports generate over 1 million U.S. jobs both on and off the farm.[3]

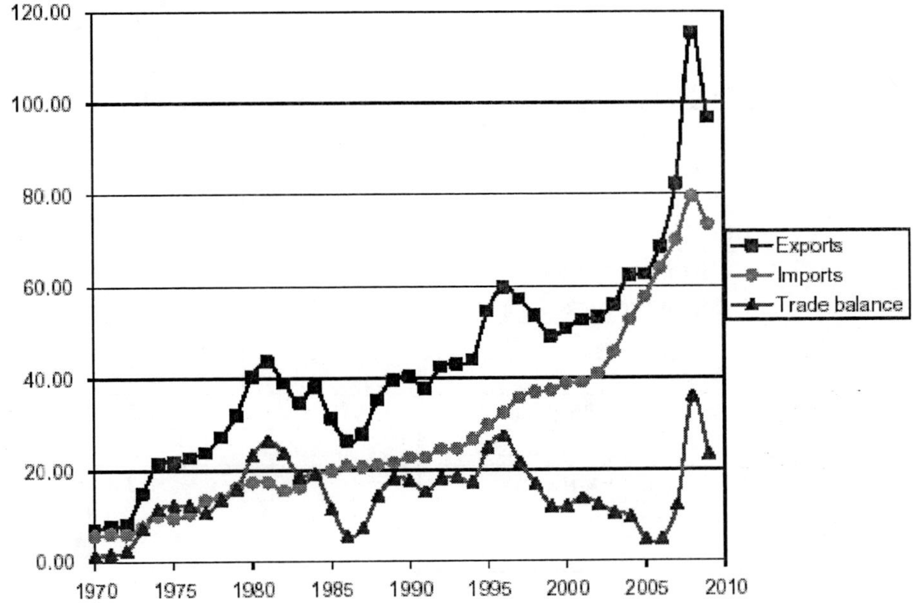

Source: USDA Economic Research Service (ERS)
Notes: U.S. foreign agricultural trade data can be obtained at http://www.ers.usda.gov/Data/FATUS/

Figure 1.Value of U.S.Agricultural Trade, FYI 970-2009 (US$ billions)

Table I. Top U.S.Agricultural Export Destination, by Value FY2009

Rank	Country	US$ millions	% of Total
I	Canada	15,518	16.0
2	Mexico	13,459	13.9
3	Japan	I 1,22 I	11.6
4	China	11,157	11.5
5	EU	7,6 I 9	7.9
6	South Korea	3,825	4.0
7	Taiwan	2,891	3.0
8	Hong Kong	1,789	1.9
9	Indonesia	1,667	1.7
10	Russia	1,429	1.5
II	Egypt	1,420	1.5
12	Turkey	1,387	1.4
13	Philippines	1,246	1.3
14	Venezuela	1,051	1.1
15	Colombia	954	1.0

Source: USDA Economic Research Service, http://www.ers.usda.gov/Data/FATUS/
Notes: In FY2009, the total value of U.S. agricultural exports was $96.6 billion.

Table 2. Top U.S.Agricultural Export Commodities, by Value, FY2009

Rank	Commodity	US$ millions	% of Total
I	Soybeans	16,454	14.0
2	Corn	8,775	9.6
3	Wheat Unmilled	5,374	6.2
4	Other Feeds & Fodder	4,028	4.0
5	Soybean Meal	3,484	3.7
6	Misc Horticultural Products	3,414	3.5
7	Cotton Products	3,383	3.4
8	Pork Products	3,178	3.3
9	Chicken Products	3, I 32	3.0
10	Other Grain Products	2,619	2.7
II	Beef & Veal Products	2,481	2.5
12	Rice-Paddy Milled	2,174	2.3
13	Almonds	1,923	1.9
14	Other Veg Oils/Waxes	1,319	1.5
15	Essential Oils	1,264	1.3

Source: USDA Economic Research Service, http://www.ers.usda.gov/Data/FATUS/
Notes: In FY2009, the total value of U.S. agricultural exports was $96.6 billion.

Table 3. Top Exporting States of Agricultural Commodities FY2008

Rank	State	US$ millions	% of Total
I	California	13,691.0	11.9
2	Iowa	7,859.5	6.8
3	Illinois	7,540.8	6.5
4	Texas	6,006.8	5.2
5	Nebraska	5,944.6	5.1
6	Kansas	5,902.1	5.1
7	Minnesota	5,461.4	4.7
8	North Dakota	3,949.5	3.4
9	Indiana	3,778.2	3.3
10	Missouri	3,2 I 9.2	2.8

Source: USDA, FAS
Notes: For FY2008, the total value of U.S. agricultural exports was $ 115.5 billion.

The top ten country destinations for U.S. agricultural exports in FY2009 are given in **Table 1**. While Canada and Mexico have continued to be the largest two markets for U.S. agricultural exports over the past few years, China and other Asian markets have become increasingly important trading partners over the past few years.

The top exported commodities in FY2009 are given in **Table 2**. With record production levels and higher demand from China, soybean exports are expected to drive the U.S. gain in exports in FY2010. Dairy, livestock, and cotton exports are also forecasted to be higher for FY2010. For more information about U.S. agricultural trade, see CRS Report 98-253, *U.S.*

Agricultural Trade: Trends, Composition, Direction, and Policy, by Charles E. Hanrahan, Carol Canada, and Beverly A. Banks.

Nearly every state exports agricultural commodities. **Table 3** gives the top ten states with the greatest shares of U.S. agricultural exports by value in FY2008. These 10 states accounted for 56 percent of total U.S. agricultural exports in FY2008.[4]

USDA'S AGRICULTURAL EXPORT PROGRAMS

The USDA's Foreign Agricultural Service (FAS) works to improve the competitive position of U.S. agriculture in the global marketplace.[5] To that end, FAS administers several export programs aimed at improving foreign market access for U.S. agricultural goods. The trade title of the 2008 farm bill, the Food, Conservation, and Energy Act of 2008 (Title III of P.L. 110-246), authorized and amended USDA's foreign agricultural export programs, which are funded through the borrowing authority of the Commodity Credit Corporation (CCC).[6] These programs include:

- direct export subsidy programs;
- export market development programs;
- export credit guarantee programs.

The 2008 farm bill made changes to a number of programs that assist with financing U.S. agricultural exports or that help develop markets overseas.[7] Changes include modifying export credit guarantee programs to conform with U.S. commitments in the World Trade Organization (WTO), making organic products eligible for export market development programs, and increasing the funds available to address sanitary and phytosanitary barriers to U.S. specialty crop exports. In addition, the 2008 farm bill repealed the major U.S. export subsidy program (the Export Enhancement Program), and repealed two export credit guarantee programs (the GSM- 103 program and the Supplier Credit Guarantee Program).

Direct Export Subsidy Programs

The 2008 farm bill authorized only one direct export subsidy program for agricultural products, the Dairy Export Incentive Program (DEIP), and repealed authority for the historically largest export subsidy program, the Export Enhancement Program (EEP).

Dairy Export Incentive Program (DEIP)[8]

The Dairy Export Incentive Program (DEIP) was established under the 1985 farm bill (P.L. 99-198) to assist in the export of U.S. dairy products. DEIP was most recently reauthorized in the commodity program title, not the trade title, of the 2008 farm bill (P.L. 110-246). DEIP aims to develop international export markets in regions where U.S. dairy products are not competitive due to the presence of subsidized products from other countries. The original purpose of the program was to counter the adverse effects of foreign dairy product subsidies, primarily those of the European Union (EU). Eligible commodities under

DEIP include milk powder, butterfat and various cheeses. DEIP can potentially increase the U.S. price of milk if enough dairy products are removed from the domestic market. Early bonus payments were in the form of sales from CCC-owned dairy stocks, and later they were in the form of generic commodity certificates from CCC inventories. Currently, USDA pays cash to exporters as bonuses. Each year, USDA's Foreign Agricultural Service (FAS) announces amounts of dairy products that may be subsidized under the program. Actual Invitations for Offers may or may not be issued depending on market conditions for dairy product exports.

The DEIP program has strong support in Congress, though the program is only used when dairy prices fall. Dairy producers consider DEIP an integral part of U.S. dairy policy, and an important adjunct to domestic support programs.[9] The program level for DEIP has varied over the past few years depending on the dairy price situation. In FY2003, DEIP levels were at $32 million, and in FY2004, they were at $3 million No DEIP bonuses were awarded from FY2005 through FY2008. Starting in late 2008 and continuing through most of 2009, U.S. dairy farmers experienced low returns due to a sharp decline in milk prices and relatively high production costs.[10] As a result, USDA reactivated DEIP in July 2009 to provide support in FY2009-2010. With dairy prices stabilizing in early 2010, no DEIP payments are expected in FY2011. Legislative authority for DEIP expires on December 31, 2012.

Agricultural export subsidies are on the agenda of currently stalled WTO multilateral trade negotiations, the Doha Round. In these negotiations, the United States, along with other trading partners who have subsidized exports, has tentatively agreed to phase out all agricultural export subsidies by 2013.[11] The elimination of agricultural export subsidies has been a longstanding objective of U.S. agricultural trade policy. These WTO export subsidy commitments would apply to DEW

Export Enhancement Program (EEP) - Repealed

Under the Export Enhancement Program (EEP), exporters were awarded generic commodity certificates which were redeemable for commodities held in CCC stores, thus enabling them to sell commodities to designated countries at prices below those on the U.S. market. The 2008 farm bill repealed legislative authority for EEP. EEP, which mainly subsidized exports of wheat and wheat flour (around 80% of EEP subsidies), had been little used as U.S. and world prices moved closer together. The last year of significant EEP subsidies was 1995. There were no EEP subsidies during the five years of the 2002 farm bill. The repeal of EEP reflected the fact that the program had been little used since 1995 and is also consistent with the U.S. position to adhere to its promised WTO commitment to eliminate export subsidies by 2013.

Market Development Programs

USDA's Foreign Agricultural Service (FAS) supports U.S industry efforts to build, maintain, and expand overseas markets for U.S. food and agricultural products. FAS administers five market development programs including the following:

- Market Access Program (MAP);
- Foreign Market Development Program (FMDP);
- Emerging Markets Program (EMP);
- Quality Samples Program (QSP); and
- Technical Assistance for Specialty Crops Program (TASC).

In general, these programs provide matching funds to U.S. organizations to conduct a wide range of activities including market research, consumer promotion, trade servicing, capacity building, and market access support. FAS also facilitates U.S. participation in a range of international trade shows. The 2008 farm bill extended legislative authorization of CCC funds for the market development programs until the end of FY2012. All of these programs are funded through the borrowing authority of the CCC.

Market Access Program (MAP)[12]

The Market Access Program (MAP), which aids in the creation, expansion, and maintenance of foreign markets for U.S. agricultural products, was originally authorized by the Agricultural Trade Act of 1978 (P.L. 95-501, as amended) and is administered by FAS.[13] MAP provides funding to non-profit U.S. agricultural trade associations, non-profit U.S. agricultural cooperatives, non-profit state-regional trade groups, and small U.S. businesses for overseas marketing and promotional activities, such as trade shows, market research, consumer promotions for retail products, technical capacity building, and seminars to educate overseas customers. MAP funds assist primarily value-added products and can be used to support both generic promotions and brand-name promotions. Generic promotions are undertaken by non-profit trade associations, state regional groups, and state agencies to increase demand for a specific commodity with no emphasis on a particular brand, e.g. peas, lentils, and cotton. MAP funds may be spent by the participating organizations themselves (direct funding) and/or can be redistributed to entities that have applied to participating organizations for MAP assistance (indirect funding). Since FY1998, USDA policy has been to prohibit the allocation of MAP funds to large U.S. companies, regardless of whether they are distributed directly or indirectly. Agricultural cooperatives and small U.S. companies[14] can receive assistance under the brand program, which seeks to establish consumer loyalty for their brand-name products. To conduct branded product promotion activities, individual companies must provide a funding match of at least 50 percent of the total marketing cost. For generic promotion activities, trade associations and others must meet a minimum 10-percent match requirement.

Although MAP is a mandatory program and hence does not require an annual appropriation, agriculture appropriations acts have on occasion capped the amounts that could be spent on the program or imposed other restraints on programming. For example, the FY1999 agriculture appropriations act imposed no limits on total MAP funding levels, but did prohibit MAP spending in support of promotion of exports of mink pelts or garments, a provision that was first adopted in the FY1996 agriculture appropriations law. Since 1993, no MAP funds may be used to promote tobacco exports. MAP has often been targeted for cuts by some Members of Congress who maintain that it is a form of corporate welfare, or to help offset increased expenditures on other programs, but such efforts have been unsuccessful. FAS usually announces MAP allocations early in the fiscal year.[15] MAP funding steadily increased from \$90 million in FY2000 to \$200 million in FY2006, where it has remained. MAP was reauthorized most recently in the 2008 farm bill, the Food, Conservation, and Energy Act of 2008 (P.L. 110-246), at \$200 million annually through FY2012. The FY2010 agriculture appropriations act (P.L. 111-80) placed no restrictions or limitations on current year spending. For FY2011 the Administration requested \$160 million for MAP.

Foreign Market Development Program (FMDP)[16]

The Foreign Market Development Program (FMDP) was originally authorized in 1955, and similar to MAP, has the primary objective to assist industry organizations in the expansion of export opportunities. The 2008 farm bill reauthorized CCC funding for FMDP for FY2008 through FY2012 at an annual level of \$34.5 million FMDP funds industry groups with a match requirement, to undertake activities such as consumer promotions, technical assistance, trade servicing and market research by the government and industry groups. Like MAP, FMDP is exempt from current WTO negotiations related to export subsidy commitments. Unlike MAP, which mainly promotes consumer goods and brand-name products, FMDP mainly promotes generic or bulk commodities.

The 1996 farm bill provided new statutory authority for the program and authorized it through 2002. Funds allocated for FMDP in FY2001 were \$28 million The 2002 farm bill increased the annual funding level to \$34.5 million The 2008 farm bill maintained the funding level authorized in the 2002 farm bill. For FY2011, the Administration is also requesting \$34 5 million in discretionary spending as part of the National Export Initiative for FMD, in addition to the \$34.5 million in mandatory funding provided through the CCC. (See Section on "Obama Administration's National Export Initiative")

Emerging Markets Program[17]

The Emerging Markets Program (EMP) provides funding for technical assistance activities intended to promote exports of U.S. agricultural commodities and products to emerging markets in all geographic regions, consistent with U.S. foreign policy. An emerging market is defined in the 2008 farm bill (P.L. 110-246) as "any country that is taking steps toward a market-oriented economy through food, agricultural, or rural business sectors of the economy of the country." Additionally, an emerging market country must have the potential to provide a viable and significant market for U.S. agricultural commodities or products. FAS limits EMP projects to countries with per capita incomes below \$11,455, and whose populations are greater than 1 million [18] The 2008 farm bill authorized funding for EMP at \$10 million each fiscal year from FY2008 through FY2012.

Quality Samples Program[19]

The Quality Samples Program (QSP) assists U.S. agricultural trade organizations to provide small samples of their agricultural products to potential importers in emerging markets overseas. The QSP focuses on industrial and manufacturing users of products, not end-use consumers, and allows manufacturers overseas to do test runs to assess how U.S. food and fiber products can best meet their production needs. Priority is given to projects targeting developing nations or regions with a per capita income of less than \$10,725 and a population greater than 1 million Priority is also given to projects designed to expand exports where a U.S. commodity's market share is 10 percent or less. Under the authority of the CCC Charter Act of 1948, FAS uses up to $2 million of CCC funds to carry out the program.

Technical Assistance for Specialty Crops (TASC) Program[20]

The Technical Assistance for Specialty Crops (TASC) Program aims to assist U.S. organizations by providing funds for projects that address sanitary, phytosanitary and technical barriers that prohibit or limit U.S. specialty crop exporters. The 2008 farm bill defines specialty crops as all cultivated plants, and the products thereof, produced in the United States, except wheat, feed grains, oilseeds, cotton, rice, peanuts, sugar, and tobacco. The types of activities covered include seminars and workshops, study tours, field surveys, pest and disease research, and preclearance programs. Under the 2002 farm bill, TASC funding was authorized at $2 million per fiscal year. The 2008 farm bill extended authority for TASC from 2008 through FY2012 and increased funding levels to $4 million in FY2008; $7 million in FY2009; $8 million in FY2010; and $9 million in each of FY20011 and FY2012.

Export Credit Guarantees

From FY2008 through FY2012, the 2008 farm bill reauthorizes USDA-operated export credit guarantee programs, which were first established in the Agricultural Trade Act of 1978 (P.L. 95501) to facilitate sales of U.S. agricultural exports. Under these programs, private U.S. financial institutions extend financing at prevailing market interest rates, to countries that want to purchase U.S. agricultural exports and are guaranteed by the CCC that the loans will be repaid. In making available a guarantee for such loans, the CCC assumes the risk of default on payments by the foreign purchasers on loans for U.S. farm exports. The 2008 farm bill extends authority for two export credit guarantee programs, the GSM-102 short-term guarantee program and the Facility Guarantee Program (FGP).

GSM-102 Program[21]

The GSM-102 program guarantees repayment of short-term financing (typically six months to three years) extended by approved foreign banks, mainly in developing countries, for purchases of U.S. food and agricultural products by foreign buyers. The GSM-102 program aims to encourage U.S. agricultural exports to buyers in countries where credit is necessary to maintain or increase U.S. sales, but where financing may not be available without CCC guarantees. Eligible countries are those that USDA determines can service the debt backed by guarantees. Use of guarantees for foreign aid, foreign policy, or debt rescheduling purposes is prohibited. CCC selects agricultural commodities and products according to market potential and eligibility based on applicable legislative and regulatory requirements. All products must be entirely produced in the United States.[22] The GSM-102 program helps ensure that credit is available to finance commercial exports of U.S. agricultural products to developing countries, while providing competitive credit terms in these countries.

The biggest recipients of export credit guarantees over the years have been Mexico, South Korea, Iraq, Algeria, and the former Soviet Union (FSU). Iraq is in default of more than $2 billion of previously extended guarantees. In FY2009, the major beneficiary countries were South Korea ($1,290.6 million), Turkey ($478.6 million), and Russia ($368.1 million). On a regional basis,[23] the largest allocation of guarantees in FY2009 went to Central America ($607 2 million), South America ($590.3 million), and Southeast Asia ($522.8 million). Guarantees facilitate sales of a broad range of commodities, but in FY2009 mainly benefitted exports of wheat, meat and poultry, oilseeds, feed grains, protein meals and cotton. **Table 4** provides GSM-102 funding by country or region for FY2010.

The 2008 farm bill authorized export credit guarantees of up to $5.5 billion worth of agricultural exports annually from FY2008 through FY2012, and provided for an additional $1 billion targeted to "emerging markets," countries and/or regions that are in the process of becoming commercial markets for U.S. agricultural products. The 2008 farm bill also capped the credit subsidy for the GSM-102 program at $40 million annually.[24] The actual level of guarantees depends on market conditions and the demand for financing by eligible countries. A provision in the statute allows guarantees to be used when the bank issuing the underlying letter of credit is located in a country other than the importing country. The farm bill permits credit guarantees for high value products with at least 90% U.S. content by weight, allowing for some components of foreign origin. The 2008 farm bill also removed the 1 percent cap on loan origination fees for the GSM-102 program.

Facility Guarantee Program[25]

The CCC also provides funding to guarantee financing under the Facility Guarantee Program (FGP). FGP guarantees financing of goods and services exported from the United States to improve or establish agriculture-related facilities in emerging markets. Eligible projects must improve the handling, marketing, storage, or distribution of imported U.S. agricultural commodities and products.

The 2008 farm bill reauthorized FGP and extended authority through the end of FY2012. It also provided that the Secretary of Agriculture may waive requirements that U.S. goods be used in the construction of a facility under this program, if such goods are not available or their use is not feasible. The new law also permits the Secretary to provide a guarantee for this program for the term of the depreciation schedule for the facility, not to exceed 20 years.

Table 4. GSM- 102 Allocation By Country & Region FY2010

Region	US$ millions
China, Hong Kong	125
Eurasia	250
Mexico	225
Middle East & North Africa	175
South America	225
South Asia	75
South Korea	450
Southeast Asia	225
Sub-Saharan Africa	175
Turkey	300

Source: USDA, Foreign Agricultural Service

Notes: FY2010 allocation was announced by USDA on March 8, 2010 - http//www.fas. usda.gov/ excredits/expcred-guar.asp; Major individual country recipients of export credit guarantees, such as Korea, Turkey and Russia, are not included in the regional funding figures.

Other Export Guarantee Programs - Repealed

Two other export guarantee programs, previously authorized, were repealed by the 2008 farm bill. These were the GSM-103 program, which guaranteed longer-term (3-10 years) financing, and the Supplier Credit Guarantee Program (SCGP), which guaranteed very short-term (up to 1 year) financing of exports without bank intermediation. The repeal of the GSM-103 program (and lifting the cap on origination fees for the GSM-102 program) was done in response to a WTO dispute panel decision in a case brought by Brazil against U.S. cotton policy (see "**Issues for Congress**" below). Legislative authority for the SCGP was suspended largely because of a high rate of defaulted obligations and evidence of fraud.

FUNDING

As mentioned above, USDA's agricultural export programs are funded through the authority of the CCC at levels established in statute. Annual appropriations acts, however, sometimes amend the spending limits on these mandatory programs. **Table 5** shows USDA foreign export budget authority levels for FY2001 through FY2010, and also includes the Administration's FY2011 request for these programs.

Table 5. USDA International Export Program Activity, FY2001-2011 (US$ millions)

Program	FY2001	FY2002	FY2003	FY2004	FY2005	FY2006	FY2007	FY2008	FY2009	FY2010 (est)	FY2011 (req)
DEIP[a]	8	55	32	3	0	0	0	0	100	25	0
MAP[b]	90	100	110	125	140	200	200	200	200	200	160
FMDP[C]	28	34	34	34	34	34	34	34	34	34	69
EMP[d]	–	–	10	10	10	10	4	10	10	10	10
TASC[e]	–	2	2	2	2	2	I	4	7	8	9
QSP[f]	2	2	2	2	2	2	I	1.4	2	2	2
GSM-102[g]		2,936	2,545	2,926	2,170	1,363	1,445	3,115	5,357	5,400	5,400

Sources: USDA, *Annual Budget Summaries,* various issues, and personal communication. These data are budget authority levels, except GSM-IO2 program, which include the value of exports financed through the program.

Note: FY2010 data are an estimate and FY2011 numbers reflect the Administration's request.

a. Dairy Export Incentive Program

b. Market Access Program

c. Foreign Market Development Program. For FY201 I, the Administration is also requesting $34.5 million in discretionary spending as part of the National Export Initiative for FMD, in addition to the $34.5 available through the CCC.

d. Emerging Markets Program

e. Technical Assistance for Specialty Crops — In FY2006, an additional $0.6 million was provided for TASC activities through a FAS direct appropriation.

f. Quality Samples Program

g. General Sales Manager (GSM) Export Credit Guarantee Program. The values given represent the value of exports financed through the program, not budget authority.

RECENT DEVELOPMENTS

U.S. and global trade are greatly affected by the growth and stability of world markets.[26] Changes in world population, economic growth, and income are most likely to alter global food demand. According to the World Bank, the volume of global trade in 2009 declined for the first time since 1982. The 2009 value of total and agricultural commodities show a broad-based decline in the value of exports and imports compared with a year earlier. In addition to current economic factors, other broader variables also influence the level of U.S. agricultural exports: income and population growth; tastes and preferences in foreign markets; and exchange rates. U.S. domestic farm policies that affect price and supply, and trade agreements with other countries, also influence the level of U.S. agricultural exports. While many of these factors are beyond the scope of congressional action, farm bills have typically included programs that promote commercial agricultural exports or provide foreign food aid. Some important factors affecting U.S. agricultural exports are discussed in greater detail below.

Macroeconomic Conditions

- **Global recession.** According to the USDA's Economic Research Service (ERS), the global economic crisis that started in late 2008 led to a sharp curtailment of international trade, including a short-term decline in the value of global agricultural trade of around 20 percent.[27] While not uniform across commodities and regions, the trade impact appears to have a greater effect on crops than on livestock. In the short term, with declining world economic activity in 2009, overall global trade declined for the first time since 1982 and agricultural trade fell as well.[28] The economic crisis affected international agricultural trade primarily through the realignment of real (adjusted for inflation) exchange rates and that realignment's effect on real incomes. The economic crisis resulted in major recessions in most of the world, with world GDP expected to have declined by more than 2 percent in 2009. The slowing of the growth in demand for agricultural commodities worldwide resulting from the fall in global income led to a slowing of the growth in the volume of agricultural commodities traded. An economic recovery is predicted to occur in 2010, which accounts for the favorable outlook for U.S. agricultural trade in FY2010.
- **U.S. currency depreciation.** Since 2002, the U.S. dollar has depreciated in value and this trend is expected to remain over the next decade. The depreciation of the dollar makes U.S. agricultural exports increasingly competitive in international markets by lowering the price of U.S. goods in global markets relative to competing goods priced in appreciating currencies. Similarly, a weak dollar tends to dampen imports by raising the price of foreign goods priced in appreciating currencies relative to U.S. domestic goods. Combined with a return to global economic growth, with gains in developing countries particularly important for agricultural demand, prospects for U.S. agricultural exports are improved.[29]
- **Global economic growth, particularly in developing countries.** Despite a drop of two percent in 2009, global economic growth is projected to average 3.3 percent annually in 2010 through 2019, mostly due to resumed high growth rates in emerging

market countries such as China and India and a return to strong growth in other developing countries and countries of the former Soviet Union. Developing countries account for the primary portion of projected increase in world agricultural imports. According to USDA-ERS, renewed economic growth is expected to occur beginning in 2010, providing the foundation for gains in world demand and trade for agricultural products. Countries in Africa and the Middle East account for 60 percent of the growth in poultry and meat imports and are projected to account for 50 percent of the increase in the world wheat imports, 40 percent of the growth in rice and coarse grain imports, and 13 percent of the rise in soybean oil imports. Food consumption and feed use are particularly responsive to income growth in those countries, with movement away from staple and traditional food crops and toward an increased diversification of diets. Demand from developing countries is further reinforced by population growth rates that are nearly twice those of developed countries.

Biofuels

Over the past few years, biofuels have grown in significance as an alternative to petroleum-based fuels in the United States and globally.[30] With recent high energy prices, the passage of major energy legislation in 2005 (P.L. 109-58) and 2007 (P.L. 110-140), and the passage of a new farm bill in 2008 (P.L. 110-246), there is growing interest in the United States for the expansion of farm production for biofuel crops. U.S. biofuel policies were seen by some observers to be a fundamental cause of the recent surge in agricultural commodity prices.[31] Commodities such as corn, sugar cane, soybeans and other vegetable oil crops, can be used either as food, feed or to make biofuels. Many observers argued that the biofuel policies diverted U.S. agricultural output to ethanol and biodiesel production, leading to lower quantities of U.S. commodities available for export and consequently causing higher world prices. They argue that the increased demand for commodities for biofuel production has led to significant impacts on the agricultural sector, including heightened competition for available cropland (and a subsequent increase in farmland value); intensification of agricultural activity on U.S. cropland to meet growing demand for food, feed, and fuel resources; and a rise in commodity prices.[32] Continued support for biofuels could result in additional impacts on food prices and subsequently on agricultural trade, they say.

However, the extent that the global demand for biofuels is responsible for the recent food price spikes (as opposed to other factors, such as exchange rates, petroleum prices, crop growing conditions in key areas, private stock holding, etc) is still widely debated. Other studies have attributed the spike in commodity prices in 2008 to factors other than increased biofuels demand, implicating instead overall increased costs of production due to high oil prices.[33] These studies conclude that while most medium-term economic models find that biofuel demand has and will put upward pressure on prices for biofuel commodities, available evidence suggests that biofuels had a relatively small contribution to the 2008 spike in food prices. In addition, these studies point out the fact that while commodity prices have fallen steeply from their peak in 2008, biofuel demand has remained steady indicating that a casual link between biofuel demand and short-term crop prices is relatively week.

Obama Administration's National Export Initiative

In his first State of the Union speech on January 27, 2010, President Obama launched a National Export Initiative, which he described as a plan to "double exports over the next five years, an increase that will support two million new jobs in America." On March 11, 2010, President Obama issued an Executive Order that officially launched the National Export Initiative, which directs agencies across his Administration to coordinate a "jobs-oriented policy and promotion effort."[34] Agriculture Secretary Vilsack spoke about the importance of exports for the agriculture sector and USDA's involvement in the National Export Initiative and the importance of trade for agriculture in remarks made in March 2010, at an industry trade show. [35]

The President's FY2011 budget request includes an additional $53.5 million request for the Foreign Agricultural Service for the National Export Initiative, and includes an increase of $10 million to expand FAS exporter assistance and in-country promotion activities, and to meet higher operating costs of FAS's 90 overseas posts; $34 5 million in new discretionary funding, which would be in addition to the $34 5 million of CCC funding, for the Foreign Market Development Cooperator Program (FMDP) to broaden program participation and to support new, innovative program activities; and a $9 million expansion of the Technical Assistance for Specialty Crops Program, which assists U.S. organizations in overcoming sanitary, phytosanitary and related technical barriers that limit the export of specialty crops, and "reflects the growing importance of specialty crops as a growing share of total U.S. agricultural exports." FAS plans to work in coordination with the interagency Trade Promotion Coordinating Committee (TPCC), and through U.S. farm groups, state departments of agriculture and state regional trade groups (SRTGs), agricultural trade and industry organizations, and other USDA agencies to execute the initiative.

Issues for Congress

Public Sector Role and Effectiveness in Export Promotion

Historically, many Members have been highly supportive of the Market Access Program (MAP) and cite the benefits the program brings to U.S. agricultural industries through export market development abroad. In fact, last year several Members expressed concern to the Administration about its proposed 20 percent reduction in MAP funding in the FY2010 agriculture budget request. Congress rejected the Administration's proposal and maintained MAP funding at its authorized level for FY2010. The Administration has again proposed to reduce MAP funding by 20 percent ($40 million) for FY2011.

At the same time, a frequent concern raised by some Members of Congress with respect to MAP and the Foreign Market Development Program (FMDP) is whether the federal government should have an active role at all in helping agricultural producers and agribusinesses market their products overseas. Some argue that MAP and FMDP are forms of corporate welfare in that they fund activities that private firms would and could fund for themselves.[36] Other critics argue that the principal beneficiaries are foreign consumers and that funds could be better spent, for example, to educate U.S. firms on how to export.

Program supporters emphasize that foreign competitors, especially EU member countries, also spend money on market promotion, and that U.S. marketing programs help keep U.S. products competitive in third-country markets.

In the early 1990s, some Members raised specific concerns about the effectiveness of MAP operations, specifically questioning the program's cost-effectiveness and impact, and citing its lack of support for small businesses and displacement of private sector marketing funds. In response to these concerns Congress directed USDA to enact significant changes to MAP. In 1996, Congress through the appropriations process prohibited FAS from providing direct assistance for brand-name promotions to companies that are not recognized as small businesses under the Small Business Act. In 1997, Congress prohibited large companies from receiving indirect assistance from MAP as well. Giving priority to small businesses did result in a substantial increase in the small business share of MAP assistance for brand-name promotion by 1997. FAS also established a five-year limit (graduation requirement) on the use of MAP funds for companies that use funds to promote a "specific branded product" in a "single market," unless FAS determined that further assistance was still necessary to meet program objectives (generic marketing was not subject to the graduation requirement). FAS later revised the regulations in 1998 to limit each company to no more than five years (consecutive or nonconsecutive) of MAP funding for brand-name promotions per country, which some participating companies currently feel is too restrictive. Lastly, a requirement was added that each participant certify that MAP funds supplement, not supplant, its own foreign market development expenditures. Though FAS regularly audits the participants and verifies that the certification statement has been completed, FAS also admits that it is difficult to verify whether MAP funds are additional to what a company would have spent in the absence of MAP funds.

A 1999 GAO study reviewed a number of studies looking at MAP's effectiveness and concluded that while changes had been made to the program, the economic benefits of export programs (including MAP) were unclear. It stated that "few studies show an unambiguously positive effect of government promotional activity on exports."[37] In addition, GAO recently testified to Congress that U.S. export promotion activities were in need of strengthened performance management systems.[38]

Congress will be considering the Administration's request for reduced MAP funding for FY2011. Some may question the exclusion of MAP from the President's National Export Initiative. Currently, some Members urging greater fiscal responsibility on the part of the federal government have introduced legislation to eliminate MAP. H.R. 4683 would amend the Agricultural Trade Act of 1978 to repeal MAP.

WTO Trade Dispute

Brazil has had a long-running dispute against the United States over U.S. cotton programs. In 2005 and again in 2008, the World Trade Organization (WTO) found that certain U.S. agricultural programs are inconsistent with WTO commitments including payments to cotton producers under the marketing loan and countercyclical programs; and export credit guarantees under the GSM- 102 Program.[39]

In December 2009 Brazil announced that it was authorized by the WTO arbitrators to impose trade countermeasures against the United States in excess of $800 million in 2010 (based on 2008 data). The WTO arbitration awards provided the level of countermeasures that Brazil could impose against U.S. trade annually in two parts: 1) a fixed amount of $147 3 million for the cotton payments; and 2) an amount for the GSM-102 program that varies based upon program usage. In March 2010, Brazil released a list of 102 goods of U.S. origin valued at $591 million that would be subjected to import tariffs and released a preliminary list of U.S. patents and intellectual property rights it could restrict, barring a joint settlement.

After several meetings between U.S. and Brazilian officials, the Government of Brazil agreed not to impose any countermeasures on U.S. trade and the United States agreed to work with Brazil to establish a fund of approximately $147 3 million per year on a pro rata basis to provide technical assistance and capacity building for Brazilian farmers until the passage of the next farm bill or a mutually agreed solution to the cotton dispute is reached, whichever is sooner. The United States also agreed to make some near-term modifications to the operation of the GSM-102 Export Credit Guarantee Program, and to engage with the Government of Brazil in technical discussions regarding further operation of the program. The U.S. hope is that continuing negotiations will lead to an agreement which avoids having Brazil impose retaliatory measures under WTO rules. Congress will likely continue to monitor developments in the WTO cotton case and its implications for the GSM-102 program.

Addressing Trade Barriers

On March 31, 2010 the U.S. Trade Representative (USTR) released to Congress a new report that outlines key sanitary and phytosanitary (SPS) barriers that American agricultural and food producers face when trying to export their products.[40] Key trade barrier issues addressed in the report include avian influenza; biotechnology; bovine spongiform encephalopathy (BSE); H1N1 influenza; maximum residue limits (MRLs) for pesticides; pathogens, and ractopamine, a veterinary drug used to promote lean meat growth in pigs, cattle and turkeys. In addition to monitoring how USTR addresses SPS issues, Congress will be considering the Administration's request to increase funding for the Technical Assistance for Specialty Crops (TASC) program, which focuses on SPS barriers to exports.

For more information about trade issues related to fruit and vegetable commodities, see CRS Report RL34468, *The U.S. Trade Situation for Fruit and Vegetable Products,* by Renee Johnson. For trade issues related to livestock and meat commodities, see CRS Report RS22948, *U.S.Russia Meat and Poultry Trade Issues,* by Renee Johnson and Geoffrey S. Becker. For more information about trade issues related to agricultural biotechnology, see CRS Report RL33334, *Biotechnology in Animal Agriculture: Status and Current Issues,* by Tadlock Cowan and Geoffrey S. Becker.

End Notes

[1] USDA Economic Research Service, Outlook for U.S. Agricultural Trade Feb 18, 2010, http://usda.mannlib. comell. edu/usda/current/AES/AES-02-18-2010.pdf.

[2] See USDA Foreign Agricultural Service Factsheet: http://www.fas.usda.gov/info/factsheets/tradevalue.pdf

[3] William Edmondson, *U.S. Agricultural Trade Boosts Overall Economy,* USDA Economic Research Service, FAU124, Washington, DC, April 2008, http://www.ers.usda.gov/Publications/FAU/2008/04 Apr/FAU124/ FAU124.pdf.

[4] Agricultural export data by state is available from USDA's Economic Research Service at http://www.ers.usda.gov/ data/stateexports/.
[5] An overview of the Foreign Agricultural Service is available at http://www.fas.usda.gov/aboutfas.asp.
[6] The CCC is a U.S. government-owned and -operated corporation, created in 1933, with broad powers to support farm income and prices and to assist in the export of U.S. agricultural products. Toward this end, the CCC finances USDA's domestic price and income support programs and its export programs using its permanent authority to borrow up to $30 billion at any one time from the U.S. Treasury.
[7] For more information about agricultural export provisions in the 2008 farm bill, see CRS Report RS22905, *Agricultural &port Provisions of the 2008 Farm Bill,* by Charles E. Hanrahan.
[8] Additional information on DEIP is available at http://www.fas.usda.gov/excredits/deip/deip-new.asp.
[9] For background about dairy policy issues see CRS Report R41141, *Previewing Dairy Policy Options for the Next Farm Bill,* by Dennis A. Shields.
[10] For background about the dairy sector and policy see CRS Report R40205, *Dairy Market and Policy Issues,* by Dennis A. Shields.
[11] For a discussion of agriculture and Doha Round negotiations, see CRS Report RS22927, *WTO Doha Round: Implications for U.S. Agriculture,* by Randy Schnepf and Charles E. Hanrahan.
[12] Additional information on MAP is available at http://www.fas.usda.gov/mos/programs/map.asp.
[13] MAP has had two predecessor programs. In 1996, MAP replaced the Market Promotion Program, which was established in 1990 to replace the Targeted Export Assistance Program authorized in 1985.
[14] As defined by the Small Business Administration.
[15] A list or MAP program participants and allocation amount for FY2010 is available at http://www.fas.usda.gov/info/ factsheets/mapfact.asp.
[16] Additional information on FMDP is available at http://www.fas.usda.gov/mos/programs/fmdprogram.asp.
[17] Additional information on the Emerging Markets Program is available at http://www.fas.usda.gov/mos/em-markets/ em-markets.html.
[18] This is the current ceiling on upper middle income economies as determined by the World Bank.
[19] Additional information on the QSP is available at http://www.fas.usda.gov/mos/programs/QSP.asp.
[20] Additional information on the TASC program is available at http://www.fas.usda.gov/mos/tasc/tasc.asp.
[21] The acronym GSM refers to the General Sales Manager, an official of FAS who administers the credit, and other, export programs. Additional information on GSM-102 export credit guarantees is at http://www.fas.usda.gov/ excredits/ exp-cred-guar-new.asp.
[22] A list of eligible commodities and products under the GSM-102 program can be found at http://www. fas. usda. gov/ excredits/gsmcommodities.html.
[23] Major individual country recipients of export credit guarantees, such as Korea, Turkey and Russia, are not included in the regional funding figures.
[24] The credit subsidy is the available budget authority for the cost of the program.
[25] Additional information on the FGP is available at http://www.fas.usda.gov/excredits/facility-new.asp.
[26] For more information about U.S. agricultural trade, see CRS Report 98-253, *U.S. Agricultural Trade: Trends, Composition, Direction, and Policy*, by Charles E. Hanrahan, Carol Canada, and Beverly A. Banks.
[27] May Peters, Mathew Shane, and David Torgerson, *What the 2008/2009 World Economic Crisis Means for Global Agricultural Trade,* USDA Economic Research Service, WRS-09-05, Washington, DC, August 2009, http://www.ers.usda.gov/Publications/WRS0905/WRS0905.pdf.
[28] Peters, Shane and Torgerson, 2009 op. cit.
[29] May Peters, Mathew Shane, and David Torgerson, *What the 2008/2009 World Economic Crisis Means for Global Agricultural Trade*, USDA Economic Research Service, WRS-09-05, Washington, DC, August 2009, http://www.crs.gov/Pages/Reports.aspx?ProdCode=R41091.
[30] Biofuels are essentially any transportation fuels produced from plants and other organic materials.
[31] Use mandates, biofuel use tax credits, and ethanol import tariffs represent the three main elements of US biofuel policy at present. For more information about these policy mechanisms, see CRS Report R40110, *Biofuels Incentives: A Summary of Federal Programs*, by Brent D. Yacobucci.
[32] For instance, see http://www.foodbeforefueLorg/files/Role%20oP/020Biofuels%206-19-08.pdf and http://www.ers.usda.gov/AmberWaves/march09/Features/Biofuels.htm.
[33] Simone Pfuderer, Grant Davies, and Ian Mitchell, *Annex 5 - The role of demand for biofuel in agricultural commodity price spike of 2007/08*, Department for Environment, Food and Rural Affairs (DEFRA), London, UK, April 1, 2010, http://www.defra.gov.uldfoodfarm/food.
[34] http://www.whitehouse.gov/the-press-office/executive-order-national-export-initiative.
[35] http://www.usda.gov/wps/portal/!ut/p/s.7_0_A/7_0_10B/.cmd/ad/.ar/saselrievecontent/.c/6_2_1UH/.ce/7_2_5JM/.p/52_4TQ/A/1/_th/J_2_9D/_s.7_0_A/7_1OB?PC_725JMcontentid=2010/03/0121.xml&PC_7_2_5JM_parent hav=TRANSCRIPTS_SPEECHES& fiC:i f 5JMnavid=fRAN—SCRIPT#725JM.
[36] See for example, http://www.fpif.org/articles/corporate_welfare_and_foreign http://councilfor.cagw.org/site/ News2?page=NewsArticle&id=11742

[37] U.S. General Accounting Office (GAO), *Changes Made to Market Access Program, but Questions Remain on Economic Impact*, NSIAD-99-38, Washington, DC, April 1999, http://www.gao.gov/archive/1999/ns99038.pdf.

[38] Yager, L. "International Trade: Observations on U.S. and Foreign Countries' Export Promotion Activities," GAO Testimony to Subcommittee on International Trade, Customs, and Global Competitiveness, Senate Committee on Finance. December, 2009.

[39] For more information see CRS Report RL32571, *Brazil's WTO Case Against the U.S. Cotton Program*, by Randy Schnepf, Brazil's WTO Case Against the U.S. Cotton Program, by Randy Schnepf

[40] See U.S. Trade Representative website at http://www.ustr.gov/about-us/press-office/fact-sheets/2010/march/keysanitary-and-phytosanitary-barriers-american-export.

In: U.S. Export Programs and Promotion Tools
Editor: Steven D. Braghoff
ISBN: 978-1-60741-328-8

Chapter 4

EXPORT PROMOTION: OBSERVATIONS ON THE EXPORT-IMPORT BANK'S EFFORTS TO ACHIEVE U.S. POLICY GOALS

Loren Yager

Mr. Chairmen and Members of the Subcommittees:

Thank you for the opportunity to appear today before the subcommittees to provide our perspective on the role of the U.S. Export-Import Bank (Ex-Im) in promoting exports and achieving other U.S. policy goals. As Congress considers policies to achieve more robust growth in the U.S. economy, it must consider the full range of tools available to further growth and create new jobs for U.S. workers. Some of these tools are related to promoting exports, which can have broad benefits to the U.S. economy. As the official export credit agency of the United States, Ex-Im has a key role in helping many U.S. firms achieve sales in foreign markets. In addition to establishing Ex-Im's broad mandate of supporting U.S. employment through exports, Congress has laid out specific, targeted goals for the bank in areas such as increasing financing for environmentally beneficial exports and expanding services to small and minority-owned businesses.

Today, I will provide some broad observations regarding Ex-Im's contribution to the export promotion goals announced in the President's National Export Initiative. I will also describe progress Ex-Im has made in achieving the specific targets set by Congress, as well as some challenges the bank faces in meeting those targets. In my statement, I will also provide some background information concerning the ways in which exports can enhance U.S. economic output, and I would be happy to provide insights from our recent work on other key agencies' export promotion efforts.

These observations are based on a range of work that we have conducted for Congress over recent years on Ex-Im as well as on the numerous other U.S. agencies involved in export promotion.[1] We conducted this work in accordance with generally accepted government auditing standards. Those standards require that we plan and perform the audit to obtain sufficient, appropriate evidence to provide a reasonable basis for our findings and conclusions based on our audit objectives. We believe that the evidence obtained provides a reasonable basis for our findings and conclusions based on our audit objectives.

SUMMARY

The President's National Export Initiative has put forth an ambitious goal of doubling exports in the next 5 years. Ex-Im has been identified as having a key role in the initiative, and a recent administration report identifies a number of specific actions for Ex-Im. Our work on Ex-Im's financing with respect to small business found areas where Ex-Im needed to improve its data systems for accurate reporting as well as its tracking of efforts to increase small business financing. Regarding Ex-Im's environmentally beneficial exports financing, we found that the bank could benefit from more consistently following strategic planning practices. Ex-Im has taken a number of steps in response to GAO recommendations, but opportunities for improvement remain. Additional attention to these issues will enable Ex-Im to develop better communication with Congress and other stakeholders regarding the balance between the small business and environmental export targets and the broader priorities in the National Export Initiative.

BACKGROUND

Ex-Im's mission is to support U.S. exports and jobs by providing export financing on terms that are competitive with the official export financing support offered by other governments. It had about 350 full-time staff positions in fiscal year 2010. Between fiscal years 2003 and 2008, Ex-Im authorized financing averaging $12.8 billion annually. In fiscal year 2009, Ex-Im had a record year, financing more than $21 billion in 2,891 authorizations. Since fiscal year 2008, Ex-Im has been "self-sustaining" for appropriations purposes, financing its operations from receipts collected from its borrowers.

Exports, and trade more broadly, contribute to the U.S. economy in a variety of ways. Trade enables the United States to achieve a higher standard of living by exporting goods and services that are produced here relatively efficiently and importing goods and services that are produced here relatively inefficiently. An indication of this is that firms engaged in the international marketplace tend to exhibit higher rates of productivity growth and pay higher wages and benefits to their workers than domestically oriented firms of the same size. U.S. exports of goods grew from $820 billion in 2004 to $1.30 trillion in 2008, and were $1.1 trillion in 2009.[2]

In addition to the longer-term benefits of trade and exports, exports can serve as a countercyclical force for the U.S. economy—that is, strengthening the economy when other parts of it are relatively weaker. For a number of years, as the United States increasingly imported more than it exported, the U.S. economy was an engine of growth for other nations. In contrast, from December 2007 through June 2009—what has been officially labeled a recession period—U.S. economic growth was boosted by an improving trade balance. More recently, strong U.S. exports have been outpaced by import growth.

The National Export Initiative Sets Ambitious Goals for Increasing U.S. Exports and Contains a Key Role for Ex-Im

The President created the National Export Initiative on March 11, 2010, with an ambitious goal of doubling exports in the next 5 years to support job creation. To facilitate achieving this goal, the National Export Initiative established an Export Promotion Cabinet that includes Ex-Im as well as 15 other agencies and executive departments. On September 16, 2010, the White House released a report on the initiative that provides an overview of progress made and lays out a plan for reaching the President's goal.

Ex-Im has a critical role to play in one of the report's priority areas—increasing export credit. The report identifies several actions for Ex-Im. They include, for example, launching new products designed to ensure credit is available to small and medium-sized enterprises (SME); focusing efforts on high-potential industries such as medical technology, renewable power, and transportation; increasing the number and scope of partnerships with financial intermediaries; and introducing a simplified application for credit insurance. GAO has not evaluated the report or other aspects of the National Export Initiative, but would welcome the opportunity to continue its work with the Congress on oversight of these efforts.

Congress Has Set Targets Regarding the Composition of Ex-Im's Export Financing

GAO has reported on Ex-Im's efforts to achieve specific targets set by Congress regarding the composition of Ex-Im's export financing. For example, Congress has shown interest in the level of financing Ex-Im provides to small businesses, including those owned by women and minorities, and Ex-Im's efforts to increase that financing. Congress has also given Ex-Im directives regarding the share of its financing for environmentally beneficial exports, including renewable energy.

Congress Has Asked Ex-Im to Increase Financing for Environmentally Beneficial Exports

Congressional interest in Ex-Im's financing of environmentally beneficial exports span many years. In 1989, Congress directed that Ex-Im should seek to provide at least 5 percent of its energy sector financing for renewable energy projects and should undertake efforts to promote renewable energy. In 2008, Congress directed Ex-Im to provide not less than 10 percent of its annual financing for environmentally beneficial exports; in 2009-2010, Congress narrowed the targeted environmentally beneficial categories.[3] Congress has also required Ex-Im to develop a strategy for increasing its environmental export financing, and to report on this financing and how the bank tracks it.

GAO recently reviewed Ex-Im's environmentally beneficial export financing and its efforts to meet congressional directives in this area.[4] We found, first, that Ex-Im had fallen far short of achieving the 10 percent environmentally beneficial financing targets set by Congress. However, we also found that Ex-Im's financing for renewable energy has recently increased; the level of renewable energy financing in the first two quarters of fiscal year 2010 exceeded its renewable energy financing for all of fiscal year 2009, which in turn represented a large increase over 2008 financing.

We also reported that Ex-Im needs to further clarify its definitions and improve its reporting on environmentally beneficial exports. For Ex-Im, the term "environmentally beneficial exports" constitutes an overarching category that includes renewable energy, energy efficiency exports including energy efficient end-use technologies, and a mix of other products with beneficial effects on the environment. Ex-Im recently sought to clarify its definitions of energy efficiency exports by publicly providing examples of products it considers to be in that category, and it began to track its financing for those exports in its internal data. However, the examples Ex-Im released do not clearly identify which energy efficient end-use technologies would count towards their 10 percent financing target. Given the congressional interest in financing in this area, it is important that Ex-Im be as clear as possible in its application of terms to facilitate communicating financing goals to potential exporters and others and communicating progress in meeting targets to Congress. GAO recommended that Ex-Im develop and provide clear definitions for its subcategories of environmentally beneficial exports and report annually on the level of financing for each of the subcategories.

We reported that while Ex-Im has taken steps to increase financing for environmentally beneficial exports, it could benefit from more consistently following strategic planning practices such as involving stakeholders and realigning resources. Ex-Im routinely shares information with stakeholders such as other U.S. agencies and lending institutions, but has not generally involved them in communicating goals or discussing strategies for achieving them. Ex-Im has considered reorganizing some staff into more focused teams to target priority industries and countries, but this effort has not included an analysis of the resources required to accomplish the goal of increasing certain types of environmentally beneficial exports. On the other hand, Ex-Im has taken some steps to assess factors that affect its financing of environmentally beneficial exports such as conducting analysis of the renewable energy markets to identify the best sectoral and geographic opportunities for Ex-Im financing. In order for Ex-Im to provide valuable information for the Congress and key stakeholders, GAO recommended that the bank consistently implement key practices for effective strategic planning, including clearly communicating the bank's priorities for increasing financing of renewable energy and energy efficient end-use technologies to both internal and external stakeholders. Ex-Im agreed with our recommendations and stated that it would strive to implement them promptly.

Small Business Exports are a U.S. Trade Priority, and Congress has Required Ex-Im to Provide a Certain Level of Support for these Exports

Promoting exports by small business has been a long-time priority of Congress as well as the executive branch, given these exports' role in generating growth and employment. While many small businesses export, it is widely recognized that they face a number of challenges in exporting. For example, they typically do not have overseas offices and may not have much knowledge regarding foreign markets. Export promotion agencies have developed various goals with respect to their small business assistance, and in some cases Congress has mandated specific requirements for supporting small businesses.

Since the 1980s, Congress has required that Ex-Im make available a certain percentage of its export financing for small business. In 2002, Congress established several new requirements for Ex-Im relating to small business, including increasing from 10 to 20 percent the proportion of Ex-Im's aggregate loan, guarantee, and insurance authority that must be made available for the direct benefit of small business. When reauthorizing the bank's charter in 2006, Congress again established new requirements for Ex-Im. These included creating a small business division with an office of financing for socially and economically disadvantaged small business concerns and small business concerns owned by women, designating small business specialists in all divisions, creating a small business committee to advise the bank president, and defining standards to measure the bank's success in financing small business.

For the past 4 fiscal years—2006-2009—Ex-Im has met the Congressional requirement to make available not less than 20 percent of its financing authority for small businesses. Percentages have ranged from almost 27 percent in fiscal year 2007 to about 21 percent in fiscal year 2009. The financing amount for small business was actually highest in 2009, given Ex-Im's overall record financing that year. In fiscal years 2002-2005, Ex-Im did not reach the goal, with its small business financing share ranging from 16.9 percent to 19.7 percent.

GAO has reported on several aspects of Ex-Im's financing for small business exports. In 2006, we identified weaknesses in Ex-Im's data systems for tracking and reporting on its small business financing and made recommendations for improvement.[5] Ex-Im has implemented those recommendations. For example, Ex-Im moved to an electronic, web-based process that allows exporters, brokers, and financial institutions to transact with Ex-Im electronically. This contributed to more timely and accurate information on Ex-Im's financing, and thus a greater level of confidence in Ex-Im's reporting on its efforts relative to congressional goals.

More recently, we reported on the performance standards that Ex-Im established for assessing its small business financing efforts.[6] We found that Ex-Im had developed performance standards in most, although not all, of the areas specified by Congress, ranging from providing excellent customer service to increasing outreach. We also found that some measures for monitoring progress against the standards lacked targets and time frames, and that Ex-Im was just beginning to compile and use the small business information it was collecting to improve operations.

GAO made several recommendations to Ex-Im for improving its performance standards for small business. Ex-Im has provided to GAO information on actions and specific steps it is taking to implement certain of these recommendations. For example, Ex-Im has identified targets for reducing the average turnaround time for processing certain types of small business transactions. GAO looks forward to continuing to work with Ex-Im in documenting that the recommendations have been implemented.

Conclusions

Mr. Chairmen, the National Export Initiative has focused the spotlight on U.S. agencies that assist U.S. exporters as a way of expanding economic growth and creating jobs in the

United States. As the nation's export credit agency, the Export-Import Bank is a key part of the initiative, and there are a number of detailed initiatives related to export credit in the report that was released on September 16, 2010. However, the goal of doubling U.S. exports in 5 years is an ambitious goal and would require not only increased activity by agencies such as Ex-Im but also increases in demand in key nations around the world.

This heightened emphasis on overall exports and increasing the level of Ex-Im financing takes place in the context of specific congressional directives regarding the composition of that financing. Our work on Ex-Im's financing with respect to small business—including minority and women-owned businesses—and environmentally beneficial exports has demonstrated that substantial steps have been taken, and Ex-Im continues to face substantial challenges. While Ex-Im has had more success in achieving the congressional targets for small business than for environmentally beneficial exports, opportunities remain for a more strategic use of resources and for better communication with Congress and other stakeholders. More broadly, Ex-Im faces the challenge of contributing to the doubling of U.S. exports along with meeting other congressional requirements, including operating at little or no cost to the taxpayer. How any sharp increase in Ex-Im financing levels will affect specific targets we have described is not clear, and is likely to be an area requiring further discussion on how to balance these overall priorities.

Chairman Moore, Chairman Meeks, Ranking Member Biggert, and Ranking Member Miller, this concludes my prepared remarks. I appreciate the opportunity to discuss these issues with you today. I would be pleased to respond to any questions you or other members of the subcommittees may have at this time.

For further information about this testimony, please contact Loren Yager at (202) 512-4347 or by e-mail at YagerL@gao.gov. Contact points for our Offices of Congressional Relations and Public Affairs may be found on the last page of the statement. Individuals who made key contributions to this testimony include Celia Thomas, Shirley Brothwell, Karen Deans, Emily Suarez-Harris, Richard Krashevski, Justine Lazaro, Valerie Nowak, and Jennifer Young.

End Notes

[1]See, for example, GAO, *Export Promotion: Increases in Commercial Service Workforce Should Be Better Planned*, GAO-10-874 (Washington, D.C.: Aug. 31, 2010); GAO, *Export- Import Bank: Reaching New Targets for Environmentally Beneficial Exports Presents Major Challenges for Bank*, GAO-10-682 (Washington, D.C.: July 14, 2010); GAO, *International Trade: Effective Export Programs Can Help in Achieving U.S. Economic Goals*, GAO-09-480T (Washington, D.C.: Mar. 17, 2009); GAO, *Export-Import Bank: Performance Standards for Small Business Assistance Are in Place but Ex-Im Is in the Early Stages of Measuring Their Effectiveness*, GAO-08-915 (Washington, D.C.: July 17, 2008); GAO, *Export Promotion: Export-Import Bank Has Met Target for Small Business Financing Share*, GAO-08-419T (Washington, D.C.: Jan. 17, 2008); and *Export-Import Bank: Changes Would Improve the Reliability of Reporting on Small Business Financing*, GAO-06-351 (Washington, D.C.: Mar. 3, 2006).

[2] Service exports were an additional $502 billion in 2009.

[3] For each of fiscal years 2009 and 2010, Congress specified a 10 percent target for Ex-Im financing but changed the targeted exports to renewable energy technologies or energy efficient end-use technologies.

[4] GAO-10-682.

[5] GAO-06-351.

[6] GAO-08-915.

In: U.S. Export Programs and Promotion Tools
Editor: Steven D. Braghoff

ISBN: 978-1-60741-328-8

Chapter 5

EXPORT PROMOTION: INCREASES IN COMMERCIAL SERVICE WORKFORCE SHOULD BE BETTER PLANNED

United States Government Accountability Office

WHY GAO DID THIS STUDY

Since the recent recession, policymakers have emphasized the role exports can play in strengthening the U.S. economy and in creating higher paying jobs. In March 2010 the President signed an Executive Order creating the National Export Initiative (NEI), with a goal of doubling U.S. exports in 5 years. However, since 2004 the workforce of the U.S. and Foreign Commercial Service (CS) has shrunk, calling into question the ability of this key agency to increase its activities to assist U.S. businesses with their exports.

In response to a conference committee mandate, GAO reviewed (1) how well CS managed its resources from 2004 to 2009, and (2) the completeness of CS's workforce plans and the quality of its fiscal year 2011 budget request. GAO analyzed data from the Departments of Agriculture, Commerce, and State; reviewed agency documents; and interviewed agency officials.

WHAT GAO RECOMMENDS

GAO recommends to the Secretary of Commerce that CS (1) strengthen management controls, (2) improve workforce planning, and (3) improve cost estimating related to CS's budget estimate. Commerce agreed with our findings and recommendations.

WHAT GAO FOUND

CS had management control weaknesses over its resources from 2004 to 2009. During this period, CS's budgets remained essentially flat as per capita personnel costs and administrative costs increased. However, CS leadership did not recognize the long-term implications of these changes because it lacked key financial and workforce information and risk analysis necessary for good management control. CS continued to pay fees associated with positions it maintained in U.S. embassies that were vacant but not officially eliminated. As CS's financial constraints grew, officials delayed their impact by using a variety of financial management practices. For example, the International Trade Administration (ITA), CS's parent agency, attributed some of CS's centralized costs to other units. However, as the availability of offsetting funds declined and costs continued growing, CS leadership failed to recognize the risks from these changes in accordance with good management controls, and reached a "crisis" situation in 2009. Officials froze hiring, travel, training, and supplies, compromising CS's ability to conduct its core business. CS's workforce declined by about 14 percent from its peak level in 2004 through attrition—affecting the mix and distribution of personnel.

CS intends to rebuild its workforce but lacks key planning elements for doing so, and its budget request has weaknesses that could affect its ability to meet its goals. CS will have a central role in implementing the NEI. The President's 2011 budget requested $321 million for CS, $63 million more than its 2010 appropriation. The budget would fund a major staff increase. CS is allocating $5.2 million of its 2010 appropriation to begin recruiting new staff. However, as new executive-level leadership was arriving, GAO found that CS lacked key planning elements, including a clear sense of strategic direction and an analysis to determine its workforce needs. Also, it had not updated its workforce plans to address staffing gaps since fiscal year 2007. Adding more staff could be delayed because CS's human resources office is itself understaffed and because CS requires up to 2 years to hire and train new Foreign Service Officers. GAO also found that the 2011 budget request, though sound in many respects, has weaknesses; it lacks some documentation, and it lacks risk analysis and contingency plans for highly variable program costs, which could lead to cost overruns.

CS Staff Lost from 2004 to 2009, and Planned Staff Increases in 2011

Type of staff	Number of staff in 2004	Staff lost from 2004 to 2009	Increase in staff based on 2011 request	Net change
Foreign Service Officers	246	13	59	46
Locally employed staff	944	128	138	10
Civil Service	541	98	71	-27
Total	1,731	239	268	29

Source: GAO analysis of Commerce data.

ABBREVIATIONS

CS	U.S. and Foreign Commercial Service
CSCSP	Capital Security Cost Sharing Program
FAS	Foreign Agricultural Service
FSO	Foreign Service Officer
FTE	full-time equivalent
ICASS	International Cooperative Administrative Support Services
ITA	International Trade Administration
LES	locally employed staff
NEI	National Export Initiative
OMB	Office of Management and Budget
ORAM and DRAM	Overseas and Domestic Resource Allocation Models
USDA	U.S. Department of Agriculture
USEAC	U.S. Export Assistance Center

August 31, 2010

The Honorable Barbara A. Mikulski
Chairwoman
The Honorable Richard C. Shelby
Ranking Member
Subcommittee on Commerce, Justice, Science, and Related Agencies
Committee on Appropriations
United States Senate

The Honorable Alan B. Mollohan
Chairman
The Honorable Frank R. Wolf
Ranking Member
Subcommittee on Commerce, Justice, Science, and Related Agencies
Committee on Appropriations
House of Representatives

With the recent recession and high unemployment rate, U.S. policymakers are looking for ways to improve the economy and create jobs. One avenue they are exploring is expanding exports. U.S. exports of goods and services[1] have grown steadily in recent years. In 2009, U.S. exports of goods and services reached about $1.5 trillion, approximately a $0.5 trillion or 55 percent increase since the beginning of the decade. Policymakers believe that investing more in promoting U.S. exports can strengthen the economy and generate higher paying jobs. On March 11, 2010, President Obama signed an Executive Order creating the National Export Initiative (NEI), with a presidential cabinet to oversee trade promotion and a goal of doubling exports in the next 5 years.[2] The Secretary of Commerce committed to supporting this goal by employing the U.S. and Foreign Commercial Service (CS) in assisting more U.S. companies to export, with a 2-year goal of helping more companies that already export to one country to start exporting to new markets. However, since 2004 the workforce of CS, a key agency in promoting the export of U.S. manufactured goods and services, has declined, calling into question its ability to increase its activities and represent U.S. business interests internationally.

In response to a conference committee mandate,[3] we reviewed (1) how well CS has managed its resources over the past 5 years, and (2) the completeness of CS's workforce plans and the soundness of its fiscal year 2011 budget request. In addition, we are providing information on how CS export promotion funding compares with funding for the Department of Agriculture (USDA) and Department of State (State) for analogous activities from 2004 to 2009.[4]

We used GAO's standards for internal control[5] to assess how well CS managed its resources from 2004 to 2009. We analyzed data provided by CS on staffing losses and gains domestically and overseas by post, identifying the number of civil servants, political hires, Foreign Service Officers (FSO), and locally employed staff (LES). We also analyzed CS's appropriations and full-time equivalent (FTE) staffing levels from 2004 through 2009 and supporting information, and interviewed CS officials. To determine how complete CS's plans for rebuilding its workforce are, we reviewed CS's 2010 and 2011 budget requests and available workforce planning and human capital resource information, interviewed CS officials about their practices and how decisions were made, and evaluated their efforts using GAO's five key principles of effective strategic workforce planning.[6] (Further information on our scope and methodology is provided in app. I.) To evaluate the soundness of CS's 2011 budget request, we assessed the request using the 12 elements GAO has identified as best practices for an effective cost estimate in our *GAO Cost Estimating and Assessment Guide*.[7] Appendix III explains the 12 principles and associated characteristics in detail. We also interviewed the agency officials responsible for developing the request and reviewed related information. We conducted this performance audit from September 2009 to August 2010, in accordance with generally accepted government auditing standards. Those standards require that we plan and perform the audit to obtain sufficient, appropriate evidence to provide a reasonable basis for our findings and conclusions based on our audit objectives. We believe that the evidence obtained provides a reasonable basis for our findings and conclusions based on our audit objectives.

BACKGROUND

CS Plays a Major Role in Export Promotion

CS plays a major role in U.S. export promotion activities as the primary agency providing export assistance to individual businesses, especially small- and medium-sized businesses. It is a unit of the Department of Commerce's (Commerce) International Trade Administration (ITA), and its services include the following:

- *Counseling and intelligence.* CS assists U.S. businesses in understanding foreign markets and developing export marketing plans including overseas product pricing, best prospects, market entry strategies, and distribution channels, and facilitates access to export financing and public and private export promotion assistance.

- *Matchmaking.* CS organizes and participates in trade events and forums, and introduces U.S. businesses to qualified overseas agents, distributors, end users, and other partners.
- *Advocacy services.* CS alerts U.S. firms to major overseas projects and procurement, and advocates on behalf of U.S. firms bidding on projects.

CS has about 300 staff members in U.S. Export Assistance Centers (USEAC) located throughout the United States who work with firms that are new to exporting or want to expand their exporting efforts. USEACs provide counseling and planning services, such as working with firms to select target markets and develop marketing plans. They also coordinate with CS posts overseas, which provide matchmaking, advocacy, and market intelligence services in the target markets. About 1,000 CS international field staff—made up of FSOs and LES—are located at posts around the world to provide these services. LES are generally natives of the countries in which they are located, making them well-suited to help U.S. companies make local connections.[8] USEAC staff and overseas post staff are supported by about 180 staff at headquarters in Washington, D.C.

For the purposes of this report we reviewed CS activities related to providing information, counseling, and assistance for exports of services and manufactured goods, which is CS's main focus. USDA and State also conduct export promotion activities.[9] USDA's Foreign Agricultural Service focuses on promoting commodities produced by U.S. farmers and ranchers. State supports CS's efforts in countries where CS does not have a presence (see app. II).[10] However, U.S. export promotion activities are multifaceted and also include reducing trade barriers, government-to-government advocacy, financing and other monetary assistance, and other activities.

Export Promotion Is a Priority of the Current Administration

U.S. plans to increase exports are generally articulated in the Trade Promotion Coordinating Committee's National Export Strategy, which is issued annually. Established in 1993, the Trade Promotion Coordinating Committee is an interagency group established to provide a framework to coordinate the export promotion and export financing activities of the U.S. government.[11] As of 2010, 20 U.S. agencies have a role in export promotion.[12] However, we have reported for a number of years that the annual National Export Strategies have limitations that affect the Coordinating Committee's ability to coordinate trade promotion activities. For example, National Export Strategies provide limited information on member agencies' goals and progress, relative to broad national priorities, to guide future efforts.[13]

Another effort is under way that could facilitate better interagency coordination. On January 27, 2010, President Obama announced the NEI in an effort to support U.S. economic recovery following the recession. A newly created Export Promotion Cabinet that reports to the President will coordinate and implement the goals of the NEI, and is expected to deliver a report to the President with a plan to implement the goals of the NEI in September 2010.

While many aspects of the NEI are still in the planning stages, the NEI will have three main components:

- Educating U.S. companies about export opportunities; directly connecting them with new customers, partners, and distributors overseas; and advocating for their interests.
- Providing access to credit through the Export-Import Bank of the United States with a special focus on small- and medium-sized businesses.
- Removing trade barriers.

The first component of the NEI, educating U.S. companies about export opportunities, will be carried out in large part by the Department of Commerce through CS.[14]

CS's Budget Is Driven by Personnel and Administrative Costs

The majority of CS's costs are related to the personnel that staff CS's headquarters and its domestic and overseas export assistance posts. According to CS, 60 percent of its budget in 2009 was associated with personnel costs, including salaries, benefits, and FSO support costs for officers posted overseas. FSO support costs include relocation, travel, training, home leave allowances, and shipping and storage of household goods. Administrative payments to State associated with having personnel stationed overseas, including International Cooperative Administrative Support Services (ICASS) and Capital Security Cost Sharing Program (CSCSP) charges,[15] as well as payments to ITA, CS's parent agency, for shared overhead totaled 29 percent.[16] The remaining 11 percent included CS-specific overhead costs including rent, communications, utilities, program-related travel, supplies, printing, and equipment costs as well as costs for developing and enhancing software for CS worldwide.

CS charges fees for export promotion services that benefit individual companies, such as connecting them with potential buyers and distributors. CS uses the fees it collects to cover the costs of the related program expenses. CS reported that it collected approximately $10 million in fees in 2008.

CS's Management of Increasing Costs and Declining Staff Levels from 2004 to 2009 Had Weaknesses

CS leadership lacked systematic information about CS's workforce, and did not fully recognize or adequately respond to program risks created by growing administrative costs and declining staff levels from 2004 to 2009. Management control standards require entities to ensure that program managers have systems to provide needed operational and financial information in a timely manner to carry out their management and oversight responsibilities.[17] In the case of CS, the most important management responsibilities were related to workforce decisions, since workforce expenses are the largest portion of CS's budget. Additionally, these standards require management to identify and analyze the relevant risks an agency faces from internal and external sources so it can proactively manage them. From 2004 to 2009, CS's budgets remained essentially flat as per capita personnel costs and administrative costs increased.[18] Although CS leadership was aware of this trend, they did not have processes in place to analyze and respond to the long-term financial implications of these costs on CS's workforce. Additionally, CS was not fully aware of the costs associated with positions it maintained in U.S. embassies that were vacant but not officially eliminated and did not take steps that would have saved money on them. As CS's financial constraints grew, officials delayed their impact through a variety of financial management practices such as using unobligated funds from prior years' appropriations. However, as the availability of these offsetting funds declined and costs continued growing, CS leadership failed to recognize the risks entailed by the financial problems, and the organization reached a "crisis" situation in 2009. Officials froze hiring, travel, training, and supplies, compromising CS's ability to conduct its core business. CS's workforce declined by about 240 staff from its peak level in 2004 through attrition—affecting the mix and distribution of personnel.

CS's Budgets Were Flat as Costs Increased

From 2004 to 2009, CS's budgets remained essentially flat, while at the same time the agency faced increasing per capita personnel costs. CS appropriations grew about 1.9 percent on average per year during that time frame. This represented a total increase of about 10 percent from 2004 to 2009, as shown in table 1.

Although CS's budget was adjusted for inflation and other increases such as pay raises and changes in benefit contribution rates, its annual increases did not cover its full costs, according to CS officials. For example, administrative costs grew from 20 percent ($44 million) of its obligations in 2004 to 30 percent ($72 million) in 2009.[19] CS officials calculated the total cumulative funding gap for 2004 to 2009—the difference between its annual appropriations and full costs—to be $24 million.

Since 2004, CS faced increased administrative payments to State that consumed larger shares of its funds. One factor increasing costs was State's CSCSP, which began in 2005 to support the building of new secure embassies and consulates. The fee was phased in over a 5-year period, with the full annual charge levied for the first time in 2009. In 2005, the fee for CS was about $3.1 million, and in 2009 it was $23.7 million. Other factors included increasing costs for personnel, benefits, and rent, which include adjustments for inflation.

Table 1. CS's Appropriations and Obligations, Fiscal Years 2004-2009

Dollars in millions	2004	2005	2006	2007	2008	2009
CS appropriations	$217	$222	$232	$232	$237	$238
CS prior year funding obligated	12	12	12	11	7	5
CS funds obligated	$225	$227	$236	$235	$242	$243

Source: Presidents' budgets, appropriations bills, and internal CS budget documents.

Note: In internal CS budget documents, funds obligated are equal to the sum of appropriations and prior year funding obligated. However, with the exception of 2009, CS appropriations in appropriations legislation, which are listed here, differ from the amounts listed in CS internal budget documents.

Table 2. CS's Estimated and Actual FTE Levels, Fiscal Years 2004-2009

	2004	2005	2006	2007	2008	2009
FTEs in budget justification (estimated/ requested)	1,286	1,386	1,386	1,254	1,254	1,137
FTEs actual	1,254	1,238	1,149	1,106	1,061	1,041
Difference between requested and actual FTEs	32	148	237	148	193	96

Source: Congressional budget justifications.
Note: FTE numbers in this table include some, but not all, LES.

CS made up the difference by not filling positions. CS budget requests were based partly on an estimated number of FTEs. CS overestimated the number of FTEs it would support with its budget every year, as shown in table 2. The actual numbers averaged 142 FTEs, or 11 percent, less than their estimates. CS used the funds it was provided based on these overestimated FTE levels to pay expenses such as administrative costs. The fact that this happened over so many years indicates that CS did not fully recognize how its workforce was being affected by increasing administrative costs.

CS Lacked Financial and Workforce Information Necessary to Manage Its Programs

CS leadership had information about growing costs as early as 2006, but they did not recognize the severity of the situation. CS had data about the growth in unfunded adjustments to base, which are essentially the difference between what CS needed in terms of funding to cover increased costs and the appropriation it received. However, CS leaders said they were not fully aware of the long-term financial and workforce implications of increasing costs until 2009 when CS switched to a new financial management system, which according to CS officials illuminated how little discretionary funding was available. In 2009, they undertook an exercise to analyze and more fully understand the costs that affected the CS budget. Additionally, CS lacks an automated workforce information system to provide up-to-date staffing information, which also has financial implications. For example, without this information CS could not easily review ICASS and CSCSP charges in order to confirm whether State's charges for these activities were correct. Currently, CS officials compile information from quarterly reports supplied by the posts to determine staffing totals. The lack of risk assessment and the lack of workforce information are both management control weaknesses.

CS Did Not Eliminate Vacant Positions or Restructure Its Operations

CS has incurred costs for administrative payments related to overseas staff that officials consider to be "fixed costs," but which can be reduced by eliminating vacant positions, downsizing, or eliminating offices. For example, CS incurs CSCSP charges for positions officially established at overseas posts, regardless of whether there is a person in the position. CS has access to information on the number of positions at its overseas posts through State's Executive Agency Personnel Support system, which tracks the number of positions at posts. The information is used to determine the number of positions CS is paying for including the number of vacant positions at posts. However, Commerce officials indicated they find the system difficult to use, and they do not use the information to manage their overseas workforce. The only way to eliminate a CSCSP charge is to officially eliminate the position.[20] In 2010, there were about 200 unfilled positions at posts incurring CSCSP charges that CS did not eliminate. Charges for vacant positions cost CS approximately $2 million annually, according to a CS budget official. The last time CS eliminated a significant number of vacant positions was in 2004. According to a senior CS official, CS recognized that State's CSCSP charge would put a cost on every overseas position whether or not it was filled, so in 2004 before the new charge was implemented, the Office of International Operations reviewed its global presence and eliminated all non-essential positions. CS may also have incurred ICASS charges for vacant positions. To avoid ICASS charges for vacant positions, CS must inform State that the position will not be filled in the upcoming fiscal year.

Regarding office closures, CS last eliminated offices under its Transformational Commercial Diplomacy Initiative, which was planned beginning in 2006 and implemented starting in 2007. The initiative was focused both on realigning CS's efforts with its mission to focus on emerging markets, and on rightsizing its operations. Under the initiative, 23 offices were closed, mainly in Europe, and 8 offices were supposed to be opened. However, as of the end of 2009, only 3 of the 8 offices were open and staffed.

Financial Management Practices Temporarily Offset Funding Constraints

Several financial management practices temporarily helped mitigate CS's growing funding constraints. These included using unobligated funds from prior years' appropriations, redistributing centralized costs to other ITA units, and redirecting user fees to ensure CS did not spend more funds than were authorized.

First, CS used its balance of unspent funds from prior years' unobligated appropriations to cover funding shortfalls. However, Congress changed CS's appropriations from no-year funding to 2-year funding in 2006. Whereas CS obligated $12 million in unspent funds in 2004, in 2009 it obligated only $5 million, as unobligated funds from prior years were depleted and some funds were no longer available.

Second, ITA officials told us they attributed some centralized costs that would have been charged to CS to other ITA programs in order to help CS with its financial problems. For example, in 2009, ITA redistributed $3 million of CS's centralized costs to other ITA units (Market Access and Compliance, Manufacturing and Services, and Import Administration) to assist CS. Centralized costs include headquarters rent, utilities, information technology support, and secretarial travel. ITA normally apportions these costs based on individual staffing levels.

Third, CS fee collections were an additional source of revenue that CS used to address its resource constraints. CS obligations of fees and reimbursements averaged $9.8 million a year from 2004 through 2009.[21] CS's domestic and overseas offices create surplus fees when they charge exporters for services, and funds remain after the bills associated with the service are paid.[22] Historically, surplus service fees were used at the location where they were earned to pay for program activities in support of CS's mission such as travel with an ambassador to another city to promote exports. As funding constraints increased, CS management began centrally controlling these fees, requiring posts to seek permission to use them. CS officials told us they took control over these surplus fees to ensure they would not spend more money than Congress authorized and violate the Antideficiency Act.[23]

CS Froze Hiring, Travel, Training, and Supplies, which Compromised Operations

Once the growth in costs reached what CS officials characterized as a "crisis" situation, CS took a number of actions such as imposing a hiring freeze in 2008 and 2009.[24] CS also cut travel funds by 28 percent from 2008 to 2009, and saved money by asking FSOs to stay in their current locations rather than relocating to them to new posts. CS also cut training and supplies. According to a senior CS official, currently CS has no discretionary travel or training funds. Although CS took actions to mitigate the impact of increasing costs as noted above, they were not timely and reflected management control weaknesses. These weaknesses include the lack of a process for promptly identifying risks as they emerge and lack of analysis of the possible effect these mitigating actions could have on CS's ability to effectively and efficiently carry out its operations. CS did not identify a long-term sustainable solution to the change in its financial situation.

Staff in both the domestic and the foreign field offices commented in a 2009 assessment of their operations that staff shortages and budget constraints, including a lack of travel funds, compromised CS's ability to conduct its core business.[25] In the domestic field offices, staffing shortages and budgetary constraints were mentioned as weaknesses or threats in seven of eight regions. One domestic region stated, "With a hiring freeze in place and severe budget limitations, current vacancies cannot be filled in USEACs on a timely basis. As well, important travel necessary to reach clients/partners, engage in professional development, and lead efforts on trade missions and at trade shows cannot be funded." Likewise, all six regions overseas indicated that lack of resources was a weakness, and four of the six identified staffing shortages as a problem. For example, one overseas region stated that "budget limitations constrict the extent to which posts can travel, which directly impacts their ability to find and assist clients." Additionally, the capacity to keep up with ever-growing demand for services was mentioned as a problem by some domestic and overseas locations.

CS's Workforce Declined by Almost 14 Percent

As a result of CS's flat budget, the size of its workforce declined through attrition from 2004 to 2009, and the composition and location of personnel shifted. During this period, CS's workforce declined by over 200 staff, from 1,731 to 1,492. The number of FSOs declined by 5 percent, LES by 14 percent, and civil servants by 18 percent (see table 3). The number of staff in foreign field offices declined by 12 percent, in domestic field offices by 9 percent, and at headquarters by 28 percent (see table 4).

CS Lacks Key Planning Elements to Rebuild Its Workforce, and Its 2011 Budget Request Has Some Weaknesses

Although CS is taking steps to rebuild its workforce, it lacks key elements in its workforce planning, and its 2011 budget request has some weaknesses that could affect its ability to meet its goals. In 2010, CS received an appropriation of $258 million, of which CS planned to use $5.2 million to begin reversing CS staffing declines. In addition, the President's 2011 budget asks for a major CS staffing increase. The 2011 budget requests $321 million for CS, $63 million more than its 2010 appropriation. Although CS began the process of reversing its previous years' staffing declines through these funding increases, we found that CS has not been following workforce planning principles and lacks current workforce plans for utilizing the new staff. CS's understaffed Office of Foreign Service Human Resources and the long lead time needed to hire and train FSOs could delay staffing increases. Additionally, we found that its budget development methodology was sound in many respects, but had a few weaknesses that could affect CS's ability to meet its goals, such as not assessing potential risks of estimated costs, which if overly optimistic could lead to cost overruns.

Table 3. Change in CS Staff by Type, Fiscal Years 2004-2009

	Number of staff in 2004	Number of staff in 2009	Change in staff, 2004 to 2009	Percent change, 2004 to 2009
FSO	246	233	-13	-5.3%
LES	944	816	-128	-13.6
Civil Service	541	443	-98	-18.1
Total	1,731	1,492	-239	-13.8%

Source: GAO analysis of Commerce data.

Table 4. Change in CS Staff by Location, Fiscal Years 2004-2009

	Number of staff in 2004	Number of staff in 2009	Change in staff, 2004 to 2009	Percent change, 2004 to 2009
Foreign field offices	1,190	1,049	-141	-11.8%
Domestic field offices	286	260	-26	-9.1
Headquarters	255	183	-72	-28.2
Total	1,731	1,492	-239	-13.8%

Source: GAO analysis of Commerce data.

CS Plans to Rebuild Its Workforce

CS Is Increasing Staff to Implement the NEI

CS is rebuilding its workforce and taking other measures to fulfill its major role in implementing the NEI in 2011.[26] Commerce, through the Trade Promotion Coordinating Committee, leads the administration's trade promotion efforts and will "operationalize" the NEI, according to the Secretary of Commerce. To that end, the Secretary indicated that with the additional resources requested in 2011, ITA expects to hire new trade experts—mostly in foreign countries—to advocate and find customers for U.S. companies, allowing CS to help more than 23,000 clients to begin or grow their export sales in 2011. Additionally, CS will focus on increasing the number of small- and medium-sized businesses exporting to more than one market by 50 percent over the next 5 years.

CS already began the process of rebuilding its workforce by designating $5.2 million of its 2010 appropriations to expand its presence in critical emerging markets. CS planned to use the funds to develop a more robust presence in challenging and developing markets in Africa, Eastern Europe, and Asia, where its presence was limited. CS projected hiring a total of 30 new positions in 2010—8 FSOs and 22 LES. In April 2010, CS approved 17 hiring freeze exemptions. It extended offers to 14 certified applicants; 11 individuals accepted the offers, according to a CS official. CS hopes to bring them on in August 2010 and anticipates they will fill vacancies in domestic and overseas locations.[27] These individuals are filling positions created by retirements and attrition that occurred in 2008 and 2009. CS also expects that at least another 7 current officers will leave the service in 2010. CS may fill those potential vacancies as it completed the process of identifying and creating a list of certified applicants, on July 12, 2010.

However, a senior CS official noted that rather than using funds to hire people in 2010, CS is focused on creating more exports sooner by increasing marketing, the number of companies going on trade missions, the number of potential trade partners brought to the United States on reverse trade missions, and matchmaking efforts. The rationale was to focus on activities that could provide quick results, according to CS officials, as it takes about 18 months to prepare a company to export, whereas it takes about 6 to 9 months to assist a company that has already exported to one market with exporting to a second market.

CS Requested a Major Staffing Increase for 2011

CS requested a major staffing increase for 2011, seeking to hire a total of 268 staff in support of the NEI. CS plans to hire 130 FSOs and civil servants, a 20 percent increase over its 2010 level of 659 staff in these categories. Additionally, CS plans to hire 138 LES, a 17 percent increase over its 2010 level of 795 staff.[28] The requested increase would reverse the 239-person decline in CS's overall staffing that occurred from 2004 to 2009. Table 5 identifies the staff CS lost over the past 5 years and the number of staff it plans to hire in 2011.

Whereas staffing declines overseas for both FSOs and LES may be addressed if the budget request is approved, there will still be fewer staff compared with 2004 in Washington, D.C. and the domestic field offices, which are generally staffed by civil servants. Additionally, the 63 FSOs and 84 civil servants who are eligible to retire as of March 2010 may not be replaced by the staff requested in the 2011 budget request.

Table 5. CS Staff Lost Over the Past 5 Years and Planned Increase in Staff Based on 2011 Budget Request

	Staff lost, 2004 to 2009	Planned increase in staff based on 2011 budget request	Net change
FSO	13	59	46
LES	128	138	10
Civil Service[a]	98	71	-27
Total	239	268	29

Source: GAO analysis of Commerce staffing data.
[a] Civil Service includes staff serving both in Washington, D.C. and at USEACs.

Table 6. FSOs Serving in the United States in the Fourth Quarter of Fiscal Year 2009

	USEACs	Multilateral Development Banks	Headquarters	Language and other training	Total
Number of FSOs	27	5	10	12	54
Percent of all FSOs (domestic and overseas)	12%	2	4	5	23%

Source: GAO analysis of Commerce staffing data.
Note: FSOs in headquarters are in positions supporting the Foreign Service, e.g., one is the Deputy Assistant Secretary for International Operations and another is a Career Development and Assignment Officer.

Another factor affecting overseas staffing is the use of FSOs in domestic positions. FSOs are sometimes assigned to work in USEACs, serve in multilateral development banks, or work in headquarters (see table 6). For example, in the fourth quarter of 2009, 23 percent of 233 FSOs were in domestic positions, with 27 FSOs specifically in USEACs. CS expects FSOs to serve a 2-year assignment at a USEAC, usually within the first 7 years of their service.[29] CS believes that what FSOs learn in their domestic rotations improves their ability to serve clients overseas.

CS Lacks Complete Strategic Workforce Plans to Utilize New Staff

Although CS requested a significant increase in funding to hire new staff in the 2011 budget request, it has not followed key principles in workforce planning to guide its use of these staff. Strategic workforce planning addresses two critical needs: first, aligning an organization's human capital program with its current and emerging mission and programmatic goals, and second, developing long-term strategies for acquiring, developing, and retaining staff to achieve programmatic goals. While agencies' approaches to workforce planning vary, the five key principles that strategic workforce planning should address irrespective of the context in which the planning is done are (1) setting strategic direction, (2) conducting workforce needs analysis, (3) developing workforce strategies to fill the gaps, (4) evaluating and revising strategies, and (5) involving management and employees throughout the process.[30] We focused our review on steps one through three, because it was premature for us to evaluate steps four and five given the status of CS's efforts during our review. CS executive-level leadership was new and was just beginning to assess CS operations.

CS Lacked Executive-Level Leadership and Strategic Direction

Until recently, CS lacked executive leadership and strategic direction in its workforce planning efforts because of key vacancies between administrations. One of the lessons from our prior work on human capital issues is the importance of having leadership that is clearly and personally involved in strategic workforce planning and provides organizational vision in times of change. Effective organizations integrate human capital approaches as strategies for accomplishing their mission. They stay alert to emerging mission demands and human capital challenges and remain open to reevaluating their human capital practices in light of their demonstrated successes or failures in achieving the organization's strategic objectives.

According to a senior CS official, the lack of political leadership hampered efforts to analyze and make decisions regarding the organization's longer term workforce needs and to ensure its ability to undertake its mission and achieve its goals. Instead, CS's recent workforce planning efforts have primarily focused on short-term responses to its constrained budget situation, such as not hiring new staff, and extending FSO tours at some posts to avoid the cost of moving them to different posts.

While ITA and CS experienced key leadership vacancies for more than a year, CS now has new executive-level leaders who are focused on determining CS's direction and resource needs. In February 2010, the new Assistant Secretary for Trade Promotion and Director General of the U.S. and Foreign Commercial Service was confirmed, and in March 2010, the new Undersecretary for International Trade was sworn in. In addition, Commerce announced the creation of a new Director's position to coordinate and direct the Department's NEI efforts, filling the position in April 2010. The new Assistant Secretary is currently reviewing all of CS's budgets, activities, and personnel to determine what its structure should be to accomplish its goals, including those of the NEI.

CS has also lacked a clear sense of strategic direction. For example, the Trade Promotion Coordinating Committee did not issue a 2009 National Export Strategy, which has a role in directing the nation's export promotion priorities and goals of CS; the last National Export Strategy was issued in October 2008 by the previous administration.[31] A plan to carry out the NEI is due in September 2010. The NEI may have important implications for CS workforce planning, especially for the locations of staff and offices.

CS has already developed several initiatives that include staff allocations and a list of "candidate" countries for new offices, which also appears in its budget request. These are preliminary plans for how CS will pursue activities in support of the NEI's goals. However, CS did not have support for how the staffing allocations were developed and the countries were identified; we therefore are unable to determine how these decisions were made.

CS Has Not Conducted a Workforce Needs Analysis to Determine Staff Levels or Placement

CS has not conducted a systematic workforce needs analysis to determine the number or type of staff (FSOs, LES, or civil servants) needed or where those staff would be located domestically and overseas. Our prior human capital work has found that a fact-based, performance-oriented approach to human capital management is crucial for maximizing the value of human capital as well as managing risk.[32] High-performing organizations identify their current and future human capital needs, including the appropriate number of employees, the key competencies and skills mix for mission accomplishment, and the appropriate deployment of staff across the organization and then create strategies for identifying and filling gaps. Valid and reliable data are critical to assessing an agency's workforce requirements and heighten an agency's ability to manage risk by allowing managers to spotlight areas for attention before crises develop and identify opportunities for enhancing agency results. Although the costs of collecting data may be significant, the costs of making decisions without the necessary information can be equally significant. In preparing its 2011 budget request, CS did not make staffing decisions based on an overall analysis of its needs, according to CS officials. Rather, it made decisions based on anecdotal information about the demand for services.

Additionally, CS only recently began to systematically monitor how many vacancies it had and how many positions it might need to carry out its mission in the future. CS took approximately 3 months to provide us with data on staffing, in part because it lacks an automated personnel system and had to use data sources such as quarterly staffing reports. A Commerce official told us that the number of staff requested in the 2011 budget request was not based on vacancies.

CS's lack of a workforce needs analysis also has implications for staff placement. Whereas CS's strategic focus has been on priority markets such as Brazil, China, and India as well as emerging markets in countries such as Azerbaijan and Qatar, staff placements may change under the NEI. As mentioned above, CS's budget request includes a list of 22 countries that are "candidates currently being considered for new overseas offices," where CS is considering placing staff. Commerce officials told us the list was not comprehensive, and the reasons for selecting those countries were not well documented. Among the "candidates" were offices that were closed under the Transformational Commercial Diplomacy Initiative such as Amsterdam, Netherlands; Barcelona, Spain; Kingston, Jamaica; Hamburg, Germany; Port of Spain, Trinidad and Tobago; and Lyon, France. Additionally, according to a State official, the NEI may target Colombia, Indonesia, Saudi Arabia, South Africa, Turkey, and Vietnam. Shifting CS's focus could change the skills and experience its workforce needs to be effective in those markets. For example, even though CS is hiring 11 new FSOs in 2010, three important posts in Brasilia, Algiers, and Kuwait are being filled with limited non-career appointments, because of a shortage of experienced officers. None of the new candidates has the necessary skills, abilities, and knowledge to take one of these positions as a first post.

CS Has Not Systematically Addressed Staffing Gaps Since 2007

CS has not followed workforce planning principles such as developing a plan to address its staffing gaps. Once an agency identifies its needs, it can develop strategies tailored to address gaps in the number, skills and competencies, and deployment of its workforce and the alignment of human capital approaches that will sustain the workforce in the future. Strategies include programs, policies, and practices that enable an agency to recruit, develop, and retain staff needed to achieve program goals.[33] In addition, agencies need to understand the strengths and weaknesses of their current human capital program.

According to a senior CS official, CS does not plan to fill all of its vacant positions. Rather, it will fill what it considers to be priority vacancies, including staffing new offices with seasoned officers. The official told us they have a reasonably good idea of where those priority locations are; one such possibility was Baku, Azerbaijan, where CS planned to open an office under the Transformational Commercial Diplomacy Initiative but did not due to a lack of funds. However, when asked if the 22 locations in the 2011 budget request were the priority locations, we were told they are possible locations but are not necessarily where people would be placed.

It is also important for agencies to align their workforce to achieve their program goals. However, since the implementation of the Transformational Commercial Diplomacy Initiative, CS workforce strategies have not been based on a systematic analysis, but were ad hoc according to Commerce officials. Commerce officials told us that in some instances they asked FSOs to extend their overseas tours at their current locations as a cost-saving measure rather than being moved somewhere else, at substantial cost, based on a systematic determination of where they are most needed.[34] CS also made decisions to leave some posts without an FSO. Instead, these posts were managed by LES—there were 25 such posts at the end of the last quarter of 2009.[35]

CS has not used its available staffing allocation model to make overseas staffing decisions since 2007, as part of its Transformational Commercial Diplomacy Initiative.[36] Under the initiative, CS used its staffing allocation model to identify locations to close, open, or add staff. The model analyzed CS's staff allocations using quantitative factors such as the macroeconomic strength of each country and other factors related to each market's size and structure. It also integrated qualitative factors including foreign and trade policy priorities, levels of economic development, geographic coverage, and commercial environments. A similar model exists for the placement of staff domestically at USEACs. The model's goal is to create a starting point for determining which U.S. locations have the highest export potential. Other factors affecting the placement of staff at USEACs include geographic coverage, policy initiatives, locations of commercial centers, and the skills and abilities of local staff.

CS's Understaffed Human Resources Office and the Long Lead Time Needed to Hire and Train FSOs Could Delay Staffing Increases

Besides the lack of a quality workforce plan, CS's capacity to implement what CS officials said may be the biggest hiring effort in CS history is compromised because its human resources office is understaffed.[37] CS's Office of Foreign Service Human Resources, which manages the hiring process for FSOs, only had staff in 10 of its 19 positions in 2009. However, CS planned to increase the number of staff in 2010. According to a senior CS official, the office recently received permission to fill 5 of the 9 vacant existing positions. As of June 2010, 3 of the 5 positions were filled, although the office also just lost another staff person.

CS needs a lead time of approximately 2 years to accomplish the major staffing increase requested in the 2011 budget request. It takes about 1 year to put together a list of qualified applicants, which involves advertising the position, identifying qualified candidates, interviewing candidates, selecting candidates, and making offers. Once a candidate is selected, he or she must obtain security and medical clearances. Commerce started the hiring process for 59 new FSOs in July 2009 and CS hopes to make offers to qualified candidates in summer 2010. Additionally, depending on the post, some positions require language training, which can take up to a year. Thus, it could take almost 2 years to hire, train, and field a new FSO. The process for hiring LES is much shorter, generally 6 weeks to 5 months, according to a senior CS official. CS is not responsible for hiring LES, who are hired overseas by State on CS's behalf.

The 2011 Budget Request Has Weaknesses That Could Affect CS's Ability to Meet Its Goals

For 2011, ITA developed a $321 million budget request for funding to support CS's activities and hire new staff.[38] The request was $63 million higher than its 2010 appropriation. We evaluated the methodology that ITA used to develop this request using best practices identified in the *GAO Cost Estimating and Assessment Guide.*[39] See Appendix III for more information on our evaluation, including detailed descriptions of the best practices criteria. ITA's methodology was sound in many respects, with good calculations for current costs such as overseas administrative fees, a good amount of detail for certain costs such as the purchase of vehicles, as well as error-checking processes that helped to ensure accuracy. However, the request also has weaknesses that could affect CS's ability to meet its goals. Among the weaknesses we identified using the *GAO Cost Estimating and Assessment Guide* are (1) a lack of information regarding potential risks associated with the costs presented in the budget request, such as changes in exchange rates, which could lead to overly optimistic estimates and cost overruns, and (2) the lack of sufficient documentation, specifically back-up data, to clearly track costs over time, allow for the budget request to be validated, and enable new staff members to understand the request in the event of staff turnover.

The 2011 Budget Request Is Sound in Many Respects

The methodology used to develop the budget request is sound in many respects, and CS took steps to ensure its accuracy. ITA budget analysts made many of their calculations in ways that are endorsed by the *GAO Cost Estimating and Assessment Guide.* They also broke the request down to an appropriate level of detail based on the standards in the guide, which both improves accuracy and facilitates good management.

In an effort to determine the accuracy of the estimate, we reviewed ITA's calculations for technical soundness and found them to be acceptable. ITA used rigorous budgeting practices to develop many parts of the request. For example, officials used relevant historical cost data and incorporated adjustments for inflation. They also followed best practices by varying their estimation methodologies as appropriate for different situations, which increased the request's accuracy. For example, based on Office of Management and Budget (OMB) guidance, ITA estimated that the personnel they anticipated hiring in 2011 would come on board 3 months after the start of the fiscal year, on average, and the request reflected this hiring lapse.

Additionally, ITA performed thorough error checking on its request, enabling CS management to make hiring and spending decisions with reasonable confidence that no costs had been forgotten or miscalculated. CS's process in developing the request included multiple reviews to ensure accuracy, including internal reviews by various stakeholders within Commerce and external reviews by OMB. CS used the feedback from these reviews to update the request as needed. Also, CS routinely updated the costs in the budget with actual costs as they became available, enabling them to see if the estimate was on track.

CS's 2011 budget request also broke down costs to a level of detail that met the standards in the *GAO Cost Estimating and Assessment Guide* in most cases, ensuring that activities and costs were broken down into small pieces that management could individually plan for, schedule, and control. For example, salaries were calculated separately for several different types of employees rather than using one salary cost as the basis for all the calculations, and the cost of replacing 37 vehicles was identified separately. One of the benefits of including this level of detail is ensuring that cost elements are not omitted or double counted.

The 2011 Budget Request Lacks a Risk Analysis and Contingency Plans

ITA did not perform a risk analysis on its budget request for CS, which could lead to overly optimistic estimates of costs and cost overruns.[40] We have found that most agency budget requests are overly optimistic, underestimating average costs.[41] A risk analysis would help correct for this tendency by providing levels of confidence so that ITA would understand the probability of executing the budget successfully given the risks that were assessed. The risk analysis would identify the assumptions driving the estimate, and provide a range of costs that span the best and worst case scenarios. This would inform CS management of the probability that costs for salaries or other key items might exceed funding levels requested, and enable them to develop contingency plans for making spending and hiring decisions accordingly. For example, new staff will be located in different locations with vastly different costs. According to an ITA official, salaries for LES range from $12,000 in Vietnam to $100,000 in Frankfurt, Germany. However, the budget request did not provide a range of possible LES salary costs. Instead, ITA used an overly simplistic averaging approach to estimate LES costs, failing to give management perspective on how these costs might vary with different staff placement scenarios, changing exchange rates, etc. Although ITA is not required to perform a risk analysis by OMB's annual budget development guidelines, it is a best practice according to the *GAO Cost Estimating and Assessment Guide.*[42]

Assumptions that drive the budget request were not fully explained, contributing to the inability to perform a risk analysis. Major assumptions in the 2011 budget request include salary estimates, annual salary increases, currency fluctuation, and travel costs, none of which were fully explained. Since ITA prepares its budget 2 years in advance, e.g., drafting its 2011 budget request in 2009, there is substantial uncertainty in these assumptions. Some assumptions were documented, such as using 2009 amounts with appropriate adjustments to estimate costs for 2011, but others were not explained. For example, travel costs were presented with a single number, without further explanation of how they arrived at this figure. Also, the reasoning behind estimating a particular exchange rate was not explained. Exchange rates can vary substantially. For example, over the course of 2009, the average monthly exchange rate of the dollar to the Brazilian real varied from a low of 1.8 to a high of 2.4, a difference of 30 percent. Likewise, the Mexican peso's average monthly exchange rate with the dollar varied by 16 percent, the euro varied by 12 percent, the Japanese yen varied by 11 percent, and the Indian rupee varied by 7 percent. Without details and explanations, CS could not calculate risk distributions for assumptions like these, which would enable it to understand how much costs might vary if the situation changes.

ITA's Budgeting Methodology Lacks Some Documentation

ITA's budget request lacks sufficient supporting documentation, making it difficult for Congress or other parties to understand how the budget request was developed. For example, the budget request broke down changes in the budget for 2011, and these changes were added to 2010 costs to arrive at the total request. However, the budget request did not include the 2010 cost information. According to the *GAO Cost Estimating and Assessment Guide,* it is a best practice to provide sufficient detail so that the documentation allows for clear tracking of cost estimates over time.[43] By documenting all steps in the development of its budget request, ITA would be able re-create its estimates in the event of budget staff turnover. This is particularly important since only a small number of people develop the budget. Additionally, thorough documentation of calculations and back-up data would allow the request to be checked and validated. Without this information, it is impossible for an outside reviewer to corroborate the information in the request.

ITA briefed department-level officials in Commerce as well as the Office of Management and Budget on the 2011 budget request. However, we were unable to obtain any documentation of what was presented at the briefings, so we could not determine whether the briefings contained enough detail for management to understand the level of accuracy, completeness, and quality of the estimate, which is a best practice.

CONCLUSIONS

In the wake of growing financial constraints and staffing declines, CS's leadership faces significant challenges in its efforts to rebuild its workforce and play a major role in the President's NEI. Additionally, depending on the direction set by the current administration, CS officials may need to make significant changes such as realigning CS's workforce and offices. While the President's plan is being finalized, the Assistant Secretary has opportunities to improve management controls over CS's resources and proactively address the issues that led to their "crisis" situation in 2009. These opportunities include improving long-term financial and workforce information necessary to recognize significant changes affecting the organization; routinely reviewing operations to identify potential cost savings, such as administrative fees related to overseas posts; and recognizing risks and considering alternative responses to significant resource changes in a systematic manner so as to minimize actions such as freezing hiring, travel, and training that compromise CS's ability to conduct its core business.

CS currently lacks two key capabilities that would better position it to implement its 2011 budget and rapidly respond to any new priorities. The first is a workforce plan developed in accordance with workforce planning principles that is linked to the agency's strategic goals and that would enable agency managers to regularly identify workforce gaps and develop a workforce strategy that fills them, including using or adopting its current staffing model. The implementation of such planning needs to be supported by adequate human capital management resources. The second capability is to estimate the budgetary costs of any changes in its operations according to best practices. This includes risk analyses to ensure that factors that could negatively impact its ability to fully fund its operations are understood and considered; contingency plans to address possible funding shortfalls; and documentation in support of the costs used to construct the estimate, so that future management and new budget staff can understand the estimate's assumptions, costs, and contingencies.

RECOMMENDATIONS FOR EXECUTIVE ACTION

To better ensure CS effectively and efficiently uses its resources in support of its strategic goals and the President's National Export Initiative, we are making the following three recommendations:

The Secretary of Commerce should direct the Undersecretary for International Trade to

- strengthen management controls over CS's financial and workforce resources,
- improve workforce planning and better align CS's workforce with its strategic goals and available resources on a routine basis, and
- improve cost estimating to better ensure that CS's budget estimate includes sufficient resources to support its planned operations and addresses potential risks.

APPENDIX I: OBJECTIVES, SCOPE, AND METHODOLOGY

In response to a Congressional mandate,[44] GAO reviewed (1) how well the U.S. and Foreign Commercial Service (CS) managed its resources from 2004 to 2009, and (2) the completeness of CS's workforce plans and the quality of its 2011 budget request. In addition, in appendix II, we provide information on how CS export promotion funding compares with the funding for Department of Agriculture (USDA) and Department of State (State) for analogous activities from 2004 to 2009.

To determine the changes in CS's workforce from 2004 to 2009, we analyzed data provided by CS on staffing losses and gains by type of position, identifying the number of civil servants, political hires, Foreign Service Officers (FSO), and locally employed staff (LES) during that 5-year period of time. We also identified staff losses and gains by location at foreign posts, U.S. Export Assistance Centers (USEAC), and CS headquarters in Washington, D.C. We traced CS data back to source documents where possible and found them sufficiently reliable to report on the loss of staff throughout CS. We used the staffing data provided by CS to identify where FSOs were serving in domestic positions.

To determine how much funding CS had available, what the major cost components of its budget were, how administrative costs changed over time, and what impact changing costs had on CS, we reviewed CS's appropriations and full-time equivalent (FTE) levels from 2004 through 2009. We used internal CS budget documents, ITA Congressional Budget Justifications, President's budgets, and appropriations bills to gather and corroborate budget data, and based on consistency among these documents, we found these data to be sufficiently reliable to report on CS's budget history. We also interviewed CS officials responsible for managing the budget. We analyzed the foreign posts' and USEACs' 2009 written comments to determine weaknesses and threats that were commonly reported.

To determine the completeness of CS's plans to rebuild its workforce, we reviewed CS's 2010 and 2011 budget requests to ascertain whether the staffing increases CS requested were sufficient to cover its staffing changes from 2004 to 2009. We interviewed CS officials who were involved in developing the requests. We also interviewed CS officials regarding their process for hiring and placing new staff overseas, and reviewed CS policy requiring FSOs to serve in domestic positions. To determine whether CS had conducted workforce planning, we evaluated its efforts using GAO's five key principles of effective strategic workforce planning.[45] We reviewed CS's previous workforce planning efforts under its 2006 Transformational Commercial Diplomacy Initiative including CS's use of its Overseas and Domestic Resource Allocation Models (ORAM and DRAM), and its cost benefit model. We interviewed CS officials regarding how workforce planning decisions were made since the ORAM and DRAM models were last used. We also interviewed a senior CS official about the human resource office's potential to handle the projected large increase in FSOs that is contained in CS's budget requests for 2010 and 2011.

To determine the quality of the International Trade Administration's (ITA) 2011 budget request for CS, we determined the extent to which ITA followed the best practices outlined in the *GAO Cost Estimating and Assessment Guide*.[46] The guide identifies 12 practices that are the basis for effective cost estimation, including cost estimation for annual budget requests. It associates these practices with four characteristics: accurate, well documented, comprehensive, and credible. The Office of Management and Budget (OMB) endorsed this guidance as being sufficient for meeting most cost estimating requirements, including for budget formulation. If followed correctly, these practices should result in reliable and valid budgets that (a) can be easily and clearly traced, replicated, and updated, and (b) enable managers to make informed decisions. In performing this analysis, we examined the 2011 budget request and supporting documentation provided by ITA, and we conducted interviews with ITA budget staff. After conducting this assessment, we identified major strengths and weaknesses of the 2011 budget request.

To describe the level of funding CS received compared with State and USDA for analogous export promotion activities in appendix II, we worked with State and USDA to determine which of their programs and activities were analogous to CS's export portfolio. We jointly agreed on what elements of their budget could be attributed to export promotion. We focused on (1) marketing and market research, (2) technical assistance and training for exporting businesses, and (3) advocacy that benefits individual companies. We reviewed the President's budget requests and agency budget justifications for CS, which are included in the budgets of the Department of Commerce's ITA, as well as the budgets for USDA's Foreign Agricultural Service and State's Office of Commercial and Business Affairs to identify those programs and activities in their budgets that supported those functions in order to develop the comparison. We determined that USDA's budget summaries were reliable by reviewing financial audits for the 6-year time period of our review. Audits for 2 of the years found that the financial statements fairly presented USDA's finances with some adjustments needed to internal controls, and the audits for the other 4 years found that the financial statements fairly presented USDA's finances without caveat. There is one limitation to USDA's budget summaries, which is that salaries and expenses are listed by function rather than by program. To address the limitation, we included these amounts, because it seemed sufficiently clear which functions related to export promotion, although the labels were different from the program names. State was not able to provide sufficient budget data for 2004 to 2008, so we only reported on 2009.

We conducted this performance audit from September 2009 to August 2010, in accordance with generally accepted government auditing standards. Those standards require that we plan and perform the audit to obtain sufficient, appropriate evidence to provide a reasonable basis for our findings and conclusions based on our audit objectives. We believe that the evidence obtained provides a reasonable basis for our findings and conclusions based on our audit objectives.

Appendix II: U.S. Agencies Promote Exports with Varying Levels of Funding and Different Promotion Models

The Departments of Agriculture (USDA), Commerce, and State are the three main U.S. agencies tasked with promoting exports through advocacy for individual companies, marketing, and technical assistance and training. In 2009, USDA's Foreign Agricultural Service (FAS) had 97 offices in 75 countries, Commerce's U.S. and Foreign Commercial Service (CS) had 127 offices in 76 countries, and State had 45 offices in 45 countries. Commerce, State, and USDA have different funding levels for export promotion. Additionally, USDA's export promotion model is different from the one employed by Commerce and State.

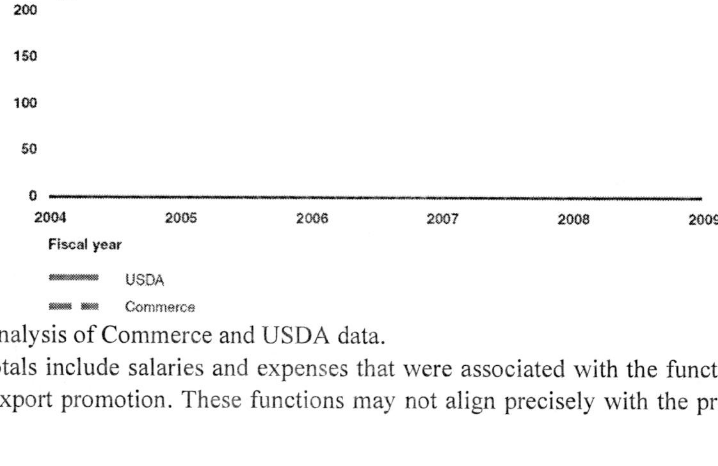

Source: GAO analysis of Commerce and USDA data.

Note: USDA totals include salaries and expenses that were associated with the functions most closely linked to export promotion. These functions may not align precisely with the programs described below.

Figure 1. Export Promotion Budgets for Commerce and USDA, Fiscal Years 2004-2009.

Commerce, State, and USDA Have Different Levels of Export Promotion Funding

In 2009, Commerce received $238 million, and USDA received $365 million for export promotion.[47] State estimated it spent $17 million in support of export promotion for 2009. See figure 1 for funding levels for USDA and Commerce from 2004 through 2009.

Funding for State is not included in the figure, as State was unable to determine the personnel costs associated for FSOs and LES who supported its export promotion efforts from 2004 through 2008. State estimated that FSO costs totaled $15 million in 2009. In addition, State funded small export promotion projects at posts and had staff in Washington, D.C., bringing the total State estimated it spent in 2009 to $17 million, excluding LES. If LES costs were included, the level of funding State spent on export promotion would be higher.

USDA Has a Different Export Promotion Approach from Commerce and State

While all three agencies conduct export promotion activities, the amount of funding the agencies receive cannot be directly compared, since USDA uses a different approach to promote exports than Commerce and State. Also, while Commerce and State use the same model, they operate in different locations and have different numbers of posts.

Commerce's model focuses on direct services to exporters, especially small- and medium-sized businesses. CS provides counseling and market intelligence, matchmaking (connecting exporters to customers), and advocacy on behalf of individual businesses. Its overseas posts coordinate with U.S. Export Assistance Centers throughout the United States.

USDA's FAS primarily promotes the export of commodities indirectly through funding for external programs, unlike CS which provides services directly to exporters. Additionally, the majority of FAS's activities are focused on promoting U.S. agricultural commodities in general, whereas Commerce's focus is on assisting individual businesses seeking to export. FAS provides funding to agricultural trade associations, state and regional trade groups, small businesses, and cooperatives that plan and carry out export promotion activities. The two largest programs are the following:

- *The Market Access Program* funds consumer promotions, market research, and technical capacity building to develop, maintain, and expand foreign markets for U.S. agricultural goods, including branded goods and generic commodities. In 2009, FAS allocated $200 million to this activity, which represented 55 percent of its total export promotion budget.
- *The Foreign Market Development Program* focuses on long-term development of foreign markets for generic U.S. agricultural commodities. In 2009, FAS allocated $34 million to this activity, which represented 9 percent of its total export promotion budget.

These programs are supplemented by smaller funding programs. One program helps trade organizations provide sample agricultural products, another provides funding to help overcome technical barriers to exporting, and a third funds development of exports in emerging markets. Additionally, FAS staff overseas provide market intelligence for U.S. firms, and work on export promotion activities including market research and trade shows.

State supports U.S. exporters in locations where CS does not have a presence.[48] Commerce and State signed a Memorandum of Understanding in January 2009, formalizing this representation. Prior to that, State acted on behalf of CS informally. Under the memorandum, State staff at these partnership posts provide services developed by CS, including matching businesses with potential customers and market research. Providing CS services at partnership posts is not a full-time job for State FSOs and LES. In a survey of the amount of time partnership post staff spent on export promotion efforts in 2009, FSOs indicated they spent about one-quarter of their time on export promotion, and LES at these posts spent about half of their time on it.

State also provides approximately $340,000 to $400,000 per year in financial support for posts' business promotion and commercial outreach activities through a Business Facilitation Incentive Fund.

Appendix III: Assessment of ITA's 2011 Budget Estimate for CS Using *GAO Cost Estimating and Assessment Guide*

To analyze the International Trade Association's (ITA) 2011 budget request for the U.S. and Foreign Commercial Service (CS), we determined the extent to which ITA followed the best practices outlined in the *GAO Cost Estimating and Assessment Guide*.[49] The guide identifies 12 practices that are the basis for effective cost estimation, including cost estimation for annual budget requests. It associates these practices with four characteristics: accurate, well documented, comprehensive, and credible. The Office of Management and Budget (OMB) endorsed this guidance as being sufficient for meeting most cost-estimating requirements, including for budget formulation. If followed correctly, these practices should result in reliable and valid budgets that (a) can be easily and clearly traced, replicated, and updated; and (b) enable managers to make informed decisions. As table 7 illustrates, we found that CS's budget development methods substantially met two, partially met one, and minimally met one of these four practices. After conducting this assessment, we identified major strengths and weaknesses of the 2011 budget request. .

The following explains the definitions we used in assessing ITA's methods for estimating costs in its annual budget submission:

- Met—ITA provided complete evidence that satisfies the entire criterion.
- Substantially met—ITA provided evidence that satisfies a large portion of the criterion.
- Partially met—ITA provided evidence that satisfies about half of the criterion.
- Minimally met—ITA provided evidence that satisfies a small portion of the criterion.
- Not met—ITA provided no evidence that satisfies any part of the criterion.

The sections that follow highlight the key findings of our assessment.

Table 7. Extent to Which CS Budgeting Methods Reflect GAO Best Practices

Best practice	Explanation	Satisfied?
Comprehensive	The cost estimates should include both government and contractor costs over the program's full life cycle, from the inception of the program through design, development, deployment, and operation and maintenance to retirement. They should also provide an appropriate level of detail to ensure that cost elements are neither omitted nor double counted and include documentation of all cost- influencing ground rules and assumptions.	Substantially met
Well documented	The cost estimates should have clearly defined purposes and be supported by documented descriptions of key program or system characteristics. Additionally, they should capture in writing such things as the source data used and their significance, the calculations performed and their results, and the rationale for choosing a particular estimating method. Moreover, this information should becaptured in such a way that the data used to derive the estimate can be traced back to, and verified against, their sources. The final cost estimate should be reviewed and accepted by management.	Partially met
Accurate	The cost estimates should provide for results that are unbiased and should not be overly conservative or optimistic. In addition, the estimates should be updated regularly to reflect material changes in the program, and steps should be taken to minimize mathematical mistakes and their significance. Among other things, the estimate should be grounded in a historical record of cost estimating and actual experiences on comparable programs.	Substantially met
Credible	The cost estimates should discuss any limitations in the analysis performed due to uncertainty surrounding data or assumptions. Further, the estimates' derivation should provide for varying any major assumptions and recalculating outcomes based on sensitivity analyses, and their associated risks/uncertainty should be disclosed. Also, the estimates should be verified based on cross-checks using other estimating methods and by comparing the results with independent cost estimates.	Minimally met

Source: GAO analysis.

2011 Budget *Substantially Met* Characteristics for Comprehensiveness

Best practices for comprehensiveness include an estimating plan that includes sufficient resources, an estimating approach with standard cost elements broken down to sufficient detail, and clear identification of ground rules and assumptions.

- *Estimating plan.* The budgeting team had the proper number and mix of resources to develop the budget request, and team members were from a centralized office. The team leader had appropriate experience and qualifications, although CS did not provide us with enough information to determine whether other team members were qualified.

- *Estimating approach.* The budget used a standard cost element structure that defined all cost elements and addressed relevant costs. CS broke down pertinent costs to an acceptable level of detail. CS properly separated contractor costs from government costs, although it detailed contractor costs more explicitly for costs that were new in 2011 than for ongoing costs.
- *Ground rules and assumptions.* CS relied on ground rules and assumptions, such as using 2010 amounts with adjustments appropriate for each cost element to estimate costs for 2011, but assumptions were not fully documented. CS did not determine risk distributions for all assumptions, which would enable it to perform an uncertainty analysis for key cost elements.

2011 Budget *Partially Met* Characteristics for Being Well Documented

Best practices for being well documented include clearly defining the estimate's purpose, defining key characteristics of the budget including primary cost drivers and systems for updating the budget, clearly identifying ground rules and assumptions, obtaining data properly, documenting the estimate so that corroborating data and calculations can be identified, and presenting clear and sufficient information to management for approval.

- *Purpose of estimate.* CS clearly defined the purpose and scope of its budget request, and all applicable costs were estimated.
- *Budget characteristics.* The number of staff is the primary driver of the cost of the 2011 budget request. CS received a $5.2 million total increase in 2010 for increasing CS's presence in emerging and developing economies. Program staff reviewed the budget and sent corrections on inaccurate items to the budget team, although there is no ongoing system for updating the budgeting team, and CS did not provide us with information on whether there was one centralized place where budget update information was stored.
- *Ground rules and assumptions.* See above under the discussion of comprehensiveness. The best practice of setting ground rules and assumptions is relevant to both being well documented and to comprehensiveness.
- *Data.* Consistent with best practices, CS used historical data to estimate key operational costs. CS performed cross-checks on its data by having program staff verify assumptions in new estimates against historical data, and developed a computer program to check for common errors. However, salaries for locally employed staff (LES) vary widely, which causes uncertainty in the cost estimate.
- *Documentation.* In some cases, we required the guidance of CS budget analysts to identify backup support because the documentation was insufficient to allow someone unfamiliar with the budget to locate detailed corroborating data. The budget documentation did not provide a step-by-step description of the budgeting process, methods, or sources. ITA staff said that documenting and chronicling the information

that was used to create it would be a best practice they aspire to but is not something they currently do.

- *Presenting to management for approval.* CS presented the budget to department-level officials in the Department of Commerce as well as to OMB and the House Appropriations Committee. However, we were unable to obtain any documentation of what was presented at the briefings, so we could not determine whether it contained enough detail for management to understand the level of accuracy, completeness, and quality of the estimate.

2011 Budget *Substantially Met* Characteristics for Accuracy

Best practices for accuracy include appropriate methodology for developing the point estimate, and updating the estimate to reflect actual costs and changes.

- *Point estimate.* CS officials used relevant historical cost data and considered adjustments for general inflation when estimating costs. They varied their estimation methodologies as appropriate for different situations. However, although they were aware that salaries were their largest cost driver, they used an overly simplistic averaging approach to reflect likely new staff salaries at hiring. Additionally, since CS did not perform a risk analysis, it is not possible to know whether its point estimate was the most likely actual reflection of costs, or was overly optimistic or conservative. We found no mathematical mistakes in the request, and CS validated the request by looking for errors. CS also crosschecked the budget estimates with program staff and with budget staff at both Commerce and OMB.
- *Update with actual costs and changes.* ITA updated the request based on feedback from program staff reviews. Additionally, actual costs were compared with estimates on a monthly basis. However, CS did not share changes to the cost estimate with us, so we were unable to assess whether changes were properly updated.

CS's 2011 Cost Estimate *Minimally Met* Criteria for Credibility

- Best practices for credibility include conducting a sensitivity analysis and conducting a risk analysis.
- *Sensitivity analysis.* CS did not perform a sensitivity analysis on each of the major assumptions to determine how outcomes would vary if they changed. Major assumptions included salary estimates, annual salary increases, impact of currency fluctuation, and travel costs.
- *Risk analysis.* CS did not perform a risk analysis to quantify the overall risk associated with changes to the assumptions that drive its budget.[50] A risk analysis would help provide CS managers with information to determine the probability that costs for key operations, such as salaries, may exceed funding levels requested in the budget, so that they could make spending and hiring decisions accordingly.

APPENDIX IV: COMMENTS FROM THE DEPARTMENT OF COMMERCE

THE SECRETARY OF COMMERCE
Washington, D.C. 20230

August 5, 2010

Dr. Loren Yager
Director, International Affairs and Trade
U.S. Government Accountability Office
Washington, DC 20548

Dear Dr. Yager:

Thank you for providing us with the draft report titled "Export Promotion: Increases in Commercial Service Workforce Should be Better Planned." In this report, GAO reviewed both (1) how well the U.S. and Foreign Commercial Service (USFCS) managed its resources from 2004 to 2009, and (2) the completeness of the USFCS' workforce plans and its fiscal year (FY) 2011 budget request. I agree with the overall findings and recommendations of your report. Indeed I have been aware of some of these issues since becoming Secretary and have been working to address them. I have directed the International Trade Administration (ITA) to use your report to develop stronger management controls, improve workforce planning, and improve cost estimates during the budget process.

As you note, President Obama announced the National Export Initiative (NEI) in January 2010. The Department of Commerce has a critical role to play in the execution of this Initiative, and I am pleased your report acknowledges that our new ITA executive leadership is on board to spearhead this effort. At my direction, ITA management has been engaged since January 2010 in a vigorous strategic planning effort to align its focus, activities, and personnel to strengthen the USFCS and support the President's NEI. Our leadership team is accelerating those efforts now as they plan implementation of the FY 2011 budget and develop contingency plans.

Our specific technical comments relating to the text of the report are enclosed; we hope you take these comments into consideration when issuing the final version of this report.

Sincerely,

Gary Locke

Enclosure

End Notes

[1] Including agricultural goods.
[2] Exec. Order No. 13,534, 75 Fed. Reg. 12,433 (Mar. 11, 2010).
[3] This report is in response to House Report 111-366, which was the conference report for the Consolidated Appropriations Act, 2010. Pub. L. No. 111-117, 123 Stat. 3034 (2009).
[4] All years in this report are fiscal years unless otherwise indicated.
[5] GAO, *Standards for Internal Control in the Federal Government*, GAO/AIMD-00-21.3.1 (Washington, D.C.: November 1999). The terms internal control and management controls are used synonymously in this report. See OMB Circular No. A-123 *Management Accountability and Control,* June 1995.
[6] GAO, *A Model of Strategic Human Capital Management*, GAO-02-373SP (Washington, D.C.: March 2002).
[7] GAO, *GAO Cost Estimating and Assessment Guide: Best Practices for Developing and Managing Capital Program Costs*, GAO-09-3SP (Washington, D.C.: March 2009).
[8] LES can also be U.S. citizens who live in the host country.
[9] See app. II for activities provided by USDA and State. While USDA has a large budget for export promotion activities, most of it is directed at promoting raw commodities rather than services and manufactured goods.
[10] The Departments of Commerce and State signed a Memorandum of Understanding in January 2009 formalizing State's role of promoting exports at U.S. embassies where CS does not have a presence. State provides designated export promotion services at 45 posts around the world.
[11] Exec. Order No. 12,870, 58 Fed. Reg. 51,753 (Sept. 30, 1993); 15 U.S.C. § 4727.
[12] The Trade Promotion Coordinating Committee has 20 member agencies. However, it generally reports in the National Export Strategy on the budgets and activities of around 10. The 2008 strategy included budget authority information for 9 agencies: the Departments of Agriculture, Commerce, State, and the Treasury; Export-Import Bank of the United States; Office of the U.S. Trade Representative; Overseas Private Investment Corporation; Small Business Administration; and U.S. Trade and Development Agency.
[13] GAO, *Export Promotion: Trade Promotion Coordinating Committee's Role Remains Limited*, GAO-06-660T (Washington, D.C.: Apr. 26, 2006).
[14] Other agencies that will play a role in the NEI include the Departments of Agriculture and State, Export-Import Bank of the United States, Office of the U.S. Trade Representative, and Small Business Administration.
[15] State charges both ICASS and CSCSP costs to U.S. agencies that are in embassies and other diplomatic and consular missions overseas. CSCSP funds the construction of new embassy compounds. ICASS charges are for services like building maintenance, vehicle operations, and travel. Payments are made by all agencies in proportion to their overseas presence.
[16] CS budget breakdown data presented in this section are based on CS's accounting system records. ICASS charges were calculated based on charges for CS only, even though other parts of Commerce also pay their ICASS through CS.
[17] GAO/AIMD-00-21.3.1.
[18] Administrative costs include centralized costs charged by Commerce as well as ICASS and CSCSP.
[19] These dollar amounts include ICASS, CSCSP, payments to ITA for shared overhead, and earmarks. ICASS amounts include charges for other parts of Commerce; all Commerce ICASS charges are paid through CS.
[20] Agencies are required to formally seek permission from the Chief of Mission to place a person overseas. Likewise, if an agency wants to eliminate a position overseas, it must formally request that the position be eliminated.
[21] CS receives reimbursements from other federal agencies for services provided through interagency agreements. CS provided us with the total obligations for fees plus reimbursements for 2004-2009.
[22] In March 2009, we reported that CS needed to ensure there was a sound basis for setting fees, which would help to ensure that user fees recover the intended portion of full costs. GAO, *Export Promotion: Commerce Needs Better Information to Evaluate Its Fee-Based Programs and Customers,* GAO-09-144 (Washington, D.C.: Mar. 4, 2009).
[23] 31 U.S.C. § 1341.
[24] ITA, including CS, had been operating under a partial hiring freeze since 2006 because of resource constraints. During this period ITA granted some exemptions that allowed CS to hire staff.
[25] The assessments conducted are referred to as Strengths, Weaknesses, Opportunities, Threats (SWOT) analyses and were based on formal feedback from CS's international and domestic field offices.
[26] The agencies implementing the NEI are to develop a plan for the initiative by September 2010.
[27] Positions in three overseas offices will be filled with limited noncareer appointments, as CS lacks staff with the necessary skills, knowledge, and abilities to fill those positions. Limited noncareer appointments are members of the general public hired for specific locations and tours of duty based on specialized skills or experience. First tours of duty are limited to 2 years, and limited appointments can not serve with CS more than 5 consecutive years.

[28] CS also had 9 Schedule C employees and 4 Personal Service Contract employees in the first quarter of fiscal year 2010. No new Schedule C or Personal Service Contract hires are planned for fiscal year 2011.

[29] CS FSOs are not the only FSOs required to serve a domestic tour. The Department of State also has a domestic tour requirement. The Foreign Service Act of 1980 includes a requirement that its FSOs serve a domestic tour at least once every 15 years. 22 U.S.C. § 3984.

[30] GAO, *Human Capital: Key Principles for Effective Strategic Workforce Planning,* GAO-04-39 (Washington, D.C.: Dec. 11, 2003).

[31] According to the Director of the Trade Promotion Coordinating Committee, a National Export Strategy is not released in transition years between administrations.

[32] GAO-02-373SP.

[33] When considering strategies, it is important for agencies to consider the full range of flexibilities available under current authorities, as well as flexibilities that might need additional legislation to be adopted.

[34] An FSO's standard overseas tour of duty is generally 4 years for nonhardship posts, and 1 to 3 years for posts in hardship locations. Officers may extend their tour of duty in 1-year increments. However, the maximum stay at a post is 5 years.

[35] Posts managed by LES are under the supervision of FSOs who are in nearby cities or countries. According to CS, it has used this arrangement to reduce costs and facilitate coordination.

[36] The model is called the Overseas Resource Allocation Model and was developed by contractors for CS.

[37] CS maintains its own Office of Foreign Service Human Resources, which hires FSOs. Hiring of civil servants for CS is conducted by Commerce's Human Resource Operations Center, and hiring of LES is handled by State.

[38] The $321 million request for CS was included in the $534 million President's budget request for all of ITA, of which CS is a unit.

[39] The *GAO Cost Estimating and Assessment Guide* was developed to establish a consistent methodology that is based on best practices that can be used across the federal government for developing, managing, and evaluating cost estimates. If followed correctly, these practices should result in reliable and valid cost estimates that (a) can be easily and clearly traced, replicated, and updated, and (b) enable managers to make informed decisions. GAO-09-3SP.

[40] A risk analysis provides a range of costs that span best and worst case scenarios. According to best practices, it is better for decision makers to know the range of potential costs that surround an estimate and the reasons behind what drives that range rather than just having a point estimate from which to make their decision.

[41] GAO-09-3SP.

[42] OMB endorsed the guidance in the *GAO Cost Estimating and Assessment Guide* as sufficient for meeting most cost-estimating requirements, including for budget formulation.

[43] CS indicated that the 2011 budget request is its cost estimate.

[44] This report is in response to a study requested in House Report 111-36, which was the conference report for Commerce, Justice, Science, and Related Agencies' fiscal year 2010 appropriations.

[45] GAO, *Human Capital: Key Principles for Effective Strategic Workforce Planning*, GAO-04-39 (Washington, D.C.: Dec. 11, 2003). Also see GAO: *A Model of Strategic Human Capital Management*, GAO-02-373SP (Washington, D.C.: March 2002).

[46] GAO, *GAO Cost Estimating and Assessment Guide: Best Practices for Developing and Managing Capital Program Costs*, GAO-09-3SP (Washington, D.C.: March 2009).

[47] In addition, CS has resources available from unobligated funds from prior years and surplus service fees. In 2009, CS spent $15 million earned from service fees, and $5 million from prior year funding that was carried over to 2009.

[48] State's economic officers at embassies and consulates around the world are also involved in government-to-government advocacy and several other areas such as negotiating reductions in foreign trade barriers. However, this report does not focus on those activities.

[49] GAO, *GAO Cost Estimating and Assessment Guide: Best Practices for Developing and Managing Capital Program Costs*, GAO-09-3SP (Washington, D.C.: March 2009).

[50] A risk analysis provides a range of costs that span a best- and worst-case spread. According to best practices, it is better for decision makers to know the range of potential costs that surround an estimate and the reasons behind what drives that range rather than just having a point estimate from which to make their decision.

In: U.S. Export Programs and Promotion Tools
Editor: Steven D. Braghoff

ISBN: 978-1-60741-328-8

Chapter 6

The Export Administration Act: Evolution, Provisions, and Debate

Ian F. Fergusson

Summary

The 111th Congress may consider legislation to renew, modify, or reauthorize the Export Administration Act (EAA). On July 31, 2009, Representative Sherman introduced the Export Control Improvements Act (H.R. 3515), co-sponsored by Representative Manzullo and Representative A. Smith, that contains provisions on export controls enforcement, integration of export control data in the AES, and diversion control. The House Foreign Affairs Committee is also reportedly working to produce as comprehensive rewrite of the EAA. As part of the Administration's export control review, Defense Secretary Robert M. Gates has proposed creating a unified export control structure merging the dual-use and munitions export control regimes, some aspects of which may require legislative consent.

Through the EAA, Congress delegates to the executive branch its express constitutional authority to regulate foreign commerce by controlling exports. The EAA provides the statutory authority for export controls on sensitive dual-use goods and technologies: items that have both civilian and military applications, including those items that can contribute to the proliferation of nuclear, biological, and chemical weaponry. The EAA, which originally expired in 1989, periodically has been reauthorized for short periods of time, with the last incremental extension expiring in August 2001. At other times and currently, the export licensing system created under the authority of EAA has been continued by the invocation of the International Emergency Economic Powers Act (IEEPA). EAA confers upon the President the power to control exports for national security, foreign policy or short supply purposes. It also authorizes the President to establish export licensing mechanisms for items detailed on the Commerce Control List (CCL), and it provides some guidance and places certain limits on that authority. The CCL currently provides detailed specifications about dual-use items including equipment, materials, software, and technology (including data and know-how) likely requiring some type of export license from the Commerce Department's

Bureau of Industry and Security (BIS). BIS administers the Export Administration Regulations (EAR), which, in addition to the CCL, describe licensing policy and procedures such as commodity classification, licensing, and interagency dispute resolution procedures.

In debates on export administration legislation, parties often fall into two camps: those who primarily want to liberalize controls in order to promote exports, and those who believe that further liberalization may compromise national security goals. While it is widely agreed that exports of some goods and technologies can adversely affect U.S. national security and foreign policy, some believe that current export controls can be detrimental to U.S. businesses and to the U.S. economy. According to this view, the resultant loss of competitiveness, market share, and jobs can harm the U.S. economy, and that harm to particular U.S. industries and to the economy itself can negatively impact U.S. security. Others believe that security concerns must be paramount in the U.S. export control system and that export controls can be an effective method to thwart proliferators, terrorist states, and countries that can threaten U.S. national security interests. Controversies have arisen with regard to particular exports such as high performance computers, encryption technology, stealth materials, satellites, machine tools, "hot-section" aerospace technology, and the issue of "deemed exports." The competing perspectives on export controls have clearly been manifested in the debate over foreign availability and the control of technology, the efficacy of multilateral control regimes, the licensing process and organization of the export control system, and the economic effects of U.S. export controls.

INTRODUCTION

Legislation to rewrite and reauthorize the Export Administration Act of 1979 (EAA)(P.L. 96-72) may be considered in the 111th Congress. In the 110th Congress, several pieces of legislation were introduced that addressed various aspects of the current system, including penalties, enforcement, diversion or transhipment of goods, and the integration of export control data into the Automated Export System. The EAA provides the statutory authority for export controls on sensitive dual-use goods and technologies, items that have both civilian and military applications, including those items that can contribute to the proliferation of nuclear, biological and chemical weaponry. The EAA, which originally expired in 1989, periodically has been reauthorized for short periods of time, with the last incremental extension expiring in August 2001. At others times, including currently, the export licensing system created under the authority of EAA has been continued by the invocation of the International Emergency Economic Powers Act (IEEPA)(P.L. 95-223).

The EAA is the statutory authority for the Export Administration Regulations (EAR), which are administered by the Bureau of Industry and Security (BIS) located in the Department of Commerce. These regulations establish the framework for regulating exports of dual-use, potentially sensitive commodities, software, computers, and technology. Exports are restricted by item, country, and recipient entity. The EAA, which was written and amended during the Cold War, focuses on the regulation of exports of those civilian goods and technology that have military applications (dual-use items). Export controls under the EAA were based on strategic relationships, threats to U.S. national security, international business practices, and commercial technologies many of which have changed dramatically in the last 20 years. Some Members of Congress and most U.S. business representatives see a need to liberalize U.S. export regulations to allow American companies to engage more fully in international competition for sales of high-technology goods. Other Members and some national security analysts contend that liberalization of export controls over the last decade has contributed to foreign threats to U.S. national security, that some controls should be tightened, and that Congress should weigh further liberalization carefully.

This report discusses the Export Administration Act in terms of its evolution in the 20th century, its major features including the types of controls authorized by the act, the Commerce Control List and export licensing procedures, and issues concerning the maintenance of export controls under IEEPA. It then highlights several controlled commodities that have been featured prominently in export control discussions. Finally, it discusses competing business and national security perspectives concerning several of more contentious themes in the export control debate: the controllability of technology, the effectiveness of multilateral control regimes, the organization of the export control system, and the impact of export controls on the U.S. economy and business.

THE EVOLUTION OF THE EXPORT ADMINISTRATION ACT

Export controls in time of war have been an element of U.S. policy for almost one hundred years.[1] The end of WWII, however, ushered in a new era in which export control policy would become an extensive peacetime undertaking. The start of the cold war led to a major refocusing of export control policy on the Soviet-Bloc countries. Enactment of the Export Control Act of 1949 (P.L. 81-11) was a formal recognition of the new security threat and of the need for an extensive peacetime export control system.

The 1949 Act identified three possible reasons for imposing export controls. Short-supply controls were to be used to prevent the export of scarce goods that would have a deleterious impact on U.S. industry and national economic performance. Foreign policy controls were to be used by the President to promote the foreign policy of the United States. The broad issues of regional stability, human rights, anti-terrorism, missile technology, and chemical and biological warfare have come to be controlled under this rubric. National security controls were to be used to restrict the export of goods and technology, including nuclear non-proliferation items, that would make a significant contribution to the military capability of any country that posed a threat to the national security of the United States.

Coincident with the establishment of the post-war U.S. export control regime was the establishment of a multilateral counterpart involving our NATO allies. The large amount of critical technology being transferred from the United States to the NATO allies, and the growing capability for technological development by the allies themselves required the establishment of a multilateral control regime. Toward this end, the Coordinating Committee for Multilateral Export Controls (CoCom) was established in 1949. CoCom controls were not a mirror image of U.S. controls but generally did reflect a uniformly high level of restrictions.

With little change in the perceived threat, the Export Control Act was renewed largely without amendment in 1951, 1953, 1956, 1958, 1960, 1962, and 1965. With the onset of the U.S.-Soviet era of "detente" in the late 1960s, however, the first serious reexamination and revision of the U.S. export control system occurred. At this time, the growing importance of trade to the U.S. economy and those of our allies began to exert significant political pressure for some liberalization of export controls. Congress passed the Export Administration Act of 1969 to replace the near-embargo characteristic of the Export Control Act of 1949. The continued shift of policy toward less restrictive export controls continued in the renewal of the act in 1974 and 1977. The act was comprehensively rewritten in 1979, and this act forms the basis of the export control system today. It was amended in 1985, and some moderate further liberalization occurred in the following years.

The collapse of the Soviet Union in 1989, an event some have partially attributed to the success of U.S. cold war export control policy, marked a dramatic change in the nature of the external threat the United States. Beginning with the George H.W. Bush Administration, the export control system has been reduced in scope and streamlined, but the basic structure of the law remains intact. There are many who see a need to revamp the act, whether to enhance exports, to shift the focus to current national security threats, or to increase penalties for violations.

The dissolution of CoCom in 1994 and its replacement by the Wassenaar Arrangement in 1997, also significantly changed the export control environment.[2] This new multilateral arrangement is more loosely structured than CoCom and members do not have the authority to block transactions of other members. Generally more liberal control practices abroad raise important questions about the ultimate effectiveness of U.S. export controls (under either the current or a revised EAA) in achieving national security objectives and the fairness of unilateral controls to American industry.

Congress has not been able to agree on measures to reform the Export Administration Act that regularly have been introduced since the 101st Congress. The export control process was continued from 1989 to 1994 by temporary statutory extensions of EAA and by invocation of the International Emergency Economic Powers Act (IEEPA). Thereafter, export controls were continued for six years under the authority of Executive Order No. 12924 of August 19, 1994, issued under IEEPA authority. Many of those who favor reforming the act, whether to liberalize or to tighten controls, contend that operating under IEEPA imposes constraints on the administration of the export control process and makes it vulnerable to legal challenge, thus undermining its effectiveness. Legislation passed by the House and Senate and signed by the President on November 13, 2000 (P.L. 106-508) extended the EAA of 1979 until August 20, 2001, temporarily removing the need to operate the export control system under IEEPA powers. Since then, export control authority has again been operating under IEEPA provisions pursuant to Executive Order 13222, issued August 17, 2001.[3]

Legislation

Legislation to rewrite the Export Administration Act has been introduced in the last several Congresses. In the 104th Congress, the House passed the Omnibus Export Administration Act of 1996 (H.R. 361) on July 16, 1996, after hearings and consideration by the Committee on International Relations, the Committee on Ways and Means, and by the Committee on National Security. On July 17, 1996, the bill was received by the Senate and referred to the Committee on Banking, Housing and Urban Affairs, which held a hearing but took no further action. Export control legislation (H.R. 1942) was introduced in the 105th

Congress, but no action was taken. In the 106th Congress, the Export Administration Act of 1999 (S. 1712) was introduced by Senator Michael P. Enzi. On September 23, 1999, the Senate Banking Committee voted unanimously (20-0) to report this legislation to the Senate floor (S.Rept. 106-180). However, action by the Senate on S. 1712 was not taken due to the concerns of several Senators about the bill's impact on national security.

107th Congress

Export control legislation was again introduced in the 107th Congress. On January 23, 2001, Senator Enzi introduced the Export Administration Act of 2001 (S. 149). Hearings were held on this legislation by the Senate Banking Housing and Urban Affairs Committee in February 2001, and the measure was reported favorably for consideration by the Senate by a vote of 19-1 on March 22, 2001 (S.Rept. 107-10). The Senate debated the legislation on September 4-6, 2001, and it passed with three amendments by a vote of 85-14. This bill was similar though not identical to S. 1712, introduced by Senator Enzi in the 106th Congress.

The House International Relations Committee held hearings on EAA and export controls on May 23, June 12, and July 11, 2002. The House version of the Export Administration Act, H.R. 2581, was introduced on July 20, 2001, by Representative Benjamin Gilman. As introduced, it was identical to S. 149, except for the additions of provisions related to oversight of nuclear transfers to North Korea. At the markup session on August 1, the House International Relations Committee passed the legislation with 35 amendments. The House Armed Services Committee (HASC) and the House Permanent Select Committee on Intelligence(HPSCI) received H.R. 2581 through sequential referral. On March 6, 2002, HASC further amended H.R. 2581 and reported out the legislation by a vote of 44-6 (H.Rept. 107-297). HPSCI held hearings on the legislation but did not alter it. The legislation received no further consideration in the 107th Congress. The Administration supported S. 149 and opposed House attempts to revise it.

108th Congress

In the 108th Congress, Representative Dreier introduced EAA legislation (H.R. 55), which was identical to S. 149, but no action was taken on it.

The National Defense Authorization Act (NDAA) has also been used periodically as a vehicle to attempt to amend the export control regime. In 2004, the House version of NDAA 2005 (H.R. 4200) contained two export control-related provisions that would have affected dual-use export controls. The first (Sec. 1404) would have required a license for dual-use goods controlled under the Export Administration Regulations (EAR) for technology and items contained in the Militarily Critical Technology List (MCTL), a list compiled by the Department of Defense (DOD) (see p. 6). The provision is in response to a March 2004 DOD study, which noted that several MCTL technologies were not controlled under the EAR or the International Traffic in Arms Regulations (ITAR). The second provision (Sec. 1405) would have required that exporters obtain licenses for items controlled under the EAR or the ITAR to a destination if that destination had previously exported such items to China. In addition, the granting of the license would be conditional on the written assurance of the foreign government or entity not to transfer the licensed item without the written consent of the President. The House NDAA report (H.Rept. 108-491) expresses concern that military embargoes on China imposed after the Tiananmen Square massacre may be repealed which may lead to the transfer of such U.S. goods or technology to China. However, neither of these provisions were contained in the conference report (H.Rept. 108-767) signed by the President on October 28, 2004.

109th Congress

In the 109th Congress, a bill to revise and extend the Export Administration Act was introduced by Representative Henry Hyde on December 16, 2005, and was referred to House International Relations Committee. It was not a comprehensive overhaul of 1979 EAA, but rather one that addressed penalties, enforcement, and the relation of the United States to multilateral control regimes. According to an administration official, the legislation reflected "targeted changes ... that all sides can be supportive of."[4] The bill also would have extended the expired EAA for two years from the date of enactment, and provided authorization of appropriations for export control activities. This bill did not receive consideration in the 109th Congress.

110th Congress

No comprehensive legislation to rewrite or reauthorized the EAA was introduced in the 110th Congress. Legislation was introduced that sought amend the enforcement and penalty structure of the Act (S. 2000, Dodd; H.R. 6828, Sherman/Manzullo), to integrate export control information into electronic filing of export data under the Automated Export System (AES) (H.R. 6828), and to target countries of diversion concern (S. 3445, Dodd/H.R. 7112, Berman; H.R. 6828). H.R. 6828 also would have required the GAO to conduct an investigation of BIS' validated end-user program. S. 2000 and parts of other legislation reflected the draft legislation that the Administration submitted to Congress on April 24, 2007. Only S. 3445/H.R. 7112 was acted upon in the 110 Congress; S. 3445 was reported out of the Banking, Housing, and Urban Affairs Committee on August 1,2008 (S.Rept. 110-443), but received no floor consideration. H.R. 7112 was both introduced and passed in the House under suspension of the rules on September 26, 2008.

111th Congress

On July 31, 2009, Representative Sherman introduced the Export Control Improvements Act (H.R. 3515), co-sponsored by Representative Manzullo and Representative A. Smith, that contains provisions on export controls enforcement, integration of export control data in the AES, and diversion control. The title on export enforcement is notable in that it does not amend the enforcement section of the expired EAA (Sec.12) and bring that section solely back in force as did H.R. 6828, or amend it with a general renewal of the existing EAA as did S. 2000. Rather, it provides additional enforcement authority for the Export Administration Regulations, which are maintained during the lapse of the EAA under authority of the International Economic Emergency Powers Act (IEEPA).

Enforcement

The draft legislation would grant investigative authority to "any department or agency exercising any function under the EAR" to conduct investigations in the United States, and with the Secretary of Commerce, any investigation outside the United States. It would allow for the search, detention, and seizure of goods by Commerce in locations within the United

States. With the concurrence of the Secretary of Homeland Security, the bill would authorize search, detention, and seizures at U.S. ports of entry or exit and overseas. It would also direct the Secretary of Commerce to publish and update best practices guidelines for effective export control compliance programs. The measure restates the confidentiality provisions of the 1979 Act. The bill includes new language governing the use of funds for undercover investigations and operations and would establish audit and reporting requirements for such investigations.

Securing Exports through Coordination and Technology Act

Title 1 of H.R. 3515 seeks to integrate the various licensing requirements, embargoes and data collection rules imposed on exporters and shippers into the Automated Export System, an electronic version of the Shipper's Export Declaration (SED) that Customs requires be submitted prior to the clearance of a shipment for export. The export control provisions of this title center on programming the AES to include export control data, and providing notification to filers of possible export control issues with their exports, in order to prevent certain improper shipments.

Diversion Concerns

The issue of evasion of U.S. export controls through the diversion of sensitive goods through transhipment hubs remains of interest to the 111th Congress. This issue first surfaced in 2006 with reports that computer circuits exported to the United Arab Emirates were diverted to Iran, where they were fashioned into bomb detonators and used in Iraq. This revelation initially resulted in licensing requirement on UAE-based Mayrow General Trading and six other entities.[5] However, the focus quickly shifted to the UAE as a transhipment hub, and the status of its export control regime. Perhaps as a means to goad the UAE into action on export controls, the BIS proposed in February 2007 the creation of a 'Country Category C', which would be made up of countries of diversion concern. Country Category C designees would face stricter licensing requirements for products thought to have a high degree of diversion concern. No country was designated as belonging to Category C, and the rulemaking was never completed.

H.R. 3515 would legislate the 'Category C' concept with regards to diversion to Iran. It would require the President within 180 days to identify all countries of concern with respect to transhipment, reexportation, or diversion of items subject to the EAR to Iran. A country could either be designated as a country of possible diversion concern or a country of diversion concern. If designated the former, the bill would require the Administration to initiate government-to-government contacts to assist in strengthening that country's export control system. If cooperation or improvements were not forthcoming within a 12-month period from that country, the Administration would be required to designate that country as a Destination of Diversion Concern. If the government of a country is directly involved with such transhipments, reexportations, or diversions, then the country would be listed forthwith as a country of diversion concern. Countries of diversion concern would be subject to additional licensing requirements, more stringent license review, and increased use of end-user checks.

A final provision of the legislation would mandate an annual report on transfers of significant dual-use U.S. technology and technical information to countries and entities of concern.

Administration Reform Efforts

On August 13, 2009, President Obama announced the launch of a comprehensive review of the U.S. export control system to be conducted jointly by the National Security Council and the National Economic Council. While the full scope of this review has yet to be released, Defense Secretary Robert M. Gates announced key elements of the administration's agenda for reform of the export control system in a speech on April 20, 2010.[6] In order to replace what he referred to as a "byzantine amalgam of authorities, roles, and missions scattered around different parts of the federal government," Secretary Gates proposed a 4-pronged approach that would create a single export control licensing agency for both dual-use and munitions exports, adopt a unified control list, create a single integrated information technology system, which would include a single database of sanctioned and denied parties, and would establish a single enforcement coordination agency.

The administration's blueprint[7] envisions that these changes would be implemented in three phases with the final tier requiring legislative action. In the first phase, preparatory work would be undertaken to harmonize the Commerce Control List (CCL) with the U.S. Munitions List (USML) and to establish a tiered control structure that would allow items to "cascade" from tier-to-tier as technology evolves. Standardized licensing processes among the control agencies would be developed, and an "Enforcement Fusion Center" to synchronize enforcement would be created along with a single electronic gateway to access the licensing system. Phase II would implement a harmonized licensing system with two identically structured tiered control lists. According to the White House fact sheet, implementing the harmonization and tiering of the control lists would "achieve a significant license requirement reduction." The factsheet also foresees that certain items would be moved from the munitions list to the dual-use list, for which congressional notification is required, unilateral controls on certain items would be examined, and consultations would take place with multilateral control regimes partners to add or remove multilateral controls on certain items.

Under the proposal, the new export control system would debut in Phase III. A single licensing agency would be established; the two harmonized, tiered control lists would be merged with mechanisms for review and update; a Primary Enforcement Coordination Agency would consolidate enforcement activities; and a single IT system for licensing and enforcement would become operational. In his speech, Secretary Gates predicted that the 3-phase plan will "will unfold over the course of the next year."

While the 3-phase plan provides a blueprint for a transition to a new export control system, it leaves many questions unanswered. Some of these proposals would require legislative action (e.g., merging the control lists; their creation is specifically mandated by statute). However, it is less clear whether legislative consent would be required to change the structure of one or both control lists, as is envisioned in Phase II. Changes to the structure of the two control lists would also entail multilateral consultations, as the CCL and USML are derived from the Wassenaar Dual-Use List and Munitions List, respectively. Changes in agency structure may also require legislation, although that it less clear. The placing of the proposed licensing agency, either within an existing Department such as Commerce, State, Defense, or Homeland Security, or as an independent entity, also has not been determined; each choice would doubtless claim proponents and detractors.

ANALYSIS OF PROVISIONS IN EAA LEGISLATION

Several principles and concepts have been common to the EAA and to efforts to renew and reauthorize the legislation. Generally, these provisions set out the types of export controls authorized (including national security, foreign policy and short supply controls), licensing procedures, the license review process, and penalty and enforcement procedures, the latter currently subject to IEEPA authority.

Types of Control Authority

Since the 1949 Act, U.S. dual-use export controls have restricted certain items based on national security, foreign policy, or for the effect of domestic exports on the national economy. These three categories form the basis by which items on the Commerce Control List (CCL) (see below, p. 7) and items subject to the Export Administration Regulations are controlled. In practice, the preponderance of items on the CCL are controlled for both national security and foreign policy reasons with different control standards determining the licensing policy of an item to a particular country.

National Security Controls

The 1979 Act restricted the export of goods or technology that could make a significant contribution to the military capabilities of any other country or groups of countries that would prove detrimental to the national security of the United States. National security control items fall under the National Security licensing requirement of the EAR. The list "Country Group D-1" presently serves as the list of controlled countries.[8] Licenses for items controlled for national security purposes are reviewed on a case-by-case basis and are approved if it is determined the item is destined for civilian use or would not make a significant contribution to the military potential of the country of destination.[9]

Pursuant to EAA, the goods and technology to be controlled for national security purposes are identified by the Secretary of Defense and other appropriate agencies. The Secretary of Defense and the Secretary of Commerce (the Secretary) are obligated by the act to periodically review and revise the list. For this purpose, the Secretary of Defense maintains the Military Critical Technology List (MCTL).[10] The national security based control list is also consistent with the control list of the Wassenaar Arrangement. U.S. national security controls, however, do not cover items that are covered under nuclear, chemical, biological or missile proliferation regimes, or to countries covered by anti-terrorism controls. These items and destinations are controlled for foreign policy purposes.

Foreign Availability

Items controlled for national security purposes are subject to a foreign availability determination. Foreign availability exists when a good is available to controlled countries from sources outside the United States in "sufficient quantity and comparable quality" so that control of the item would be ineffective.(Sec. 5(f)(1)(a)) The 1979 Act charges the Secretary, in conjunction with the Secretary of Defense and other appropriate agencies, with determining on a continuing basis whether any item currently subject to export control for reasons of national security meets foreign availability status. Under EAA, a request to make a foreign availability determination can be made by a license applicant or through the initiative of the Secretary. If the Secretary makes a foreign availability determination, the item must be decontrolled, although the President can overturn that decision with a determination that decontrolling such items would be detrimental to the national security of the United States. In such case, the President is directed to enter negotiations with multilateral control partners to eliminate the availability in question. The bill also created an Office of Foreign Availability to gather data for the Secretary to make foreign availability determinations and to report to Congress on operations and improvements on the ability to assess foreign availability. This office no longer exists. However, the Office of Technology Evaluation is now tasked with conducting foreign availability determinations. In addition, the EmergingTechnology and Research Advisory Committee (ETRAC) was created in September 2008. This committee was created to allow university experts to play greater role in helping determine which technologies should be in the control list, particularly for purposes of deemed exports. It is also meant to assist in streamlining the CCL to better reflect the narrow set of technologies that should be protected for national security reasons which are not readily available overseas. BIS conducted an overall systemic review of the CCL in 2007-8 and plans to review 1/3 of the CCL each year to create a three review cycle.

On May 22, 2009, BIS issued a final rule lifting certain licensing requirements on uncooled thermal imaging cameras to 36 U.S. allied countries. This rule decontrolled low to mid-market night vision cameras, such as those used by firefighters, when they are not incorporated into military commodities and if they are not exported or reexported to be embedded in a civilian product. The rule also tightened export controls on higher-end thermal imaging cameras, unembedded camera cores, and thermal imaging cameras embedded in a military commodity. Exporters must report the transactions to BIS on a semi-annual basis. While this action does support the notion that present mechanisms can accommodate foreign availability concerns, some remain concerned at the length of time taken to resolve the issue. According to an industry source, "it took three years to get BIS engaged on the issue and another three years for BIS to reach interagency agreement with the [Defense Technology Security Administration]. 'It's a small step too late, but it's a step nonetheless.'"[11]

Mass Market

The concept of mass market status was proposed in EAA legislation introduced in the 106th and 107th Congress. Neither the 1979 EAA nor current regulations provides for decontrol of items based on mass market criterion. Mass market status was defined to apply to items produced or made available for sale in large volume or to multiple buyers. Under legislation introduced in the 106th and 107th Congress, the item's manner of distribution; its conduciveness to commercial shipping; or its usefulness for intended purposes without modification or service were also criteria considered when determining mass market status. This feature proved to have been a controversial part of the legislation, and was cited as a stumbling block in negotiations over the bill in the 107th Congress with some Members arguing that its existence would provide for wholesale decontrol of sensitive items.

Foreign Policy Controls

The EAA authorizes the President to control exports for the purpose of promoting foreign policy objectives, complying with international obligations, or deterring and punishing terrorism.

Currently, foreign policy controls are in place for anti-terrorism, regional stability, crime control, United Nations sanctions purposes, unilateral embargoes and sanctions, and non-proliferation objectives. This latter category includes adherence to multilateral non-proliferation agreements in the areas of chemical and biological weapons, nuclear proliferation, and missile technology.

The EAA attaches limitations on the use of foreign policy controls. Foreign policy controls must be renewed on a yearly basis.[12] It requires the President to clearly state objectives and criteria for controls to be reported to Congress. It directs the President to engage in negotiations to remove the foreign availability of items controlled for foreign policy purposes, and it requires the President to impose controls to comply with international obligations or treaties. Furthermore, it requires a license for the export of certain items to countries that support international terrorism. Additionally, foreign policy controls are not authorized for sales of medicine or medical supplies, donations of food, medicines, seeds, and water resource equipment intended to meet basic human needs, or for sales of food if the controls would cause malnutrition or hardship. Controls on sales of agricultural products and medicines have been further amended by the Trade Sanctions Reform and Export Enhancement Act of 2000 (Title IX, P.L. 106-387).[13]

Enhanced Proliferation Control Initiative

Controls based on the end-use or end-user of an item (also known as catch-all controls) are also administered as foreign policy controls. They were introduced under the Enhanced Proliferation Control Initiative (EPCI) of 1991, and they are contained in Part 744 of the EAR. Catch-all controls require a license for export or reexport of any item, not just specifically controlled items, if the applicant knows or is informed by BIS that item will be used for nuclear, missile, chemical or biological proliferation activities. The Bureau of Industry and Security (BIS) maintains an end-user list of entities requiring licenses subject to EPCI.[14] Current regulations prescribe a presumption of denial for licenses to certain entities in Russia, China, Pakistan, India, and Israel and to foreign terrorist organizations as designated by the Secretary of State.

Short Supply Controls

The 1979 EAA authorized restriction on the export of goods and technology to protect domestic industry from shortages of scarce materials and the potential inflationary impact of foreign demand. Few short-supply controls remain in force; they include restrictions on exports of crude oil, petroleum derivatives, unprocessed western red cedar, and the export of horses by sea.[15] The EAA legislation proposed in the 107th Congress did not provide for short-supply control authority.

The Control List and Licensing Procedures

Within the Department of Commerce, the Bureau of Industry and Security administers the license application process. In FY2008, BIS reviewed 21,213 applications with a total value of approximately $72.1 billion, which included $50.2 billion in licenses for crude oil exports in return for refined petroleum. The value of dual-use technology licenses, approximately $21.9 billion, represented 1.7% of total U.S. exports in FY2008. BIS approved 17,945(84%), denied 177 (1.0%), and returned 3,171 (15%) license applications. Most applications for licenses are referred to other government agencies for evaluation, extending the length of the review process. The average processing time for referred license applications was 27 days, down from 28 days in FY2007. China was the largest destination for controlled goods in FY2008 with 1,990 licenses approved with a value of $2.7 billion, approximately 3.7% of the value of total exports to China that year. The greatest number of approved license applications for one commodity to all destinations in FY2008 was for chemical manufacturing facilities and equipment, accounting for 2,212 applications with a value of $294 million.[16]

Commerce Control List

The 1979 EAA directed the Secretary of Commerce (Secretary) to create a control list, known in the Export Administration Regulations as the Commerce Control List). The CCL includes items controlled for national security, foreign policy, and short-supply purposes. Under foreign policy controls, it incorporates the control lists of the multilateral non-proliferation regimes to which the U.S. adheres. TheCCL is the list of specific goods, technology, and software that are controlled by the EAR. The CCL is composed of ten categories of items: nuclear materials, facilities, and equipment; materials, organisms, microorganisms, and toxins; materials processing; electronics; computers; telecommunications and information security; lasers and sensors; navigation and avionics; marine; and propulsion systems, space vehicles, and related equipment. Each of these categories is further divided into functional groups: equipment, assemblies, and components; test, inspection, and production equipment; materials; software; and technology. Each controlled item has an export control classification number (ECCN) based on the above categories and functional group. Each ECCN is accompanied by a description of the item and the reason for control. Currently, there are about 500 ECCN listings. In addition to discrete items on the CCL, nearly all U.S.-origin commodities are "subject to the EAR." This means that any product "subject to the EAR" may be restricted to a destination based on the end-use or end-user of the product. For example, a commodity that is not on the CCL may be denied if the good is destined for a military end-use, or to an entity known to be engaged in proliferation. In addition, items on the CCL often are eligible for license exceptions, a practice that, while not requiring prior approval for an export, vests exporters with certain due diligence and record-keeping requirements related to a given transaction. Yet some products, even if shipped to a friendly nation, will require a license due to the high risk of diversion to an unfriendly destination or because of the controversial nature of the product.

Commodity Jurisdiction/Classification

A commodity jurisdiction (CJ) is used to determine whether a product is considered a dual-use item or a munition, and thus the regulatory regime that will apply to the product. CJs are determined by the Directorate of Defense Trade Controls at the Department of State. Given the more restrictive nature of defense controls, some exporters would like their products to be classified a dual-use goods and may submit their product for a BIS commodity classification. Under the commodity classification process, the exporter requests from BIS a classification for an export item if that item does not correspond to an existing CCL listing. As the exporter is making a calculated judgment that the item belongs under EAR jurisdiction by making this request, BIS is required to refer these requests to State and Defense under certain referral criteria promulgated in 1996. However, this has not always happened. Commerce was criticized by the General Accounting Office (GAO) for the low number of classifications the agency referred and the lack of criteria for referring classification requests to State and Defense.[17] In a follow-up report, GAO found that out of 5,370 commodity classification requests processed in 2005, only 10 were referred to State and Defense, and that the development of renewed referral criteria with State and Defense had not been undertaken.[18] In 2008 GAO reiterated,

> Such jurisdictional disagreements and problems are often the result of minimal or ineffective coordination between the two departments and the departments' differing interpretations of the regulations. Despite our recommendations to do so, the two departments have not yet come together to resolve these jurisdictional disputes or develop new processes to improve coordination. Until these disagreements and coordination problems are resolved, exporters--not the government--will continue to determine which restrictions apply and, therefore, the type of governmental review that will occur. [19]

License Review Procedures

The EAA and the implementing Export Administration Regulations (EAR) establish policies and procedures for the review of license applications and the resolution of interagency disputes. Procedures currently employed were created by Executive Order 12981,[20] as amended, of December 6, 1995. These procedures confer on the Secretary of Commerce (the Secretary) the power to review and to determine the disposition of export licenses. The Departments of State, Defense, and Energy have authority to review any licenses submitted, and the Secretary may refer licenses to others as he deems appropriate. These agencies may waive their right to review license applications for certain commodities or to certain destinations.

Within nine days of a license application's registration, the Secretary must seek additional information, refer the application to other agencies, assure the security classification is correct, return the application if a license is not required, grant the application, or notify the applicant of denial. In case of review by another agency, the reviewing agency must request any additional information from the Secretary within 10 days. After reviewing the file, the reviewing agency may request additional information which the Secretary shall promptly request from the applicant.

Within 30 days of receipt of the application, or of requested review information, the agency must recommend approval or denial of the application, and provide regulatory or statutory justification for a denial. If an agency fails to provide a recommendation within 30 days, the agency is deemed to have no objection to the decision of the Secretary. However, the license application is subject to several actions that can 'stop the clock' on the license application.

Dispute Resolution

The 1995 Order created a three-level interagency dispute resolution mechanism. The top tier of this structure is the Export Administration Review Board (EARB), an entity itself created by Executive Order in 1970.[21] The Board consists of the Secretary, who serves as Chair, and the Secretaries of State, Defense, and Energy. The Chairman of the Joint Chiefs of Staff and the Director of Central Intelligence are non-voting members. The Board may also invite the heads of other agencies to participate as appropriate. Under the EARB is the Advisory Committee on Export Policy (ACEP), which consists of the Assistant Secretary for Export Administration, who serves as Chair, as well as the relevant assistant Secretaries and appropriate officials from the agencies represented in the EARB. The Operating Committee (OC) of the ACEP is the third tier which is made up of representatives of the departments listed above. The Chair is selected by the Secretary of Commerce and serves as the Executive Secretary of ACEP.

The dispute resolution process begins with the OC. The Chair reviews the recommendations of the examining departments and informs them of his decision within 14 days of the deadline for receiving agency recommendations. Any reviewing department may appeal the decision of the Chair to the ACEP. An appeal may be made within five days by an appointee of the President and must state the statutory or regulatory basis for the appeal. The ACEP members review recommendations and information and vote on the application within 11 days of such an appeal. Within five days of a majority decision of the ACEP, a department head of a dissenting agency may appeal the decision to the Secretary. Within 11 days of such an appeal, the EARB must decide by majority vote on the disposition of the application. A member of EARB may appeal this decision to the President within five days of the application. The interagency appeal process must be completed within 90 days of the registration of the application. However, the Order does not set a time frame for Presidential consideration of a license decision.

BIS's denial of an export license must be supported by the statutory and regulatory basis for the denial, giving specific considerations and modifications that would allow BIS to reconsider an application. An explicit appeal procedure is specified in the EAR. One possible basis for appeal is an assessment of foreign availability (see above). If the item in question can be shown to be readily available from a non-U.S. source in sufficient quantity and of comparable quality then a license denial may, in some cases, be reversed. In FY2008, BIS reported that 422 cases were escalated to the OC, and that a further 20 were examined by the ACEP.[22]

Issues Concerning IEEPA

When the 1979 EAA first expired in September 1990, President George H.W. Bush extended existing export regulations by executive order, invoking emergency authority contained in the International Emergency Economic Powers Act (IEEPA).[23] As required by

IEEPA, the President first declared a national emergency "with respect to the unusual and extraordinary threat to the national security, foreign policy and economy of the United States" posed by the expiration of the act. IEEPA-based controls were later terminated during two temporary EAA extensions enacted in 1993 and 1994 as Congress attempted to craft new export control legislation.[24] After the second extension expired in August of 1994, President Clinton reimposed controls under IEEPA.[25] During this period, a major restructuring and reorganization of export control regulations was published as an interim rule in the March 23, 1996 *Federal Register*. On November 11, 2000, President Clinton signed legislation to extend the authority of the 1979 Act until August 20, 2001,[26] when emergency controls were renewed by President George W. Bush pursuant to Executive Order 13222. Several deficiencies have been noted in maintaining export controls under IEEPA authority:

- The police power of enforcement agents lapsed with the EAA. Under IEEPA, these agents must obtain Special Deputy U.S. Marshal status in order to function as law enforcement officers, a complication that consumes limited resources better used on enforcement.
- IEEPA does not authorize the President to limit the jurisdiction of federal courts and thus does not permit him to extend the EAA's general denial of judicial review. In addition, IEEPA does not have an explicit confidentiality provision to authorize protection from public disclosure of information pertaining to the export license applications and enforcement.[27]
- The IEEPA does not explicitly authorize the executive to implement provisions to discourage compliance with foreign boycotts against friendly countries.
- It has been argued that the United States sends the wrong message to other countries by not enacting appropriate legislation. Although the United States has been urging countries such as Russia, Kazakhstan, Ukraine, and China to strengthen their export control laws and implementing regulations, goes the argument, U.S. export controls laws have expired and U.S. credibility is diminished by its lack of a statute.[28]

In addition, penalty authorities under IEEPA were substantially lower than under the EAA and thus had less of a deterrent effect. However, the International Emergency Economic Powers Enhancement Act (P.L. 110-96), signed by President Bush on October 16, 2007, raised criminal penalties to $1 million (up from $50,000 previously) or up to 20 years' imprisonment for natural persons, or both. The act also raised civil penalties to $250,000 from $50,000 previously. Equivalent penalties under the EAA limit civil penalties to $10,000, or $100,000 for violations involving national security controls, and criminal violations to $250,000 and 10 years' imprisonment for individuals and $1 million or 5 times the value of exports for firms.

Technology and Commodities of Concern

Controversial exports have included telecommunications and advanced electronic equipment, precision machine tools (especially computer assisted machines), guidance technology (including Global Positioning System technology), aerospace and jet engine technology, synthetic materials (especially high-strength, light-weight, heat- and corrosion-resistant materials), specialized manufacturing and testing equipment (including mixers, high temperature ovens, heat and vibration simulators). In the last few years, congressional attention has focused on the following goods and technologies.

High Performance Computers (HPCs)

These technologically advanced computers can perform multiple, complex digital operations within seconds. Sometimes also called supercomputers, HPCs are actually a wide range of technologies that also include bundled workstations, mainframe computers, advanced microprocessors, and software. Until recently, the benchmark used for gauging HPC computing performance was a metric known as composite theoretical performance (CTP), measured in millions of theoretical operations per second (MTOPS). The actual MTOPS performed by an HPC over a period of time can vary, based on which operations are performed (some can take longer than others or can be performed while other operations are taking place) and the real cycle speed of the computer. However, the Wassenaar Arrangement approved a new standard for calculating computing power in December 2005, which was incorporated into a BIS final rulemaking on April 24, 2006.[29] The new standard, called adjusted peak performance (APP), is the "adjusted peak rate at which digital computers perform 64-bit or larger floating point additions and multiplications," and is measured by a metric known as "weighted teraflops"(WT).[30] The control level is set at 0.75 WT, a level which BIS states "continues to control high-end proprietary HPCs, such as those used by the Department of Defense and the Department of Energy for advanced research, development, and simulation."[31] This level replaces the 190,000 MTOPS benchmark level of January 2002. The level for computer software and technology is set at 0.04 WT and for computer development and production technology at 0.1 WT.

Since the advent of HPC technology, there have been restrictions on U.S. exports. However, some advocates have maintained that because the computing capabilities of HPCs have advanced so rapidly, and due to the foreign availability of models comparable to some of those produced in the United States, export restrictions of HPCs are neither practical or enforceable. During the Clinton Administration, HPC export thresholds—or the amount of MTOPS capability that an HPC would need to require a license—were raised several times. The last change to the MTOPS level was in January 2002, when the Bush Administration raised the threshold for HPC exports to Tier 3[32] countries to 190,000 MTOPS, up from 2,000 MTOPS in 1995.[33] (This process of decontrol has had a significant regulatory impact on BIS. It reports that in 1993 over 11,000 (42% of total license applications that year) were for computer assemblies and hardware; by 2003, that number had dropped to 14 license applications for the category that year.)[34] Despite the conversion to the WT metric, changes in the control level are still subject to the notification requirements of Title XII (B) of Division A of the National Defense Authorization Act of 1998 (NDAA98), which allows implementation of the new performance level 60 days after a report has been submitted to Congress.[35]

The National Defense Authorization Act of 1998 imposed special conditions on the export of high performance computers. This Title (a) requires the prior notification requirement for exports of HPCs above the MTOPS threshold to Tier III countries. Under this provision of NDAA, exports of these HPCs are subject to the approval of the Secretaries of Commerce, Defense, Energy, and State; (b) imposes post-shipment verification requirements for these HPCs; and (c) imposes the requirement to notify Congress of an adjustment in the MTOPS threshold levels. Each version of EAA in the 107th Congress provided for the repeal of NDAA98 provisions.

Encryption

Encryption is the process of encoding electronic messages to transfer important information and data securely. "Keys" are needed to unlock or decode the message. Encryption is an important element of e-commerce security, however this technology is also central to cryptography and could affect military code-breaking capabilities. The increased civilian importance of encryption technology resulted in the transfer in control authority of certain encryption technology from the Department of State to the Department of Commerce by Executive Order 13026 on November 16, 1996. Since that time, there have been several decontrols of encryption items and technology. The result of these actions has been the progressive decontrol of "retail" or "mass market" encryption technology. Currently, retail encryption products and technology can be exported to western countries[36], and to non-governmental end-users in other countries through a license exemption that requires notification of the transaction. Licenses for encryption products and technology continue to be required for countries covered by anti-terrorism (AT) controls.

Stealth Technology and Materials

Stealth design incorporates materials, shapes, and structures into a functional system to protect it against electronic detection. Stealth technology falls into two categories. Certain stealth materials can deflect an incoming radar signal to neutral space thus preventing the radar receiver from "seeing" the object. Conversely, other materials may absorb incoming radar signals preventing them from reflecting back to the receiver. Stealth related commodities are sensitive from an export control perspective because some materials and processes involved have civil applications that make it difficult to control dissemination and retain U.S. leadership in this technology. Concerns over the potential export of this material led the Department of State to reclassify certain stealth-related technology as munitions in the 1990s.[37]

Satellites

Congress has debated the issues of how strictly to control exports of commercial communications satellites and whether monitoring of foreign launch operations has been effective in preventing disclosures of missile secrets. In 1998, the Cox Committee found that U.S. satellite manufacturers provided missile design information and skills to China through the improper transfer of launch failure analysis.[38] Exports of satellites were licensed by the Department of Commerce from late 1996 until March 1999. In October 1998, Congress returned the authority, effective March 15, 1999, to license exports of commercial communications satellites to the Department of State which had traditionally licensed missile technology exports.[39] The satellite industry claims that this transfer has led to licensing delays and lost sales resulting from regulatory uncertainty, and they have lobbied to reverse export controls to Commerce.[40] Satellites launched for commercial communication purposes may contain embedded sensitive technology such as positioning thrusters, signal encryption, mating and separation mechanisms, and multiple satellite/reentry vehicle systems. As stand-alone items, these technologies are controlled under the U.S. Munitions List. The Foreign Relations Authorization Act of 2010-11 (H.R. 2410), passed by the House on June 10, 2009, contained a provision that would grant the President flexibility to transfer commercial satellite and satellite components from the USML back to the CCL with the approval of the congressional committees of jurisdiction.

Machine Tools

This category covers manufacturing technology such as lathes and other manufacturing equipment used to produce parts for missiles, aircraft engines and arms. This capital equipment is increasingly sophisticated, employing advanced computer software and circuitry. The industry has been vocal in claiming that its competitive position has been hampered by the lack of multilateral controls over sales of this equipment, especially the lack of consensus on controls regarding China.[41] On July 21, 2009, the BIS Office of Technology Evaluation released a critical technology assessment of 5-axis simultaneously controlled machine tools which found foreign availability for certain of these products in China and Taiwan and recommended their decontrol to these destinations.[42]

Aerospace

"Hot section" technology is used in the development, production and overhaul of jet aircraft both military and commercial. Technology developed principally by the Department of Defense is controlled by the U.S. Munitions List. However, technology actually incorporated in commercial aircraft is regulated by the Department of Commerce and falls under a separate foreign policy-based control category. During debates on EAA legislation in the 106th Congress, several senators raised concerns about the possible decontrol of this technology and sought a "carve-out" of hot section and other sensitive technologies that would prevent such items from being decontrolled.[43]

Civil Aviation Equipment

The civilian aviation industry has long been concerned that the Directorate of Defense Trade Controls (DDTC), the agency within the Department of State that controls defense goods and technology, has been increasingly asserting jurisdiction over civilian aircraft parts and components. Section 17(c) of the EAA states, in part, that "standard equipment certified by the Federal Aviation Administration (FAA), in civil aircraft and is an integral part of such aircraft, and which is to be exported to a country other than a controlled country, shall be subject to export controls exclusively under this act. Any such product shall not be subject to controls under Section 38(b)(2) [licensing requirements] of the AECA." In the aftermath of the QRS-11 case, in which DDTC asserted jurisdiction over a non-FAA component of a commercial standby instrument system (CSIS) under the jurisdiction of Commerce, commercial suppliers have complained that in order not to run afoul of the ITAR, they must submit commodity jurisdiction for items they believe are covered by 17(c).

On September 24, 2007, Representative Manzullo introduced legislation (H.R. 3633) to clarify that civil aircraft equipment, parts, component, or technology eligible for export airworthiness approval under Federal Aviation Administration regulations are to be subject only to controls under the EAA. After negotiations with Congress and industry, DDTC released a new rulemaking[44] clarifying the interpretation of Section 17(c) of the EAA. Under the regulation, Commerce will have jurisdiction over parts and components of civil aircraft when such components are standard equipment, covered by a civil aircraft type certificate issued by the Federal Aviation Administration, and is an integral part of the aircraft. For such parts and components not considered significant military equipment (SME), this means that suppliers will no longer have to submit the part or component for a commodity jurisdiction determination.

Deemed Exports

Exports of technology, know-how, and non-encryption source code is "deemed" to have been exported when it is released to a foreign national within the United States. Such knowledge transfers are regulated by the Export Administration Regulations,[45] which require that a license must be obtained by a U.S. entity to transfer technology to a foreign national in the United States if the same transfer to the home country of the foreign national would require a license. Deemed exports are not expressly mentioned in the 1979 EAA. House versions of EAA in the 107th Congress sought to explicitly define deemed exports as exports falling under the jurisdiction of the act. Processing deemed export license applications has become a larger part of BIS activity. In FY2007, BIS reviewed 1,056 deemed export licenses (5.4% of the total licenses submitted to BIS) and reports that nearly 57% of deemed licenses reviewed were for Chinese nationals.[46]

In March 2005, BIS established a rule-making procedure in response to an Inspector General's (IG) report,[47] which recommended that BIS alter the standard governing which foreign nationals are subject to export controls. Currently, foreign nationals are subject to export controls requirements based on their country of citizenship or permanent residency; however, the IG recommended that country of birth should be the standard used. According to the IG, foreign nationals from controlled destinations could access technology without scrutiny if they first establish permanent residency in a third country, and foreign nationals from controlled destinations often have dual nationalities. However, Under Secretary of Commerce David McCormick announced in December 2005 that deemed export controls would continue to be based on country of citizenship or permanent residency, not place of birth.[48]

In December 2007, BIS released the report of the Deemed Export Advisory Commission (DEAC), which was commissioned in September 2006 to conduct an independent assessment of the deemed export regulatory regime. The Commission recommended the establishment of a "trusted entity" program for academia and industrial entities to qualify for a streamlined deemed export application process. The Commission proposed an evaluation of an applicant's probable loyalties that would include consideration of an applicant's country of birth, prior country of residence, current citizenship, and an examination of a person's prior and present activities to determine eligibility for a deemed export license. The Commission also recommended streamlining certain terminology in the deemed export regulations and the establishment of an outside panel of experts to conduct an annual "sunset" review of technologies on the Commerce Control List.[49]

The DEAC recommendations were highly criticized by industry representatives and the research community with one group summing up the proposals as "unadministerable for the government and difficult-to-impossible to comply with for industry."[50] BIS published a notice of inquiry in May 2008 seeking comment on the scope of technologies on the Commerce Control List subject to deemed export controls and on the criteria used to assess country affiliation for foreign nationals.[51] While this inquiry has yet to result in a formal rulemaking, another DEAC recommendation, the Emerging Technologies and Research Advisory Committee (ETRAC) has begun to meet and has been grappling with these issues.

Competing Perspectives in the Export Control Debate

A principal theme in debates on export administration legislation is the tension between commercial and national security concerns. These concerns are not mutually exclusive, and thus it is often difficult to characterize opposing camps. For example, nearly everyone favors reform of the current system, yet no one considers themselves opposed to national security. Generally, however, many who favor reform of the current export control accept the business perspective that such reform would assist U.S. business to compete in the global marketplace. Others view the issue more from a national security perspective. To this group, reform should be concerned less with the abilities of U.S. industry to export and more with effective controls placed on potential exports to countries that threaten the security of the United States, terrorists, violators of human rights, and proliferators of weapons of mass destruction. From these different perspectives, controversies arise regarding the controllability of technology, the effectiveness of multilateral regimes, the bureaucratic structure of the licensing process and the impact of export controls on the U.S. economy.

Foreign Availability and the Controllability of Technology

The foreign availability and mass market provisions of EAA reauthorization legislation, and the underlying concept of the controllability of technology, have proved controversial in the EAA debate. Industry groups that have taken an active position on legislation to replace the 1979 EAA have considered the adoption of these provisions as a key benefit of potential EAA legislation. The foreign availability and mass market concepts are integral to their contention that the flow of technology cannot be effectively controlled, and that U.S. dominance of cutting-edge technology can no longer be assumed. According to their arguments, unilateral controls will not stop other countries from obtaining advanced technology. Advocates of this viewpoint claim that "countries of concern" will simply obtain this technology from other nations. Adherents to this view regard current multilateral controls on dual-use articles as ineffectual. From this perspective, only American business suffers from the unilateral nature of U.S. export controls. In the process, foreign business wins new markets or gains an incentive to enter new markets.[52]

According to the industry position, unilateral export controls are also becoming increasingly unworkable as the economy undergoes globalization. The current export control system is predicated on goods being manufactured or assembled in one country. In many industries, however, component parts are manufactured worldwide and are considered commodities. If these parts are not available from one source on a timely basis, they can be obtained elsewhere.[53] Purchasing managers at Daimler Chrysler Aerospace, for example, reportedly have been instructed to reduce dependence on American components for defense and space technology products because of delays associated with American licensing procedures.[54]

Other participants in the export control debate are concerned about the mass market and foreign availability arguments advanced by industry proponents. Critics charge that the mass market standard would effectively nullify the whole U.S. control regime by decontrolling any item that met the criteria under the law. They assert that virtually any product, including dual-use items used for proliferation purposes, could qualify for mass market status. Similarly, as one nonproliferation advocate testified regarding EAA legislation in the 106th Congress, the foreign availability criterion would allow the sale of "anything a controlled country can purchase from a rogue buyer."[55]

A related argument made by industry is that national security is enhanced by robust export industries. This argument is predicated on the changing nature of defense procurement, research and development. During the Cold War, the formative period of the current export control regime, the military conducted considerably technical research on its own and provided funds for research and development. Now that situation is largely reversed. The military now purchases many items 'off-the-shelf' and relies to a greater extent on commercial applications. Industry argues that it is in the national security to sell current technology to generate funds to develop future technology. If American firms are competitively hindered because of export controls, the argument goes, foreign firms will gain market share, increase profits, invest more in R&D, shrink and possibly surpass our technological lead. These circumstances, in turn, potential could affect the quality of the technology available for national security purposes. Thus, industry argues it needs a streamlined export process, one that will not needlessly impede exports.

Critics of industry's national security position reject this argument. They maintain that the United States does not promote its national security by selling advanced technology to potentially hostile states. This technology, if sold to a regime of dubious stability, could be used against the United States or allies in the future. Proponents of this argument point to the case of Iraq, which received U.S. weaponry in the 1980s when Saddam Hussein was considered a useful counterweight to Iran. Subsequently, this technology was used against

Kuwait and allied forces in the Persian Gulf War. Reliance on the civilian sector for R&D, they claim, is a policy decision brought about by declining defense budgets in the 1990s. Some further argue that R&D that advances defense capabilities should be funded within the Defense Department if it is necessary to maintain controls on technology to certain nations.

Computing Power

Industry groups and some other observers have used the rapid rise in computing power as an illustration both of the uncontrollable nature of technology and the inability of the export control system to account for such innovation. According to one national security analyst, attempting to control computing power is not "feasible or effective." He maintains that the restraint of computer trade is self-defeating because it cedes markets and profits that could be used for R&D.[56]

Increasing computing speeds combined with networking advances have blurred the distinction between super-computers and commodity computers. Microprocessors that individually comply with export regulations can be linked together to create servers with MTOPS capabilities that breach export thresholds. If enough processors are linked together, they can create a parallel processing system with capabilities that approach those of a super-computer. The Defense Science Board noted that the ability to cluster commodity computers in order to multiply computing power erodes the ability to restrict access to high-performance computing, even if high-performance stand-alone machines can be controlled.[57]

Other observers believe the United States can restrict access to the highest computer technology by limiting exports. They maintain that American-made computers are perceived as superior, and thus carry greater cachet than products from other nations. They note that the purchase of an American-made computer product also buys superior networking and service, often at a better price. Control advocates maintain that these distinctions are significant, that qualitative differences are important.[58] In addition, networking a parallel processing system, as those without access to advanced computing technology must do to increase computing capability, presents additional challenges distinct from those faced by engineers of commodity computers.

Post-Shipment Verification

One policy that has been attempted to monitor and verify the end-use of controlled goods is the post-shipment verification requirement (PSV) on the export of HPCs mandated by Sec 1213 of NDAA98 (see above). This section requires that a PSV be made for computers destined for computers controlled to tier III destinations, including China, Russia, India, Pakistan, Israel and other nations in areas of regional instability.[59] Lawmakers have been especially concerned with exports of HPCs to the People's Republic of China. The GAO has reported that China has restricted access to facilities that contain U.S. HPC exports. It has also found that BIS has made limited efforts to monitor or to verify compliance with the terms and conditions specified by the export license.[60] Reportedly, the difficulty in monitoring the end-use of HPC exports in China has been exacerbated by the close ties that Chinese state owned enterprises have with the Chinese military.[61]

The Effectiveness of Multilateral Regimes

The United States participates in several multilateral export control regimes. The principal multilateral regime related to dual-use goods and technology is the Wassenaar Arrangement (WA) on Dual-Use Goods and Munitions. The WA was created in 1996 and is the successor organization to the Coordinated Committee (CoCom), the Cold War era dual-use control regime that ended in 1994. The WA dual-use control list is generally consistent with U.S. CCL items subject to national security controls. The United States also participates in four proliferation related control regimes: the Australia Group (chemical and biological weapons and precursors); the Missile Technology Control Regime, and the Nuclear Suppliers Group.[62]

Generally, these groups are characterized by national discretion, a common control list, and regular reporting requirements. Each group has formulated a common control list and member nations control the exports of those goods under their own national laws, a policy know as national discretion. Unlike CoCom, however, these organizations do not perform a review function prior to the grant of a national export license. The regime's members do pledge disclosure of export licensing decisions, and pledge consultation on sensitive export licenses. Some groups adhere to a "no undercut" provision—that is, a member state will not license the sale of an item in which a license has been denied by another state. However, these groups operate by consensus and are hampered by limited institutional structures.

Some observers contend that the Wassenaar Arrangement, in particular, is ineffective because it relies on consensus of member states. The necessity for consensus, critics charge, results in a level of control acceptable to all. Its minimal reporting requirements mandate notification only that an item has been sold, thus preventing effective pre-export consultation among member states.

Industry representatives stress the necessity of effective multilateral controls. They argue that export controls are effective only if they are adhered to by all states capable of exporting a given technology. For example, the machine tool industry has been at the forefront in criticizing the unilateral nature of our export policies, especially concerning exports to China. It notes that there is no consensus among Wassenaar Arrangement countries on the proper limits of technology transfer to China. (Indeed, no country is explicitly targeted by Wassenaar.) Stringent domestic controls combined with minimal multilateral constraints only damage American companies, according to industry spokesmen. They fault the U.S. for having an overly rigorous licensing policy towards China, without noticeably pursuing a strategy to convince our allies to follow our lead.[63]

Proponents of tighter export restrictions note that America traditionally has taken the lead in export controls and non-proliferation efforts. These efforts included the original EAA, adopted in 1949, and the establishment of CoCom. They argue that efforts to strengthen CoCom's successor regime, the Wassenaar Arrangement, cannot succeed if Washington itself is loosening export restrictions. Thus, the United States must take the lead in order to convince other nations to follow the U.S. example. Adherents of this viewpoint argue that the successful negotiating strategy in these multilateral fora is to adopt controls first and then persuade other countries to follow suit. Hence in their view, an export control strategy pegged solely on the policies of other nations, negotiated by consensus, is ineffectual and harmful to national security.[64]

Both industry spokesmen and advocates of heightened export controls agree that the multilateral controls need to be strengthened. Yet, to do this requires consensus on which goods and which countries represent a threat. There does seem to be agreement among western nations to restrict dual-use items to a limited number of 'countries of concern,'[65] yet consensus breaks down with regard to other states, notably China. The export control dilemma in this context becomes clear. Without consensus on a particular target country, the question becomes whether the United States should impose controls unilaterally. One then needs to determine either: which non-proliferation or other foreign policy goals are sufficiently important to offset possibly damaging American business, and possibly costing American jobs; or how large an economic benefit would justify risking important national security goals.

China

Debate over export controls has often focused on China. The dilemma that encapsulates U.S. export control policy to China is how to benefit from the potentially vast Chinese market and low Chinese production costs while minimizing the risk to U.S. security interests of exporting sensitive dual-use technologies to China. Some representatives of the business community have argued that U.S. export control policy toward China is too stringent. They claim such controls have hampered technology transfers to China in the past few years while the controls of U.S. allies have not. They reported that Chinese companies will not ask U.S. companies to bid on sales because of the delays associated with the U.S. licensing process. As one industry spokesman has testified: "The result has been that the Chinese are denied nothing in terms of high technology, but U.S. firms have lost out in a crucial market. This serves neither our commercial nor our strategic interests."[66]

However, other analysts and several Members of Congress have expressed grave concerns about China's dual-use technology acquisitions. They cite findings of the Cox Commission that China evaded existing export controls to illegally obtain missile design and satellite technology and that China has circumvented end-user controls on high-performance computers.[67] According to this view, the Commission's findings show the need for both tightened controls and greater enforcement of export controls against China. In addition, China has been implicated in several nuclear, missile, and chemical proliferation activities.[68]

The "China Rule"

On June 19, 2007, BIS published the final rule entitled "Revisions and Clarification of Export and Re-export Controls for the People's Republic of China" (72 *Fed. Reg.* 33646). The final rule is composed of three parts: a new licensing requirement for certain products for military end-use in China, a validated end-user (VEU) program, and a requirement to obtain an end-user statement for certain licensed products. The proposed rule has been driven by the concern that the export of commercial technology to certain end-users is undermining the arms embargo that the United States and others maintain against China. Others, including industry, have questioned the scope and efficacy of these new controls.

The new licensing policy has two distinct components: the establishment of new military end-use controls for the PRC and a revised License Review Policy for national security controlled items destined for the PRC. The aspect that has received the most attention is the establishment of new military end-use controls on 20 product categories consisting of 31 export control classification numbers (ECCN). Currently, these items are controlled primarily for anti-terrorism reasons, thus a license is required only for exports to countries determined to be state sponsors of terrorism (Cuba, Iran, North Korea, Sudan, Syria). Under the new rule,

BIS will require a license for the export, reexport, or in country transfer of these items if the exporter knows, has reason to know, or is informed by BIS that the item is or may be intended for military end-uses in the PRC. The final rule also revises the long-standing licensing policy for National Security controlled items destined for the PRC contained in the EAR, Part 742.4(b)(7). It clarifies that there is a presumption of denial for license applications to export, reexport, or transfer items that would make a direct and significant contribution to the PRC's military capabilities in certain key weapons systems.

The second component of the Final Rule also increases the exemption threshold for obtaining End-Use Statements (EUS) from the Ministry of Foreign Commerce (MOFCOM) of the PRC. The PRC requires that MOFCOM issue an EUS before BIS can conduct a pre-license check or post-shipment verification for an export. A U.S. exporter must request that the importer obtain the EUS for a license application because the BIS inspection is often a statutory or regulatory prerequisite for approving some applications. The rule increases the amount of the value of the license exempted from the EUS requirement from $5,000 to $50,000 for most goods to the PRC. However, it expands the EUS requirement to cover all license applications to the PRC reaching this threshold. Previously, EUS were required only for items under national security controls.

Validated End-User (VEU) Program

The VEU is the third component of the China Rule. The VEU establishes a method by which trusted PRC civilian end-users can be nominated for the program, and, if approved by BIS, the eligible end-users may receive items eligible under the program without a license. The rule sets up an applications process by which an end-user can be nominated for the program. In approving a candidate for VEU status, the ERC will evaluate the entity's exclusive engagement in civilian end-use activities, its compliance record with U.S. export controls, its capability to comply with the recordkeeping requirements of the VEU authorization, agreement to on-site review prior to approval and subsequently to ensure adherence to VEU conditions, and its relationship with U.S. and foreign companies. On September 11, 2007, China's Minister of Foreign Commerce (MoFCom) announced that any company seeking VEU status would need authorization from MoFCom before allowing plant or records inspections.[69]

Not all items on the CCL are eligible for export under this program. Items controlled for crime control or missile technology by the EAR do not qualify for export under this program due to statutory reasons. In addition, not all items that are eligible for export under this program can be exported to all validated end-users. The approved VEU application will be accompanied by a list of items that can be exported to the end-user, and this list can be expanded or contracted by the ERC. Once approved , the VEU can import approved items from any exporter, not just the nominee.

According to BIS, the proposal would streamline licensing for certain companies for whom exporters routinely request and receive licenses for the same product over time. Thus, resources that currently process these routine applications could be diverted to staff more problematic license applications. On October 2, 2007, BIS announced the expansion of the VEU program to eligible companies in India, and General Electric India was named as the first eligible company on June 17, 2009.[70]

On October 19, 2007, BIS announced the first five VEU companies: Applied Materials China, National Semiconductor, Boeing Hexcel AVIC I Joint Venture, Semiconductor

Manufacturing International Corporation (SMIC), and Shanghai Hua Hong NEC Corporation (HHNEC). BIS reported that these companies had imported licensed goods valued at $54.3 million in 2006.[71] In January 2008, the Wisconsin Project on Nuclear Arms Control charged in a report that two of the entities, AVIC I and HHNEC, present diversion risks through their corporate affiliations with government-owned companies that do business with the Chinese military. The Wisconsin Project also contend that some of these entities' affiliates have run afoul of U.S. proliferation sanctions and export control laws.[72] Then BIS Undersecretary Mario Mancuso responded to the report by maintaining that the companies had a "demonstrable history of using U.S. technology in the past...We know a lot about these companies and know a lot about how they use the technologies they are authorized to receive through VEU. These technologies were previously available to these companies by license, and [the VEU] judgment was based on data, not conjecture."[73]

Controversy regarding the VEU has not abated. A GAO study of September 2008[74] recommended the suspension of the VEU program with China because BIS has not been able to reach a VEU-specific inspection agreement with China for conducting on-site reviews of validated end-users. Nor has the agency developed criteria for selecting candidates for on-sites, or the procedures for conducting the on-site review itself, according to GAO. Commerce notes that it has conducted checks under the pre-existing 2004 end-use verification understanding (EUVU). However, checks conducted under this system require the aforementioned MoFCom end-use statement, running counter to the trade facilitation rationale of the program, and if the companies do not voluntarily seek an EUS from MoFCom, then an inspection cannot take place.[75] On January 13, 2009, BIS announced full implementation of the VEU to China "with agreement on procedures to ensure the program's secure and efficient operation."[76] More recently, at a June 4, 2009, House Energy and Commerce Committee hearing, Representative Markey cited information from the Wisconsin Project claiming that another VEU approved entity, Aviza Technology China, shared an address with a state-owned firm that was sanctioned by the State Department in December 2006 for illicit sales to Iran and Syria.[77]

The Licensing Process and Organization of the Export Control System

As noted earlier, the Bureau of Industry and Security (BIS) within the Department of Commerce (DOC) is responsible for regulating dual-use exports. However, other agencies also provide input into the licensing process. BIS consults with other members of the national security community on license applications and commodity classifications. The Defense Technology Security Agency in the Department of Defense conducts national security reviews for license applications referred from Commerce and State. The Department of Energy also reviews dual-use license applications referred by BIS for nuclear uses and nuclear end-users, and it and the Nuclear Regulatory Commission license exportation of nuclear materials. In addition, the Directorate of Defense Trade Controls (DDTC) at the State Department administers the International Traffic in Arms Regulations. Through the U.S. Munitions List, DDTC controls the export of weapons and military technology.

Industry leaders identify several problems with the existing licensing system. First, overlapping jurisdiction between the Commerce and State Departments with regard to certain dual-use products makes it unclear where the exporters need to apply for licenses. Second, extended time periods required for license approval compromise the reliability of U.S. suppliers and make it hard for manufacturers and customers to plan ahead. Third, the licensing system does not reflect advances in technology, foreign availability of dual-use items, and the economic impact of export controls on the industrial base. Finally, there is no opportunity for judicial review of licensing decisions.

Others consider foreign availability and economic impact to be important considerations, yet secondary to national security. Export administration officials claim that they conduct thorough, fair, and expeditious license reviews. Time is required to check proposed export items against lists of controlled items, check end users and end uses against lists of suspect recipients, and coordinate with several government agencies. Officials say they must be able to "stop the clock" to obtain additional information and investigate certain issues on a case-by-case basis to insure that sensitive technologies do not find their way into the wrong hands.

Some analysts who see national security as the primary purpose of the export control regime question whether BIS belongs in the Department of Commerce. They claim that DOC's mission is mostly one of promoting exports and generally serving commercial interests. This, in some eyes, may create an institutional bias towards the granting of export licenses and skew the process against national security goals. Other analysts point to the full and equal participation of other agencies, particularly the Department of Defense, in the current structure to argue that such bias is unlikely to prevail.

End Notes

[1] In the first half of the 20th century, war, or the imminent threat of war, led to the Trading With The Enemy Act of 1917 and the Neutrality Act of 1935. In 1940, Congress increased presidential power over the export of militarily significant goods and technology with the passage of P.L. 76-703, "An Act to Expedite and Strengthen the National Defense." In each of these instances the rationale for control was the necessity of not giving aid and comfort to the nation's enemies.

[2] For details on Wassenaar, see CRS Report RS20517, *Military Technology and Conventional Weapons Export Controls: The Wassenaar Arrangement*, by Richard F. Grimmett.

[3] IEEPA provisions are renewed yearly through Presidential determination, the most recent being on August 13, 2009. On the occasion of this renewal, the Obama administration announced that it would be conducting a broad-based review of the U.S. export control system.

[4] Peter Lichtenbaum, former Assistant Secretary for Export Administration, "Administration Will Press Congress to Renew EAA, but no Major Reform in Sight," *International Trade Reporter*, January 19, 2006.

[5] General Order Concerning Mayrow General Trading and Related Entities, 71 *Federal Register 32272*, June 5, 2006.

[6] Secretary Gates' speech is available at http://www.defense.gov//speeches/speech.aspx?speechid=1453.

[7] "Fact Sheet on President Obama's Export Control Reform Initiative," April 20, 2010, available at: http:// www.whitehouse.gov/the-press-office/fact-sheet-presidents-export-control-reform-initiative

[8] This list currently includes Albania, Armenia, Azerbaijan, Belarus, Cambodia, China (PRC), Georgia, Iraq, Kazakhstan, Kyrgyzstan, Laos, Macau, Moldova, Mongolia, North Korea, Russia, Tajikistan, Turkmenistan, Ukraine, Uzbekistan, and Vietnam. (EAR 15 C.F.R. 740, Supplement 1).

[9] EAR, 15 C.F.R. 742.4.

[10] The list can be seen at http://www.dtic.mil/mctl.

[11] "BIS Narrowly Eases Some Thermal Imaging Camera Export Controls," *Inside U.S. Trade*, May 29, 2009; "BIS Easing Requirements for Uncooled Thermal Imaging Cameras," *Export Practitioner*, May 2009.

[12] For a description of the full range of foreign policy controls implemented, see BIS, Foreign Policy Report 2008, available at http://www.bis.doc.gov/news/2008/2008-fpr.pdf.

[13] See CRS Report RL33499, *Exempting Food and Agriculture Products from U.S. Economic Sanctions: Status and Implementation*, by Remy Jurenas.

[14] EAR, 15 C.F.R. 744, Supplement 4.

[15] EAR, 15 C.F.R. 754.

[16] BIS, 2008 Annual Report, pp. 7-8. http://www.bis.doc.gov/news/2009/bis_annual_report_08.pdf

[17] See GAO Report 02-996, *Export Controls: Processes for Determining Proper Control of Defense Related Items Need Improvement*, September 2002.

[18] GAO Report 06-638, Export *Controls: Improvements to Commerce's Dual-Use System Needed to Ensure Protection of U.S. Interests in the Post 9-11 Environment*, June 2006.

[19] GAO Report 08-710T, *Export Controls: State and Commerce Have Not Taken Basic Steps to Better Ensure U.S. Interests Are Protected,* April 24, 2008.

[20] EAR, 15 C.F.R. 750.4.

[21] Executive Order 11533, June 4, 1970; continued by Executive Order 12002, July 7, 1977.

[22] BIS 2008 Annual Report, p. 8.

[23] 50 U.S.C. §§ 1701 et seq. See Exec. Order No. 12730, 55 Federal Register 40373 (1990). The use of IEEPA authorities to extend expired export controls was anticipated by Congress in the legislative history of IEEPA. See H.Rept. 95-459 at 13.

[24] P.L. 103-10; P.L. 103-277.

[25] "Continuation of Export Controls," Exec. Order No. 12924, 59 Federal Register 43437 (1994); Message from the President, September 11. 1998, "Continuation of National Emergency Regarding the Lapse of the Export Administration Act of 1979," Ex. Com. 10845, H.Doc. 105-303.

[26] P.L. 106-508.

[27] In a recent case, however, the U.S. Court of Appeals for the District of Columbia upheld the authority of the Commerce Department to withhold information on export license applications under the Freedom of Information Act exemption for matters specifically exempted from disclosure by statute, notwithstanding the lapse of the EAA. Wisconsin Project on Nuclear Arms Control v. U.S. Dep't of Commerce, 317 F.3d 275 (D.C.Cir. 2003).

[28] Testimony of William A. Reinsch the Under Secretary for Export Administration, Department of Commerce on the Reauthorization of the Export Administration Act of 1979 (EAA), before the Senate Committee of Banking, Housing and Urban Affairs, Subcommittee on Trade and International Finance, on January 20, 1999.

[29] 71 *Federal Register* 20876, April 24, 2006.

[30] "Wassenaar Arrangement Technical Note on 'Adjusted Peak Performance'" in *The Export Practicioner*, January 2006, p. 22.

[31] 71 *Federal Register* 20878, April 24, 2006.

[32] For HPCs, the Commerce Department organized countries of destination into 4 tiers with increasing levels of export control. These range from a no-license policy for HPC exports to Tier 1 countries (Western Europe, Australia, Mexico, Japan, and New Zealand) to the virtual embargo for exports to Tier 4 countries (Cuba, Iran, Iraq, Libya, North Korea, Sudan, and Syria). Tier 3 countries, including China, Russia and other countries of the Commonwealth of Independent States (CIS), India, and Pakistan, were subject to a dual control system distinguishing between civilian and military end-users and end-uses until 2000. In January 2001, President Clinton merged the Tier I and Tier 2 categories and effectively decontrolled exports to those countries.

[33] For a summary of changes to HPC controls, see Bureau of Industry and Security, "High Performance Computer Export Controls," http://www.bis.doc.gov/HPCs/Default.htm.

[34] BIS, 2003 Annual Report, http://www.bis.doc.gov/news/2004/03annualrept/index.htm#Chap2.

[35] The National Defense Authorization Act of 2001 lowered the notification requirement from 180 to 60 days, H.Rept. 106-945, Sec. 1234, October 6, 2000. The WT metric conversion notification was sent to Congress on February 3, 2006.

[36] European Union countries, Australia, Czech Republic, Hungary, Japan, New Zealand, Norway, Poland, and Switzerland.

[37] For further discussion, see GAO Report NSIAD 95-140, Export Controls: Concerns over Stealth Related Exports (May 1995).

[38] H.Rept. 105-851, U.S. National Security and Military/Commercial Concerns with the People's Republic of China, May 25, 1999.

[39] Required by the National Defense Authorization Act for FY1999, P.L. 105-261.

[40] Satellite Industry Association, "Satellite Export Licensing: The Impact of Federal Export Control Laws on the California Space Industry," Presentation, February 2001.

[41] See Paul Freedenberg, Testimony before the Senate Banking Committee, February 7, 2001, http://www. senate. gov/ ~banking/01_02hrg/020701/index.htm (hereafter Freedenberg).

[42] http://www.bis.doc.gov/defenseindustri albaseprograms/osies/ defmarketresearchrpts/final_ machine_ tool _ report.pdf

[43] "Sen. Warner Says Agreement Near On Bringing EAA Bill to Floor This Week," 17 International Trade Reporter 340, March 2, 2000.

[44] "Amendment to the International Traffic in Arms Regulations: the United States Munitions List: Category VIII," *Federal Register*, August 14, 2008, p.47,523.

[45] EAR 15 C.F.R. 734.2

[46] BIS, 2007 Annual Report, p.17-18.

[47] *Deemed Export Controls May Not Stop the Transfer of Sensitive Technology to Foreign Nationals in the United States*, (IPE-16176, March 2004).

[48] David McCormick, "Foreign Talent Need Not Threaten Security," *Financial Times*, December 13, 2005.

[49] Deemed Export Advisory Commission, *The Deemed Export Rule in the Era of Globalization*, December 20, 2007, available at http://tac.bis.doc.gov/2007/deacreport.pdf.
[50] Letter from AeA, et al., to Secretary Gutierrez, February 15, 2008.
[51] 73 *Federal Register* 28795, May 19, 2008.
[52] For examples of this argument see, Prepared Statement of Dan Hoydosh, co-chairman of Computer Coalition for Responsible Exports, in Senate Banking Committee, Reauthorization of the Export Administration Act, S.Hrg. 106-461, March 16, 1999 (Reauthorization).
[53] Hamre, John, Testimony before the Armed Services Committee, February 28, 2000, transcript, p. 31-33.
[54] Douglass, John W., prepared testimony before the Armed Services Committee, February 28, 2000, p.3.
[55] Milhollin, Gary, prepared testimony before the Senate Governmental Affairs Committee, May 26, 2000, p. 6.
[56] Richard Perle, former Assistant Secretary of Defense for Security Policy in the Reagan Administration speaking at the Forum for Technology and Innovation, March 23, 1999, http://www.tech-forum.org/upcoming/transcripts/ CompExportsTrans.htm.
[57] Defense Science Board, Final Report of Task Force on Globalization and Security, Washington: Office of the Under Secretary of Defense for Acquisition and Technology, December 1999, p. 27.
[58] Milhollin, Gary, prepared testimony before the Senate Governmental Affairs Committee, May 26, 2000, p. 6.
[59] Originally this regulation applied to computers over 2,000 MTOPS. The benchmark was raised over the years to 190,000 MTOPS and has now been replaced by a new metric, weighted teraflops (WT) (see "High Performance Computers (HPCs)," above).
[60] GAO Report 02-468T, *Export Controls: Issues to Consider in Authorizing a New Export Administration Act*, February 28, 2002, p. 7.
[61] CRS Report 98-617, *Technology, Trade, and Security Issues Between the United States and the People's Republic of China: A Trip Report, August 1997*, by Glenn J. McLoughlin.
[62] See CRS Report RL31559, *Proliferation Control Regimes: Background and Status*, coordinated by Mary Beth Nikitin; and CRS Report RS20517, *Military Technology and Conventional Weapons Export Controls: The Wassenaar Arrangement*, by Richard F. Grimmett.
[63] See Freedenberg, p. 6.
[64] Milhollin, prepared, p. 7.
[65] Cuba, Iran, Iraq, Libya, North Korea, and Sudan.
[66] Freedenberg, p. 7.
[67] For more information on technology transfers to China, see CRS Report 98-485, *China: Possible Missile Technology Transfers Under U.S. Satellite Export Policy—Actions and Chronology*, by Shirley A. Kan.
[68] Ibid.
[69] China Ministry of Commerce, Announcement #60, 2007, September 11, 2007, http://english.mofcom. gov. cn/aarticle/policyrelease/domesticpolicy/200709/20070905091778.html; *The Export Practitioner*, October 2007, p. 27.
[70] BIS Press Release, October 2, 2007, http://www.bis.doc.gov/10-02-07%20India%20VEU%20-%20FINAL.pdf; BIS Press Release, June 17, 2009, http://www.commerce PressReleases_Fact Sheets/ PROD01_008103.
[71] "New BIS Program Changes Export Rules on Targeted Products For Select Companies in China," BIS Press Release, October 19, 2007 http://www.bis.doc.gov/news/2007/china10182007.htm.
[72] Wisconsin Project on Nuclear Arms Control, "In China We Trust?", January 2008, available at http://www.wisconsinproject.org/pubs/reports/2007/inchinawetrust.pdf.
[73] "Mancuso Defends VEU Program as Union Calls for Suspension," *Inside U.S. China Trade*, January 9, 2008.
[74] GAO Report 08-1095, *Export Controls: Challenges with Commerce's Validated End-User Program May Limit Its Ability to Ensure that Semiconductor Equipment Exported to China is Used as Intended,* September 2008.
[75] GAO-08-1095, p. 29.
[76] BIS Press Release, January 13, 2009. [http://www.bis.doc.gov/news/2009/bis_press01132009.htm] .
[77] Rep. Markey Slams New Export Rule Favoring Chinese Company, June 10, 2009. http://www. Wisconsin pubs/editorials/2009/markeyslamsnewrule-061009.htm

In: U.S. Export Programs and Promotion Tools
Editor: Steven D. Braghoff
ISBN: 978-1-60741-328-8

Chapter 7

EXPORTS SUPPORT AMERICAN JOBS

U.S. Department of Commerce

INTRODUCTION

Updated Measure will Quantify Progress as Global Economy Recovers

On March 11, 2010, President Barack Obama issued an executive order creating the National Export Initiative (NEI), which aims to double U.S. exports over the next five years in support of 2 million jobs here at home.

The NEI recognizes that exports will play a critical role in catalyzing America's near- and long-term economic growth, and it represents the first time the United States will have a government wide export promotion strategy with focused attention from the president and his Cabinet.

The report that follows is an analytical complement to the NEI, demonstrating the fundamental role that exports already play in the U.S. economy and providing the methodological framework that will be used to track progress in meeting the president's goals.

As the report lays out, in 2008 exports represented 12.7 percent of U.S. gross domestic product (GDP), the highest level in almost a century. These exports supported jobs for over 10 million Americans, making very clear that our ability to access and compete in global markets is an integral part of economies in cities and towns across the country—and became more so in the years leading up to the worldwide recession. Despite sluggish economywide job growth between 2003 and 2008, export-related jobs actually increased by nearly 3 million during this period.

It is important to note that the increase in export- supported jobs occurred despite the fact that the U.S. government lacked a comprehensive export policy, and while the budget for export promotion activities was flat. Enhanced trade promotion efforts, like those described in the NEI, will help speed a return to pre-recession export levels.

An additional finding of this report is the role that exports play in supporting a healthy, vibrant manufacturing sector. Indeed, the nearly 3.7 million manufacturing jobs supported by exports contribute to 27 percent of all employment in the manufacturing sector. This report suggests that success in supporting American manufacturing is fundamentally dependent on a successful export policy.

The report also highlights the broader implications of exports for our economic well-being. Exports are concentrated in sectors, such as manufacturing, that are a critical source of the productivity gains that increase living standards for Americans throughout the country. Now more than ever, exports are central to a strong U.S. economy.

The year 2009 was a difficult one for the global economy, which hit U.S. exporters and their employees particularly hard. This report clearly illustrates that recovery in our economy, employment, productivity, and manufacturing is tied to our ability to drive export competitiveness. For this reason, the challenge presented by the president's NEI is crucial to U.S. economic success, both in the short term and for years to come.

This examination of the relationship between U.S. exports and the jobs they support covers 1993–2008, with preliminary estimates for 2009 and 2010. Te report shows the following information:

- Exports of goods and services supported 10.3 million jobs in 2008.
- Export-supported jobs accounted for 6.9 percent of total U.S. employment in 2008. The value of total exports, as measured in this study, totaled nearly $1.7 trillion—or nearly $165,000 per export job in 2008.
- Additional analyses indicate that the number of jobs supported by exports declined sharply in 2009 from 2008. The drop reflected a large decrease in the nominal value of exports and a modest gain in the ratio of exports per job. The yearly movements in the ratio strongly correlate with that of nominal labor productivity (nominal output per hour) and with capacity utilization in the manufacturing sector.
- Further analyses indicate that the value of exports per job will increase from $175,000 to $185,000 in 2010. Regression analyses, combined with forecasts of nominal productivity and capacity utilization, yield the lower bound of the range. Extending trend growth of 5.9 percent per year suggests the upper bound.

Gary F. Locke
Secretary
U.S. Department of Commerce

Francisco J. Sánchez
Under Secretary for International Trade
U.S. Department of Commerce

INTERNATIONAL TRADE RESEARCH REPORT NO. 1

by John Tschetter

In 2008, U.S. exports supported more than 10 million full- and part-time jobs during a historic time, when exports as a percentage of gross domestic product (GDP) reached the highest levels since 1916. The new record, 12.7 percent, shows that the upward growth of trade in an expanding global market holds great opportunities for U.S. businesses whose leaders are thinking strategically about the future growth of their companies. The importance of exports and trade in the U.S. economy was accelerating during the past 7 years, but was interrupted by the economic downturn that began in December 2007. Because of the weak global economy, exports and export-supported jobs dropped sharply through the first half of 2009; however, they began to recover in the second half. Government and private-sector economists expect that the recovery in exports will continue in 2010 and beyond, which will increase the opportunities for U.S. businesses to grow.

For government and business leaders to chart their way forward, they must measure the importance of exports in the national economy by using generally accepted tools. In an analysis by the Department of Commerce's Economics and Statistics Administration (ESA) and the International Trade Administration (ITA), this interagency white paper finds that the value of exports to support one job will increase to as much as $185,000 in 2010. That figure was last officially estimated in 1996 at $92,000 per job and reflects the high and increasing productivity of the U.S. workforce in exported-related production.

This report represents the work of a panel of experts from several government agencies, led by the Working Group on Analysis and Data of the Trade Promotion Coordinating Committee (TPCC). This group included representatives of 20 federal agencies and was chaired by Mark Doms, chief economist at the U.S. Department of Commerce, and David Walters, chief economist in the Office of the U.S. Trade Representative. Among the other participating agencies were the Department of Agriculture's Economic Research Service and Foreign Agricultural Service, the Export–Import Bank of the United States, U.S. International Trade Commission, and the U.S. Small Business Administration.

This examination of the relationship between U.S. exports and the jobs they support covers 1993–2008, with preliminary estimates for 2009 and 2010. Table 1 shows the following information:

- Exports of goods and services supported 10.3 million jobs in 2008.
- Export-supported jobs accounted for 6.9 percent of total U.S. employment in 2008. The value of total exports, as measured in this study, totaled nearly $1.7 trillion—or nearly $165,000 per export job in 2008.
- Additional analyses indicate that the number of jobs supported by exports declined sharply in 2009 from 2008. The drop reflected a large decrease in the nominal value of exports and a modest gain in the ratio of exports per job. Te yearly movements in the ratio strongly correlate with that of nominal labor productivity (nominal output per hour) and with capacity utilization in the manufacturing sector.
- Further analyses indicate that the value of exports per job will increase from $175,000 to $185,000 in 2010. Regression analyses, combined with forecasts of

nominal productivity and capacity utilization, yield the lower bound of the range. Extending trend growth of 5.9 percent per year suggests the upper bound.

METHODOLOGY AND CAVEATS

Researchers have used widely different forms of economic analyses to demonstrate the relationship between exports and jobs. This study uses input–output (IO) analysis to measure the links for 1993–2008. IO analysis, sometimes referred to as *interindustry analysis*, is an economic tool that measures the relationships between various industries in the economy.[1] This research uses a time series of IO matrixes that provide detailed and consistent information on the flow of goods and services that make up the production processes of U.S. industries.[2] Findings reflect the number of jobs supported across the entire chain of export production, such as material and service inputs, final assembly, and transportation. The employment numbers are annual snapshots of the size of export contribution to overall employment. It is important to note the following:

- These snapshots reflect *average* (sometimes labeled *accounting*) *relationships*. In IO analyses, if 10 percent of an industry output is exported, then 10 percent of the industry's employment is attributed to exports. The averages tell us nothing about employment requirements for the first or last dollar of output.
- Averages derived from IO analysis should not be used as proxies for change. They should not be used to estimate the net change in employment that might be supported by increases or decreases in total exports, in the exports of selected products, or in the exports to selected countries or regions.
- The averages are not proxies because the number of jobs supported by exports usually does not change at the same rate as export value. The rate is not the same because other factors, such as prices, resource utilization, business practices, and productivity, do not usually change at the same rate. In addition, the material and service inputs and the labor and capital inputs differ significantly across types of exports. For example, the labor requirements for an exported aircraft are significantly different from those of an exported agricultural product or an educational service.
- The findings shown in Table 1 take all those factors into account. The ratio of exports per job for total exports was $165,000 in 2008. This ratio varied from $150,000 for goods to $203,000 for services. The ratio for total exports grew 5.9 percent per year from 2002 to 2008, a period of strong export growth. The ratio for goods grew 6.5 percent per year during that period, which is faster than the 4.3 percent increase for services.

The ratios reflect the stages of the business cycle in which they occurred. They are directly affected by changes in aggregate output, including the output for exports, which influence the size of the overall workforce, employment, and unemployment. During periods of slack business activity, increased output, such as exports, would tend to increase employment, to lower unemployment, and to increase labor force participation. Conversely, during periods of high business activity, when industry operates at or near full capacity and employment, increased output, including output for exports, tends to raise employment less—if at all—and instead mainly shifts employment to industries that pay higher wages.

The findings presented in this paper are only snapshots of the relationships between exports and employment. The figures do not illustrate other important dynamic links. The most important contribution of exports (and imports) to the U.S. economy is its role in increasing the industrial efficiency and standard of living of the United States. International trade encourages structural changes in domestic industries that, in turn, result in increased efficiencies, economies of scale, and more productive investments that enhance the competitiveness of foreign and U.S. producers alike.

FINDINGS

Exports of goods and services supported a record 10.3 million jobs in 2008 (see Figure 1). The number of jobs supported by exports has been increasing since 2003, when exports supported 7.6 million jobs.

Preliminary estimates suggest, however, that export- supported employment fell sharply in 2009 to 8.5 million. The drop reflects a 15-percent decline in nominal value of exports and a 4.3 percent increase in nominal productivity (nominal output per hour) in the nonfarm business sector. However, 2009 included a shift in the growth of nominal exports from a decline during the first half to a gain in the second half. It is widely expected that the recovery will continue in 2010 and beyond.

Jobs supported by exports accounted for 6.9 percent of total employment in 2008. This share has fluctuated within a narrow range over time (see Figures 2 and 3).

The value of exports totaled nearly $1.7 trillion in 2008 (as measured in the IO framework, see appendix A for historical series) or 11.9 percent of GDP (see Figure 2). Figure 3 (on page 3) shows that the export share of GDP in 2009 was a historical record dating back to the 1870s. Figure 3 also shows that the share generally went up during the past six decades, with some large swings in the middle.

The ratio of export-supported employment to total employment is smaller than the ratio of exports to GDP (Figure 3). The smaller employment ratio reflects that a significant portion of exports is produced in the manufacturing sector. Productivity levels in the manufacturing sector are well above the economy-wide average, and a significant share of the material and service inputs to manufacturing is imported. Both factors reduce the labor intensity of exports relative to labor intensity of other spending categories, such as consumer spending for services and residential construction.

Figure 4 shows that the value of exports per job was $165,000 in 2008. This ratio has trended steadily up since 2002, growing 5.9 percent per year from 2002 to 2008. The ratio began to accelerate in 2001.

Figure 5 shows that the ratio of exports per job (shown as an index) has gone up at about the same pace as nominal productivity in the nonfarm business sector. Nominal productivity is the ratio of nominal output to hours worked. The strong upward trends shown in Figure 5 are favorable long-term developments because they underlie the growth of the nation's living standards.

Table 1. Jobs Supported by Exports

	Jobs supported by exports in 2008		Exports in 2008 (billions of dollars)	Value of exports per job	
	Number (thousands)	*Percent of employment*		*2008 ratio (thousands of dollars)*	*Percent change, 2002–2008*
Total	10, 293	6.9	1,694	165	5.9
Goods	7,525	5.0	1,132	150	6.5
Services	2, 768	1.9	562	203	4.3

Source: U.S. Department of Commerce, Bureau of Economic Analysis.

Figure 6 shows that medium-term variations in the two series reflect, in part, the movements in capacity use in the manufacturing sector.

Analyses by the Office of the Chief Economist suggest that the value of exports per job increased from $170,000 to $175,000 in 2009 and will increase to $185,000 in 2010 (see Figure 4).

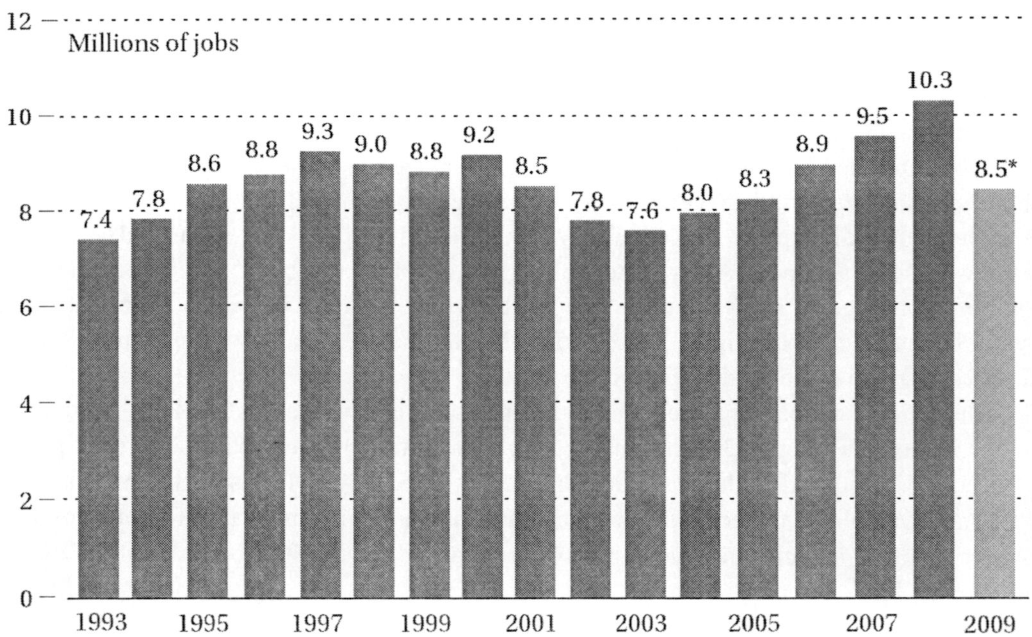

* Note: 2009 is a preliminary estimate.

Estimates compiled by U.S. Department of Commerce, Office of the Chief Economist.

Figure 1. Jobs Supported by Exports of Goods and Services, 1993–2009.

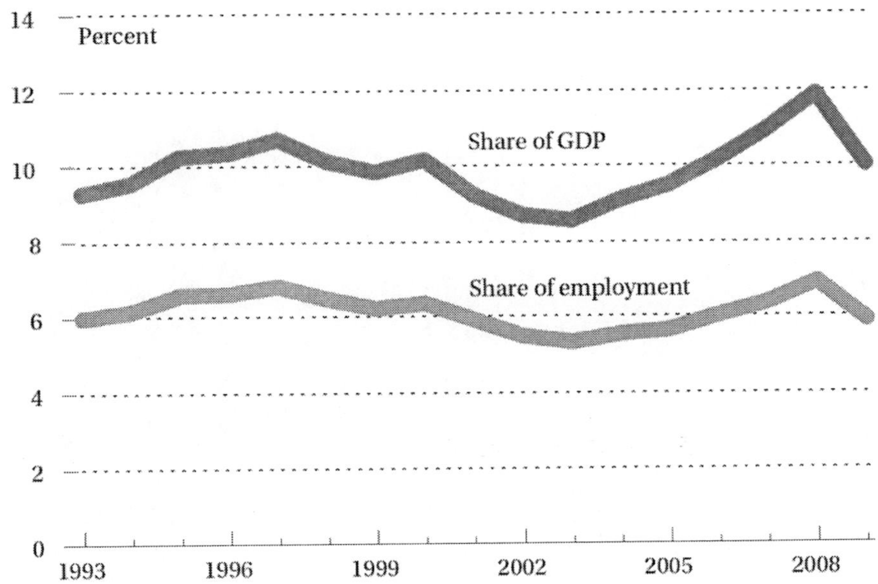

Note: data for 2009 are preliminary estimates.
Estimates compiled by U.S. Department of Commerce, Office of the Chief Economist.

Figure 2. Export Share of GDP and Employment, 1993–2008.

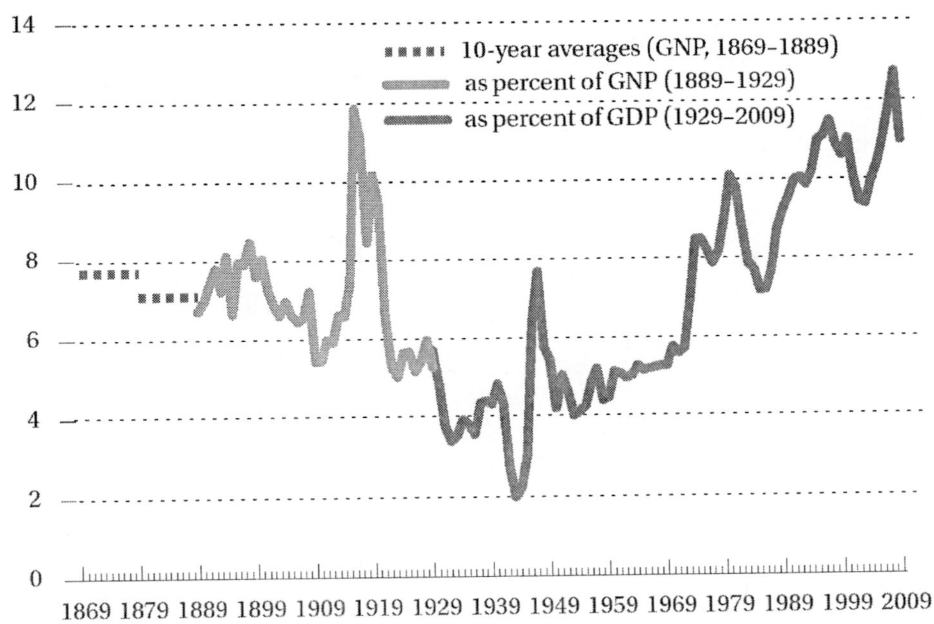

Estimates compiled by U.S. Department of Commerce, Office of the Chief Economist.

Figure 3. Exports of Goods and Services as Percent of GNP or GDP, 1869–2009 (national income accounts basis).

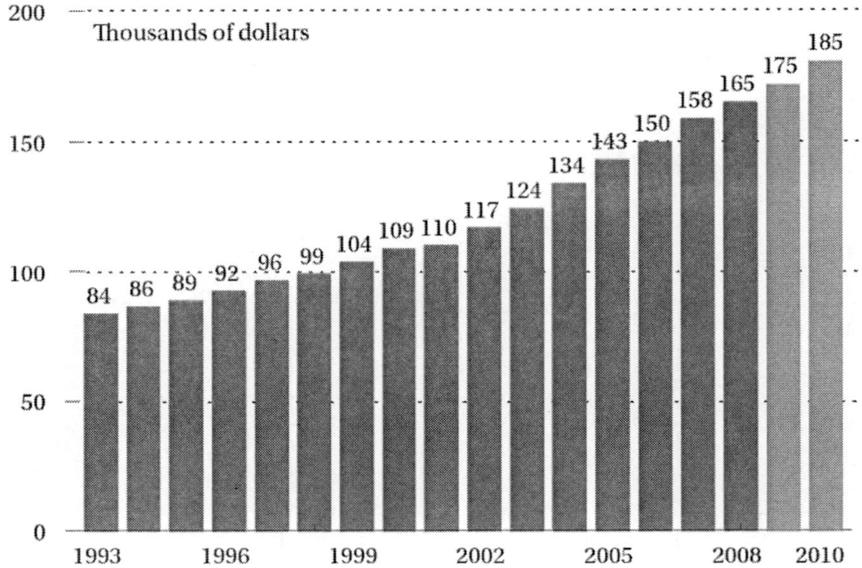

Note: Data for 2009 and 2010 are preliminary estimates.
Estimates compiled by U.S. Department of Commerce, Office of the Chief Economist.

Figure 4. Value of Exports per Job, 1993–2010: Total Exports.

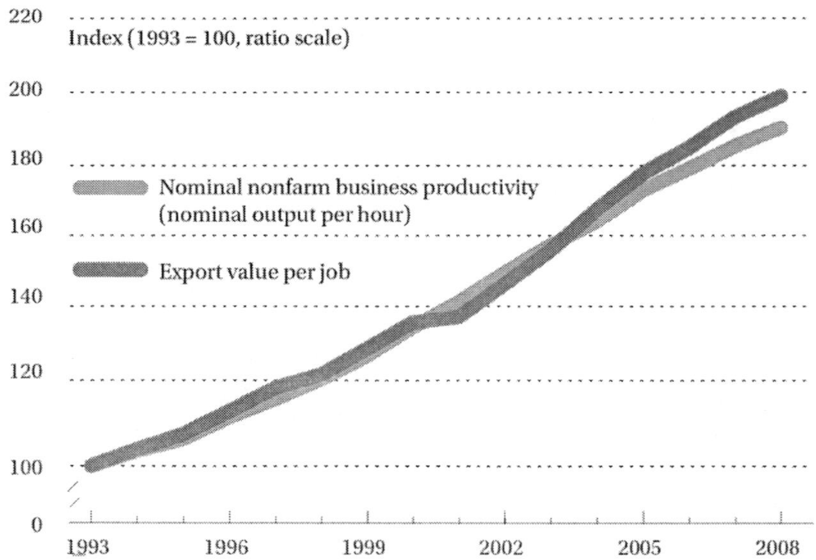

Estimates compiled by U.S. Department of Commerce, Office of the Chief Economist.

Figure 5. Exports per Job and Nominal Productivity, 1993–2008.

Regression analyses that related the yearly movements in the ratio of exports per job to nominal productivity and capacity use in manufacturing, combined with forecasts of the productivity and use series,[3] yield the lower part of the range.

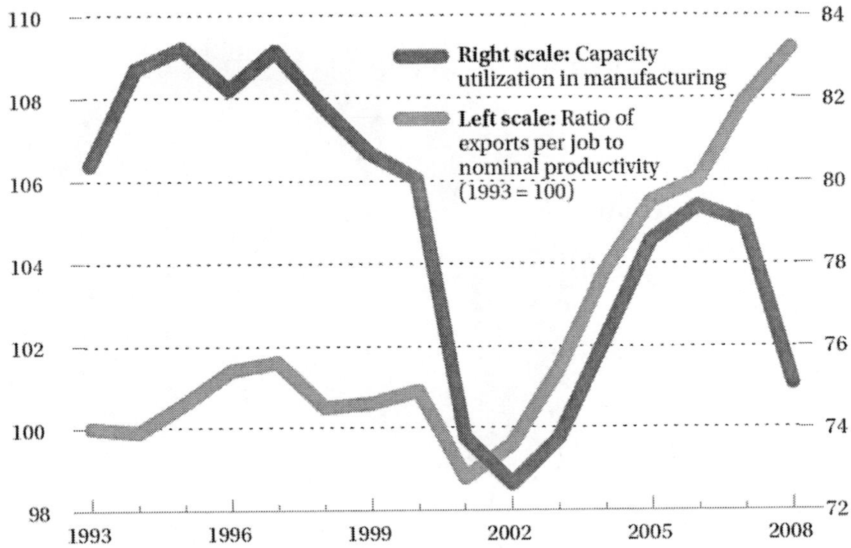

Estimates compiled by U.S. Department of Commerce, Office of the Chief Economist.

Figure 6. Ratio of Exports per Job to Nominal Productivity and Capacity Utilization, 1993–2008.

Export-Supported Jobs by Industry

More than half of the 10.3 million jobs supported by exports in 2008 occurred in two industries: (a) manufacturing and (b) professional or business services. Export-supported manufacturing jobs totaled nearly 3.7 million, or 36 percent of the total jobs supported by exports (see Figure 7). Export-supported jobs in professional and business services totaled nearly 2.1 million, or 20 percent of the total.

Manufacturing's share has gone modestly down since 1993, while the share of professional and business services has gone modestly up (see Figure 8). The nearly 3.7 million manufacturing jobs supported by exports in 2008 accounted for 27 percent of all jobs in the manufacturing sector (see Figure 9).

Exports also accounted for significant shares of employment within transport and warehousing (23 percent), agriculture (19 percent), and wholesale trade (17 percent).

The export-supported share of total manufacturing jobs rose to a record in 2008 from the 1993–2004 average of about 20 percent (see Figure 10). That share reflects jobs supported by total exports of goods and services, including manufactured goods. The increase occurred because of strong foreign demand for U.S. goods and sluggish domestic demand.

The export-supported share likely fell in 2009 because exports fell 19 percent while manufacturing shipments excluding exports dropped by 15 percent. However, the share started to recover as the year progressed. Exports of manufactured goods increased 19 percent from their low in April 2009, while shipments excluding exports rose by a much smaller 4 percent.

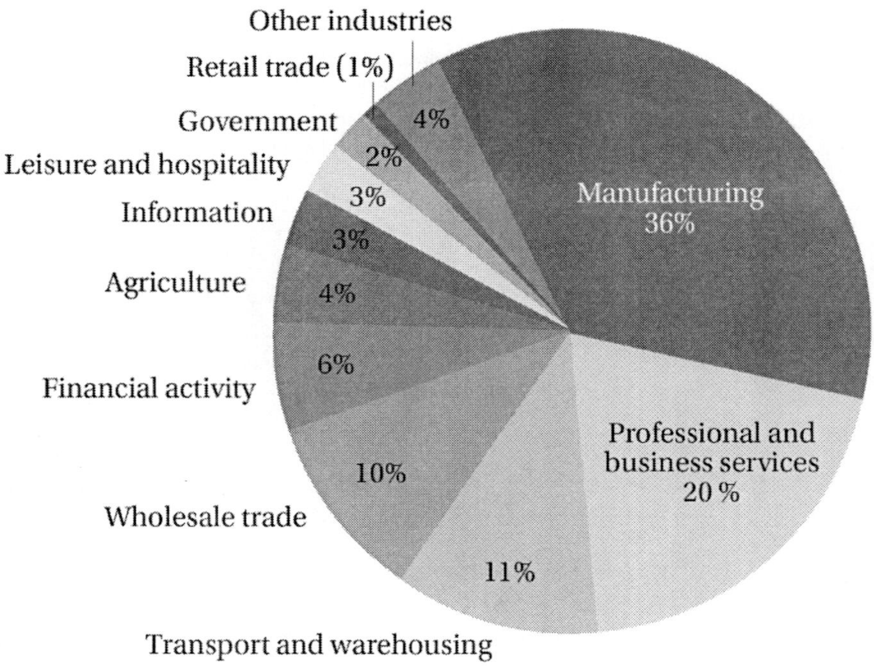

Estimates compiled by U.S. Department of Commerce, Office of the Chief Economist.

Figure 7. Export-supported Jobs in 2008, by Major Industry.

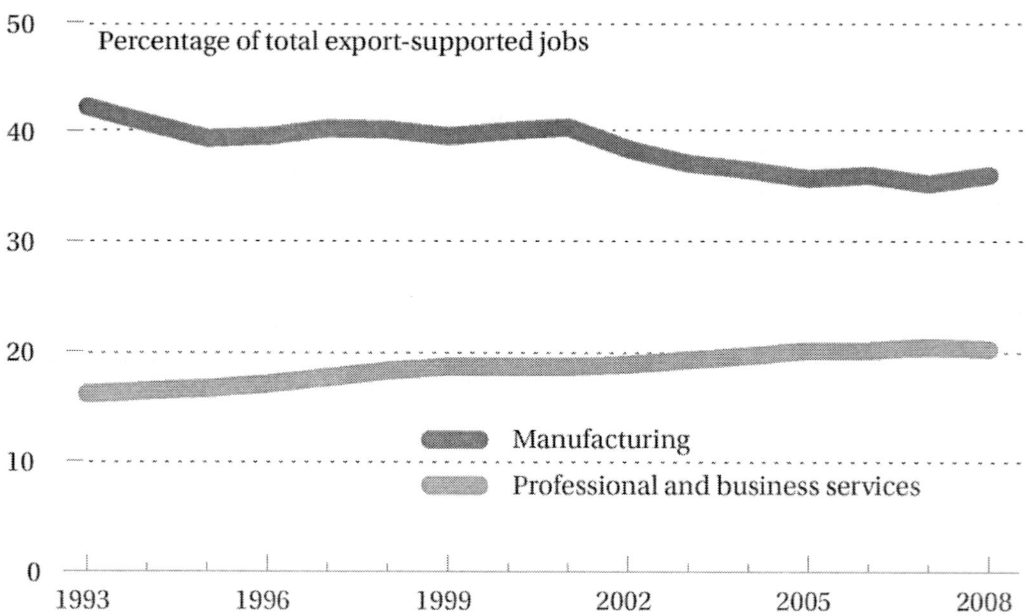

Estimates compiled by U.S. Department of Commerce, Office of the Chief Economist.

Figure 8. Export-supported Jobs in Manufacturing and Professional and Business Services, 1993–2008.

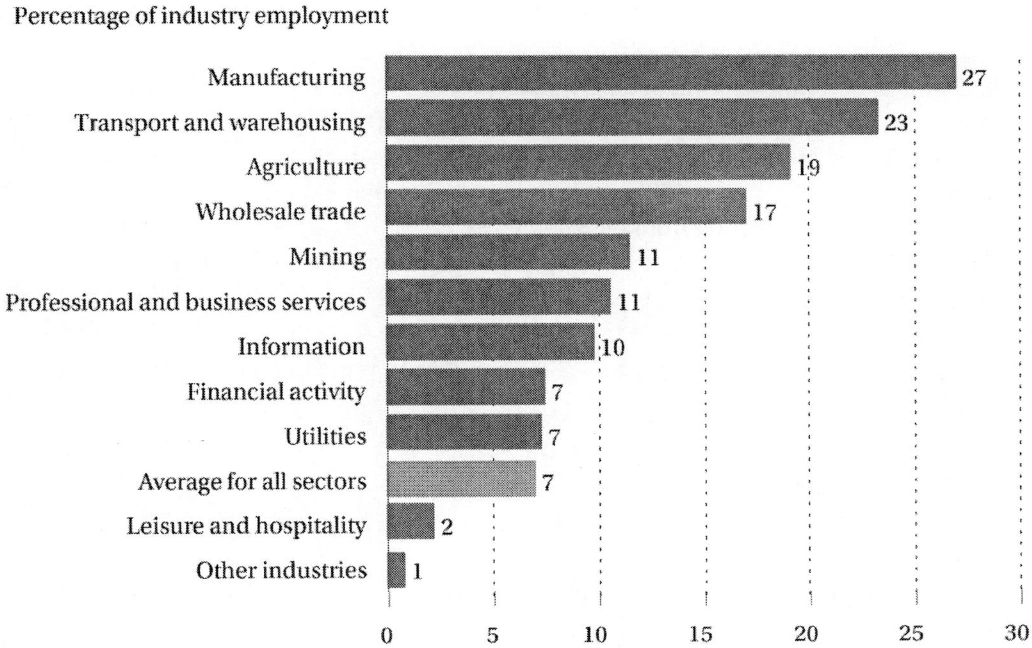

Estimates compiled by U.S. Department of Commerce, Office of the Chief Economist.

Figure 9. Shares of Industry Jobs Supported by Exports in 2008.

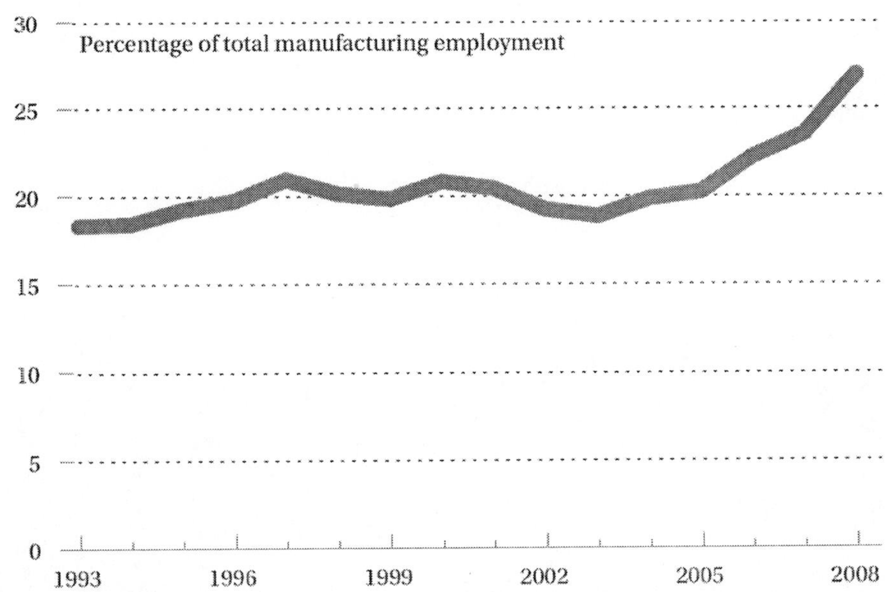

Estimates compiled by U.S. Department of Commerce, Office of the Chief Economist.

Figure 10. Export-supported Jobs in Manufacturing, 1993–2008.

Jobs Supported by Exports of Goods

In 2008, exported goods (including manufactured goods) supported 7.5 million, or 73 percent, of the 10.3 million jobs supported by total exports (see Figure 11).

The number of jobs supported by exports of goods has been increasing since 2003. But again, available data, including a 20 percent drop in nominal exports of goods, suggest that the number fell sharply in 2009 from the 2008 level.

Of the 7.5 million jobs supported by exports of goods in 2008, 3.5 million (or 47 percent) occurred in manufacturing (see Figure 12). Goods exported include agricultural products, raw materials, and manufactured goods.

The export of goods also supported 1.2 million jobs in professional and business services and 1 million jobs in wholesale trade.

Jobs Supported by the Exports of Services

Exported services supported 2.8 million jobs, or 27 percent, of all jobs supported by exports (see Figure 13).

The number of jobs supported by service exports has been increasing since 1993 (the starting point for these estimates). But again, available data, including a 7 percent drop in the nominal exports of services, suggest that the number fell in 2009.

Of the 2.8 million jobs, 0.9 million, or 32 percent, were in professional and business services (see Figure 14).

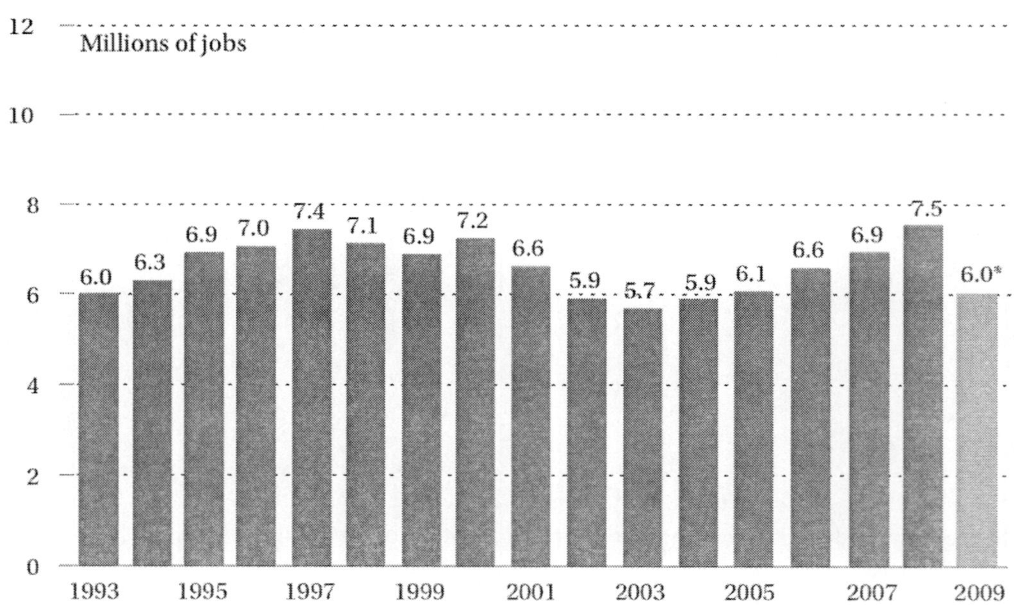

* Note: 2009 is a preliminary estimate.

Estimates compiled by U.S. Department of Commerce, Office of the Chief Economist.

Figure 11. Jobs Supported by Exports of Goods, 1993–2009.

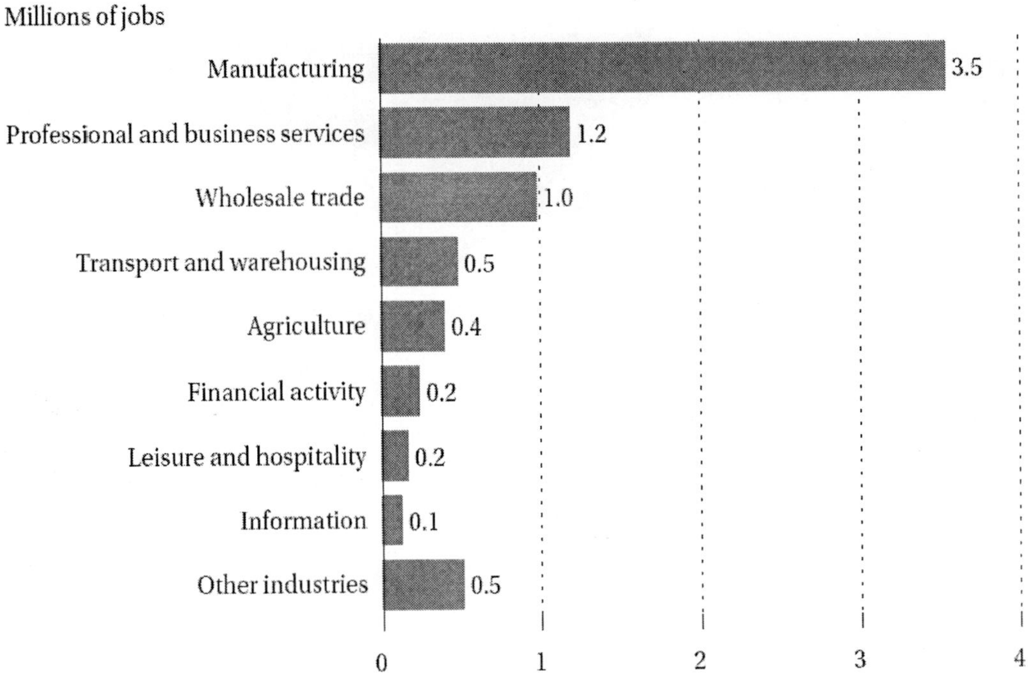

Estimates compiled by U.S. Department of Commerce, Office of the Chief Economist.

Figure 12. Jobs Supported by Exports of Goods in 2008, by Major Industry.

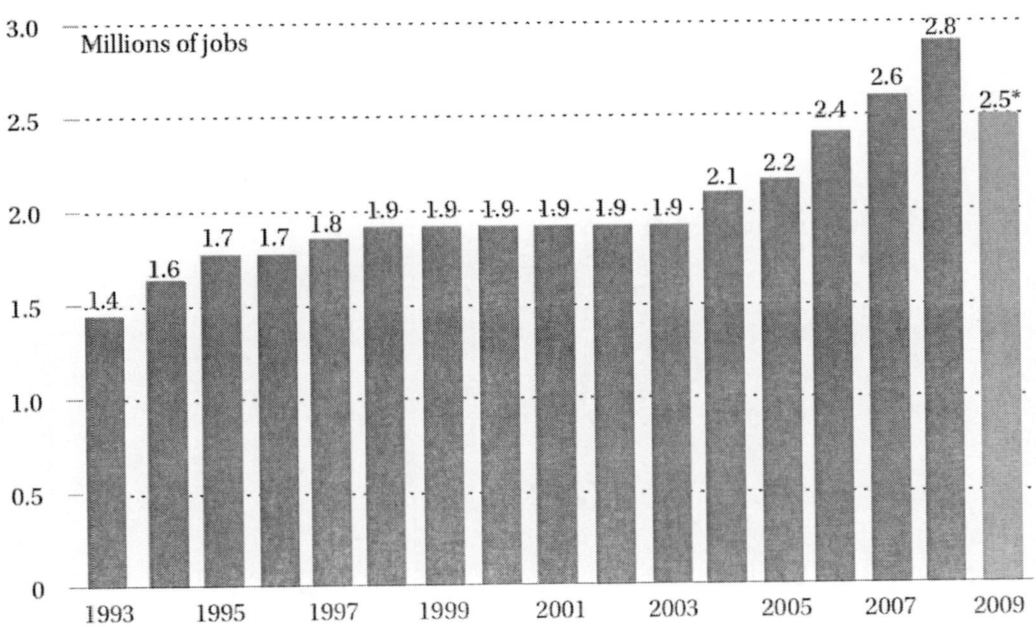

* Note: 2009 is a preliminary estimate.
Estimates compiled by U.S. Department of Commerce, Office of the Chief Economist.

Figure 13. Jobs Supported by Exports of Services, 1993–2009.

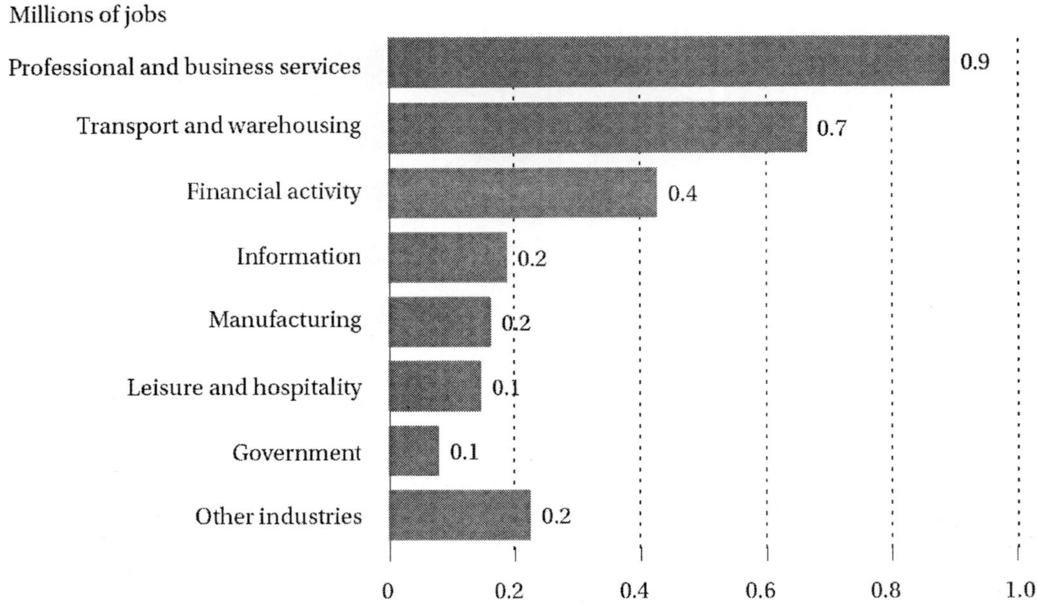

Estimates compiled by U.S. Department of Commerce, Office of the Chief Economist.

Figure 14. Jobs Supported by Exports of Services in 2008, by Major Industry.

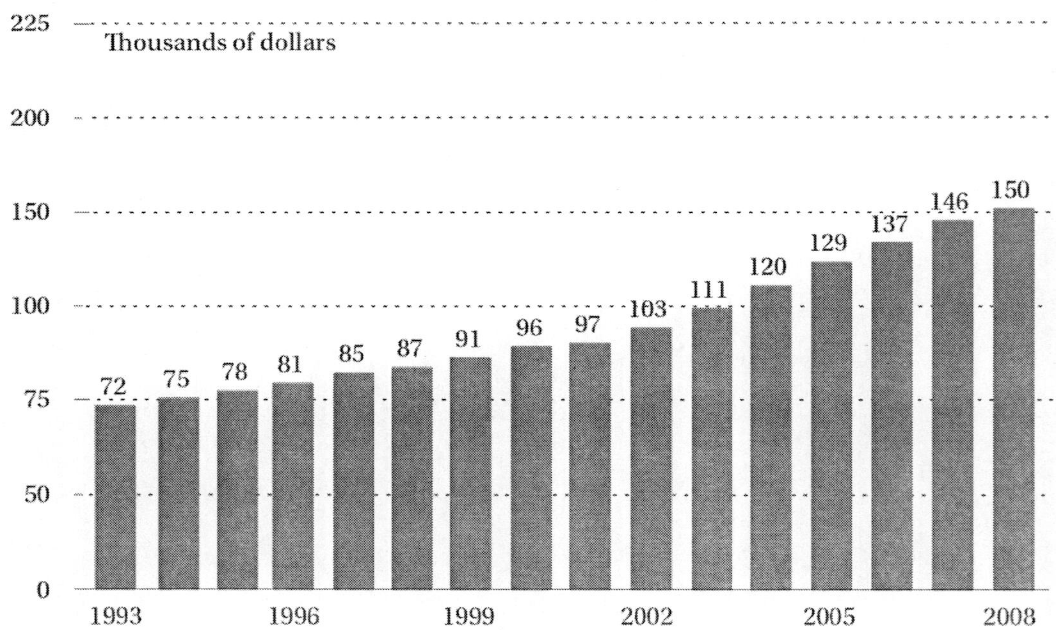

Estimates compiled by U.S. Department of Commerce, Office of the Chief Economist.

Figure 15. Value of Exports per Job for Goods, 1993–2008.

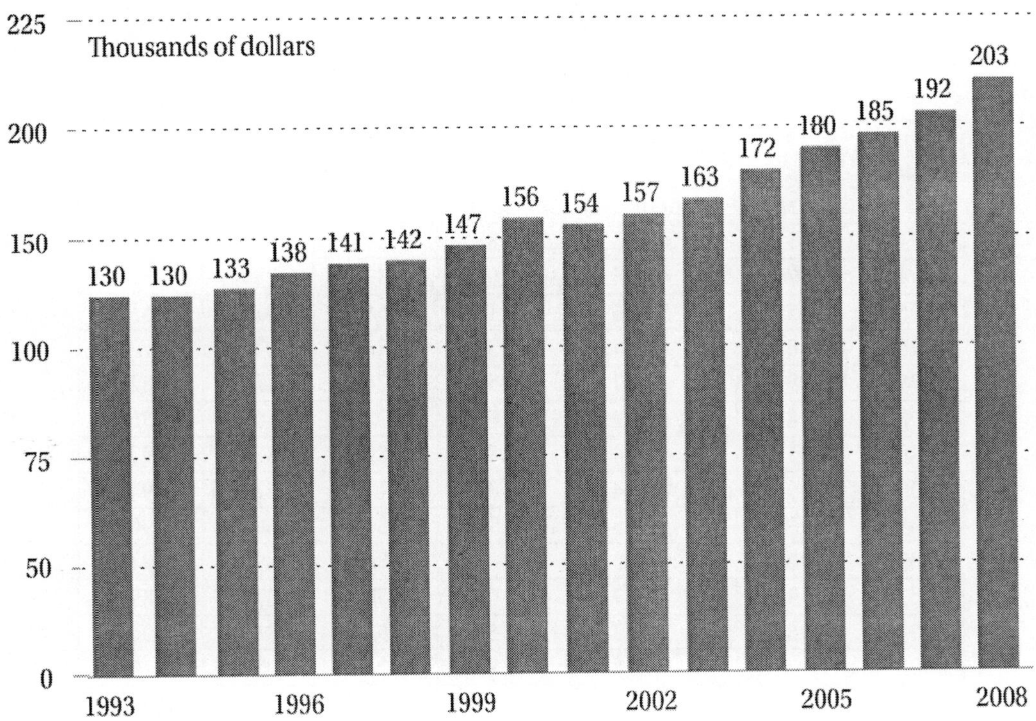

Estimates compiled by U.S. Department of Commerce, Office of the Chief Economist.

Figure 16. Value of Exports per Job for Services, 1993–2008.

A Comparison: Goods Exports per Job and Service Exports per Job

The value of goods exports per job was nearly $150,000 in 2008 (Figure 15). The ratio of service exports per job was much higher at $203,000 (Figure 16).

The ratio for service exports is boosted significantly by services such as professional and business services, which include the leasing of non financial intangible assets; the management of companies; and architectural, engineering, and related services. The ratio for goods exports per job grew 6.5 percent per year from 2002 to 2008, which is faster than the 4.3-percent growth for service exports per job. The growth in the ratio for goods exports was boosted by the productivity gains posted within the manufacturing sector and by the expanding—and important— role played by imports in manufactured goods.

APPENDIX A: EXPORTS OF GOODS AND SERVICES AND JOBS SUPPORTED BY THEM, 1993–2008

Year	Value of exports (billions of dollars)			Jobs supported by exports (thousands of jobs)		
	Total	Goods	Services	Total	Goods	Services
1993	617.9	429.8	188.1	7,394.5	5,950.7	1,443.8
1994	675.3	473.4	201.9	7,839.5	6,289.3	1,550.2
1995	759.2	539.6	219.7	8,568.1	6,911.4	1,656.7
1996	809.3	571.4	237.9	8,768.6	7,042.9	1,725.7
1997	890.6	633.7	256.9	9,245.8	7,425.0	1,820.8
1998	886.1	621.9	264.2	8,970.6	7,109.1	1,861.5
1999	911.8	628.4	283.4	8,806.0	6,879.8	1,926.2
2000	996.3	692.4	303.9	9,171.5	7,225.8	1,946.0
2001	935.1	641.5	293.6	8,514.2	6,607.1	1,907.1
2002	909.5	608.5	301.0	7,802.4	5,890.3	1,912.1
2003	937.7	629.7	307.9	7,566.2	5,671.3	1,894.9
2004	1,062.1	706.3	355.8	7,949.9	5,883.1	2,066.9
2005	1,177.6	782.6	385.0	8,249.6	6,052.4	2,197.2
2006	1,338.2	900.2	438.0	8,949.8	6,575.7	2,374.1
2007	1,510.4	1,008.2	502.2	9,539.7	6,920.1	2,619.6
2008	1,693.6	1,131.5	562.1	10,293.4	7,525.3	2,768.1

Source: U.S. Department of Commerce, Office of the Chief Economist.

APPENDIX B: IO ANALYSES—METHODOLOGY, STRENGTHS, AND WEAKNESSES

The following highlights the methodology and caveats of the IO-based figures. This research is based on the IO framework. The Bureau of Labor Statistics (BLS) developed and published the accounts used in this research.

The BLS Web site at *www.bls.gov* provides files of IO data for the U.S. economy from 1993 to 2008. The IO tables produced by the BLS are derived from IO data initially developed by the Bureau of Economic Analysis (BEA).

The BLS IO accounts provide detailed, consistent information on the flow of goods and services that are involved in the production processes of industries. For each year, the accounts show how industries interact as they provide inputs to and use outputs from each other to produce GDP.

IO accounts begin with *make* and *use* tables. The make table shows the commodities produced by each industry. The use table shows the inputs to industry production and the commodities consumed by final users (including exports to foreign customers).

Requirements tables are derived from the make and use tables. The *direct requirements* table shows the amount of a commodity that is required by an industry to produce a dollar of the industry's output. A *total requirements* table shows the production required, directly and indirectly, from each industry and commodity to deliver a dollar of a commodity to final users. A *domestic requirements* table shows the domestic output of goods and services required to meet final demand (including exports). To calculate the domestic output requirements, one must subtract imports from the use table before calculating the total requirements matrix. This subtraction is made for each industry. The ratio for the subtraction is the value of imports over domestic supply:

$$\text{Import ratio} = \text{Imports} / (\text{Commodity output} - \text{Imports} + \text{Exports}) \quad (1)$$

BLS published an additional table of domestic employment requirements. The table shows the direct and indirect effect of changes in final demand on employment. The changes stem from the domestic requirements tables. First, a ratio for jobs per dollar of output was calculated. This ratio was then applied to the domestic output requirement for each industry to derive the employment requirement. The requirement was found by multiplying the industry employment ratio with the respective domestic requirements data contained in each row.

Employment in the requirements tables is based on a count of jobs. The job count includes wage and salaried workers, self-employed workers, and unpaid family workers.

The jobs in this research are not full-time equivalents (FTEs). FTEs are estimates for adjusted industry employment for the mix of full- and part-time workers. BLS's IO accounts include substantial detail on more than 200 industries (including 84 manufacturing industries) and more than 200 categories of final demand (including exports of goods and services).

BLS data for exports of goods and services can be regrouped to allow estimates of jobs supported by exports of goods, services, manufactured items, agricultural products, and other sources.

BLS focuses on employment outlook by industry and occupations for the next decade (2008–18). The November issue of the *Monthly Labor Review* presents have comprehensive articles that describe the outlook.[4]

BLS makes the underlying data and methodology of these projections available to researchers. The details include time series of industry output and employment and interindustry relationships, including final demand expenditures and IO matrixes.

BLS presents the formulas for calculating the requirement matrixes in "Employment Outlook: 2008–2018," which is available on its Web site. The final demand and employment requirement matrixes were critical components of the findings.

Exports in this study reflect IO concepts and, as a result, exclude reexports and reimports of goods. *Reexports* are foreign-origin goods that have previously entered the United States and, at the time of exportation, have undergone no change in form, condition, or enhancement in value by further manufacturing in the United States. *Reimports* are U.S. merchandise that has been returned. *Exports o*f military goods are included in goods exports.

Exports are measured by their value at the point of leaving the country and are equivalent to their purchase price. The national income accounts and the U.S. Census Bureau data on exports of goods are also measured at the value leaving the country.

IO analysis, however, shows exports at producer prices, and the transportation costs and margins required to move the export to the port are included in the respective commodities for transport and trade.

This paper's introduction highlighted a number of caveats to IO analyses, including the following:

- IO analyses (and this analysis) reflect *average* (sometimes labeled *accounting*) *relationships*. If 10 percent (or 20 percent) of an industry output is exported, then 10 percent (or 20 percent) of its employment is attributed to exports. Those averages tell us nothing about employment requirements for the first or last dollar of output.
- The findings are sensitive to numerous factors, including macroeconomic developments. Those developments include the pace of overall economic growth; the degree of resource use; and the pace of productivity growth and industry-level developments, such as the speed of innovation, attitudes toward out- and in-sourcing shifts, and the use of imports as material and service inputs.

BLS IO and final demand data do not reflect the BEA Comprehensive National Income and Product Accounts revisions that were published in July 2009. The data also do not reflect BLS's annual revisions to the nonfarm payroll employment that were published in February 2010. Because BLS published its projections of industry and occupational employment every other year, the analyses presented in this white paper will not be updated until November 2011.

End Notes

[1] The Department of Commerce has published previous IO analyses of jobs supported by exports. This research updates Lester A. Davis, "U.S. Jobs Supported by Goods and Services, 1983–1994," U.S. Department of Commerce, Economics and Statistics Administration, November 1996. The U.S. Census Bureau also produces reports on jobs supported in each state by exports of manufacturing goods. One example is the "Exports from Manufacturing Establishments: Preliminary Report for 2006," U.S. Census Bureau, April 2008.

[2] The Bureau of Labor Statistics published this time series of IO tables, industry and commodity output, and employment in December 2009. For more information, see http:// stats.bls.gov/news.release/ecopro.toc.htm and http://bls.gov/ emp. The Office of the Chief Economist took great advantage of the considerable e orts by the Bureau of Labor Statistics. The final demand and employment requirement matrixes were critical components of the findings.

[3] Macroeconomic Advisers ("Outlook Commentary," February 2010) forecasted a 4.2 percent increase in nominal nonfarm business productivity (output per hour) in 2010 and a recovery of manufacturing capacity use from 66.8 percent in 2008 to 70.6 percent in 2010.

[4] BLS projections were summarized by Kristina J. Bartsch, "The Employment Projections for 2008–18," *Monthly Labor Review* 132, no. 11 (November 2009): 3–11.

In: U.S. Export Programs and Promotion Tools
Editor: Steven D. Braghoff

ISBN: 978-1-60741-328-8

Chapter 8

INTERNATIONAL TRADE: EFFECTIVE EXPORT PROGRAMS CAN HELP IN ACHIEVING U.S. ECONOMIC GOALS

Loren Yager

Mr. Chairman and Members of the Subcommittee:

Thank you for the opportunity to appear today before the Subcommittee to provide our perspective on the role of exports in the U.S. economy. As Congress responds to the rapid deterioration in the U.S. economy, it must consider the full range of tools available to further growth and create new jobs for U.S. workers. Some of these tools are related to promoting exports, which can have broad benefits to the U.S. economy. Today, I will lay out some observations regarding export promotion challenges from a range of work that we have conducted for Congress over recent years.

In my statement today, I will provide some background information concerning the ways in which exports can enhance U.S. economic output, and I will summarize some of the work we have conducted to address congressional interest in promoting the growth of exports and improving export promotion programs.

My remarks are based on a variety of reports and testimonies we have issued on a range of international trade issues over the past 4 years. We conducted this work in accordance with generally accepted government auditing standards. Those standards require that we plan and perform the audit to obtain sufficient, appropriate evidence to provide a reasonable basis for our findings and conclusions based on our audit objectives. We believe that the evidence obtained provides a reasonable basis for our findings and conclusions based on our audit objectives.

BACKGROUND

Exports, and trade more broadly, contribute to the U.S. economy in a variety of ways. Trade enables the United States to achieve a higher standard of living through producing and exporting goods and services that are produced here relatively efficiently, and importing goods and services that are produced here relatively inefficiently. An indication of this is that firms engaged in the international marketplace tend to exhibit higher rates of productivity growth and pay higher wages and benefits to their workers than domestically oriented firms of the same size.

U.S. exports of manufactured goods grew from $730 billion in 2004 to $1.1 trillion in 2008. U.S. exports of non-manufactured products grew from $89 billion in 2004 to $178 billion in 2008. These exports have come from every state. For example, in 2008 Illinois exported $49 billion worth of manufactured goods and $5 billion in non-manufactured goods. Similarly, California exported $127 billion in manufactured goods and $18 billion in non-manufactured goods, of which nearly $8 billion were agricultural products.

In addition to the longer-term benefits of trade and exports, exports can serve as a countercyclical force for the U.S. economy, strengthening the economy when other parts of it are relatively weaker. For a number of years, as the United States increasingly imported more than we exported, the U.S. economy was an engine of growth for other nations. In contrast, when the U.S. economy slowed in 2007 and much of 2008, U.S. economic growth was boosted by an improving trade balance. With strong global demand for U.S. goods and services, increases in net exports (exports minus imports) accounted for over half of U.S. economic growth in the past 2 years. Unfortunately, when U.S. trading partners are also experiencing economic downturns, as we are currently seeing, the potential for trade to continue to serve as a countercyclical force is diminished.

GAO Has Addressed Longstanding Concerns about Challenges to Achieving Economic Benefits through Export Promotion

Congress has expressed longstanding concerns regarding several aspects of U.S. export promotion efforts, especially regarding interagency coordination, meeting the needs of small businesses, and effectively enforcing trade agreements. We have addressed these concerns by reviewing and providing recommendations on a wide range of U.S. policies and programs that have the potential to increase U.S. exports. Effective export promotion policies are always important, but are of particular interest in the current environment. My statement today will address three policy areas: (1) coordinating export promotion programs; (2) effectively meeting the needs of small businesses; and (3) monitoring and enforcing trade agreements to broaden U.S. access to foreign markets.

Coordination of Export Promotion Efforts Can Help Maximize Benefits from Agency Activities

The Trade Promotion Coordinating Committee (TPCC) is charged with providing a unifying interagency framework to coordinate U.S. export promotion activities and develop a government-wide strategic plan. TPCC member agencies provide a wide range of export promotion activities, including the Department of Commerce's advice and advocacy to businesses during the export process, the Department of Agriculture's financing for promotional activities, and the Export-Import Bank's (Ex-Im) loan guarantees for foreign buyers of U.S. exports. According to the TPCC's 2008 *National Export Strategy*, nine member agencies had about $1.3 billion in budget authority for export promotion programs in fiscal year 2008.[1] Two agencies accounted for more than three quarters of the reported total export promotion budget—Agriculture with $644 million and Commerce with $339 million, followed by the Department of State with $184 million. Other agencies can play significant roles in export promotion, despite their smaller budget authorities. Ex-Im, for example, has recently requested no budget authority, projecting that the fees it collects will offset its costs. Nonetheless, in fiscal year 2008, Ex-Im authorized $14.4 billion in loans, guarantees, and export-credit insurance to support U.S. exports.

One of the longstanding congressional concerns we have addressed is a lack of effective coordination of trade promotion activities. We have reviewed the TPCC several times since its inception and we testified in 2006 that the TPCC had made progress over time in improving coordination.[2] However, we also testified that its *National Export Strategy* continued to provide limited information on agencies' goals and progress relative to broad national priorities. Examples of positive steps we reported on across TPCC member agencies included improvements in interagency training and joint outreach to better serve small business. We further noted that the strategies did not review agencies' allocation of resources in relation to government-wide export promotion priorities. We note now that the 2008 *National Export Strategy* contains information regarding the status of priority initiatives identified in the prior year's annual report. It also contains information on individual TPCC member agencies' export promotion strategies and results. However, the strategy still lacks an overall review of agencies' allocation of resources relative to government-wide export promotion priorities.

Broadening Trade Benefits by Increasing Small Business Exports Is a Trade Priority

Promoting exports by small businesses has been a perennial priority in the *National Export Strategy*. In addition, USTR's 2009 *Trade Policy Agenda* calls for using trade and commercial policies to help small and medium businesses become more effective competitors and exporters in the global marketplace. While many small businesses export, it is widely recognized that they face a number of challenges in exporting.[3] For example, small businesses typically do not have overseas offices and may not have much knowledge regarding foreign markets. Export promotion agencies have developed various goals with respect to their small business assistance, and in some cases Congress has mandated specific requirements for supporting small businesses.

My remarks will focus on our findings regarding Ex-Im's efforts to address congressional mandates regarding its small business financing. Since the 1980s, Congress has required that Ex-Im, which provides loans, loan guarantees, and insurance to finance U.S. exports, make available a certain percentage of its export financing for small business. Since 2002, Congress has required that share be at least 20 percent. Moreover, in Ex-Im's 2006 reauthorization, Congress directed Ex-Im to establish performance standards for assessing its small business financing efforts, including activities directed at businesses owned by socially and economically disadvantaged individuals and women.

We identified two types of challenges in monitoring Ex-Im's support for small businesses:

- *Developing effective performance measures.* We found that Ex-Im had developed performance standards for assessing its small business financing efforts in most, although not all, of the areas specified by Congress, ranging from providing excellent customer service to increasing outreach.[4] We also found that some measures for monitoring progress against the standards lacked targets and timeframes, and that Ex-Im was just beginning to compile and use the small business information it was collecting to improve operations. GAO made several recommendations to Ex-Im for improving its performance standards and Ex-Im agreed to take steps to address them.
- *Maintaining reliable data and reporting.* In 2006, we found weaknesses in Ex-Im's data and data systems for tracking small business financing and made recommendations for improvement; Ex-Im has taken steps to address those weaknesses.[5] One notable improvement has been the introduction of "Ex-Im Online," an interactive, web-based process that allows exporters, brokers, and financial institutions to transact with Ex-Im electronically. This contributed to more timely and accurate information on Ex-Im's financing, and thus a greater level of confidence in Ex-Im's reporting on its efforts relative to congressional goals.

Trade Agreements Need to Be Effectively Monitored and Enforced to Ensure U.S. Companies Can Benefit

A top trade priority for the United States is opening foreign markets for U.S. goods and services by ensuring that U.S. trading partners comply with existing trade agreements. These agreements have addressed traditional barriers to trade such as tariffs, as well as other obstacles ranging from weak intellectual property protection to selective enforcement of agricultural inspection requirements. As a result, monitoring and enforcing these agreements—which number in the hundreds and cover the vast majority of U.S. exports—is a key responsibility for U.S. government agencies.

Congress has expressed longstanding concerns regarding a number of issues, of which I will discuss two related issues:

- *Effective monitoring and enforcement of trade agreements.* We have reported on a variety of issues related to monitoring and enforcing the broad range of U.S. trade agreements with a number of countries.[6] For example, since China's accession to the World Trade Organization in 2001, Congress has been keenly interested in the extent to which China is complying with its obligations. As a result, we have performed a large body of work examining U.S. government efforts to oversee China's implementation of its trade obligations. Most recently, we reviewed USTR's annual reporting on China's compliance.[7] Our analysis of these reports identified about 180 compliance issues with China, ranging from agriculture policies to China's legal system. Of these, we found that USTR had resolved 23 percent, achieved some progress on 40 percent, and made no progress on 37 percent. We are also in the process of completing a report analyzing the results of free trade agreements between the United States and four countries.

- *Sufficiency of agencies' human capital to perform monitoring and enforcement responsibilities.* We have previously reported that the workload for agencies responsible for monitoring and enforcing trade agreements has increased significantly and that the agreements they monitor and enforce have become more complex.[8] Effective monitoring and enforcement requires significant expertise—often involving staff with expertise in trade policy, the foreign country, and the particular industry. However, we have found that trade agencies face constraints to developing and accessing necessary expertise. For example, after identifying a lack of training for U.S. government staff overseas regarding monitoring and enforcing trade agreements, we recommended that key trade agencies jointly develop a strategy for meeting those training needs to better equip staff to handle increasingly complex or technical barriers to U.S. exports. Let me also mention that while in China last week, I heard a number of examples of situations in which having specialized U.S. government personnel in the embassy and consulates can be a great benefit to U.S. firms and their ability to serve foreign markets.

Chairman Rush and Ranking Member Radanovich, this concludes my remarks. I appreciate the opportunity to discuss these issues with you today. We would be glad to work with the Subcommittee in the future on other issues related to foreign commerce. I am happy to answer any questions you may have.

End Notes

[1] TPCC has 20 member agencies. However, it generally reports in the *National Export Strategy* on the budgets and activities of around 10. The 2008 strategy included budget authority information for 9 agencies: Departments of Agriculture, Commerce, State, and the Treasury; Ex-Im, Overseas Private Investment Corporation, Small Business Administration, U.S. Trade and Development Agency, and the Office of the U.S. Trade Representative.

[2] GAO, *Export Promotion: Trade Promotion Coordinating Committee's Role Remains Limited*, GAO-06-660T (Washington, D.C.: April 26, 2006).

[3] According to the 2008 *National Export Strategy*, 97 percent of firms that export are small or medium enterprises. However, a very low proportion—less than 1 percent—of U.S. firms export.

[4] See GAO, *Export-Import Bank: Performance Standards for Small Business Assistance Are in Place but Ex-Im Is in the Early Stages of Measuring Their Effectiveness*, GAO-08-915 (Washington, D.C.: Jul. 17, 2008).

[5] See GAO, *Export-Import Bank: Changes Would Improve the Reliability of Reporting on Small Business Financing,* GAO-06-351 (Washington, D.C.: March 3, 2006) and GAO, *Export Promotion: Export-Import Bank has Met Target for Small Business Financing Share,* GAO-08-419T (Washington, D.C. Jan. 17, 2008).

[6] See, for example, GAO, *International Trade: Further Improvements Needed to Handle Growing Workload for Monitoring and Enforcing Trade* Agreements, GAO-05-537 (Washington, D.C.: June 30, 2005).

[7] GAO, *U.S.-China Trade: USTR's China Compliance Reports and Plans Could Be Improved,* GAO-08-405 (Washington, D.C.: April 14, 2008).

[8] GAO-05-537.

CHAPTER SOURCES

The following chapters have been previously published:

Chapter 1 – This is an edited reformatted and augmented version of a Congressional research Service publication, report R41495, dated Novemeber 19, 2010.

Chapter 2 – This is an edited reformatted and augmented version of a Congressional Research Service publication, report 98-569, dated February 25, 2010.

Chapter 3 – This is an edited reformatted and augmented version of a Congressional Research Service publication, report R41202, dated April 19, 2010.

Chapter 4 – This is an edited reformatted and augmented version of a United States Government Accountability Office publication, report GAO-10-1069T, dated September 29, 2010.

Chapter 5 – This is an edited reformatted and augmented version of a United States Government Accountability Office publication, report GAO-10-874, dated August 2010.

Chapter 6 – This is an edited reformatted and augmented version of a Congressional Research Service publication, report RL31832, dated April 26, 2010.

Chapter 7 – This is an edited reformatted and augmented version of a United State Department of Commerce publication, report *Exports Support American Jobs*.

Chapter 8 – This is an edited formatted and augmented version of a United States Government Accountability Office publication, report GAO-09-480T, dated March 17, 2009.

INDEX

C

D

E

F

G

H

I

N

O

P

Q

R

S

T

U

V

W

Y